Leadership, Character and Strategy

LEADERSHIP, CHARACTER AND STRATEGY

EXPLORING DIVERSITY

Keith Patching

palgrave
macmillan

First published in 2007 by
PALGRAVE MACMILLAN
Houndmills, Basingstoke, Hampshire RG21 6XS and
175 Fifth Avenue, New York, N.Y. 10010
Companies and representatives throughout the world.

PALGRAVE MACMILLAN is the global academic imprint of the Palgrave Macmillan division of St. Martin's Press, LLC and of Palgrave Macmillan Ltd. Macmillan® is a registered trademark in the United States, United Kingdom and other countries. Palgrave is a registered trademark in the European Union and other countries.

ISBN-13: 978–0–230–50084–6
ISBN-10: 0–230–50084–6

This book is printed on paper suitable for recycling and made from fully managed and sustained forest sources.

A catalogue record for this book is available from the British Library.

A catalog record for this book is available from the Library of Congress

10 9 8 7 6 5 4 3 2 1
16 15 14 13 12 11 10 09 08 07

Printed and bound in China

Contents

CHAPTER 1

Introduction

What do the following people have in common: Margaret Thatcher, Martin Luther King Jr., Mahatma Gandhi and Franklin D. Roosevelt? The obvious answer is that they were all famous and successful leaders who achieved a great deal in their lifetimes. Each can teach us something about leadership, and I shall be drawing on some of those lessons in this book.

The problem is that many of the lessons they teach us are contradictory.

From a practical point of view, trying to follow all of these leaders' examples would produce leadership behaviors at odds with each other. As role models they are all good. But as a pool of resources to draw upon they teach us contradictory lessons.

While Thatcher taught us to fight, Gandhi taught us that fighting is futile. While Roosevelt taught us to build, King taught us to dismantle.

It could be suggested that, to some extent, each leader adapted his or her approach to the context of the day. Thatcher found herself faced with what she saw as a sick economy in need of some tough remedies; Gandhi found himself confronted with the British Raj; Roosevelt with a deepening Depression, and King with racial prejudice in America's deep south.

These circumstances are, of course, relevant to their lives and histories. But it would be wrong to deduce from this that the way to lead depends solely upon the demands of circumstance. To select a leadership role model based on the fact that his or her context looks similar to yours would be mistaken or misguided.

The first is that circumstances are never just circumstances: they are how you see them. The second is that what drove the leadership strategies of these four people was their characters far more than the context of their day.

This book is written primarily for the 99 percent of people in leadership positions within the heart of organizations who are not, and probably will not get to the top. Statistically alone, few people make it there. If following carefully in the footsteps of the few, everyone could be guaranteed to get to the top, there would be no one left actually to do the work. At any one time there are thousands of leaders, most of whom could do better. And this is not because they are doing a bad job. It is because everyone has the capacity to do better the more they practice and learn. What is contained in this book has helped many people who are leaders to be better at leadership.

Leadership is not just for the very few people who head up organizations and states. It is for all those in organizations and society who have influence on others. And that means almost every one of us. You don't have to be a Chief Executive Office (CEO) to be a leader – nor a Prime Minister. You just have to interact with people. And help them to see and do things differently. That's why, day by day, in meetings and casual conversations, we all have the chance to lead.

It will help you see how your own character influences both how you see the circumstances in which you operate, and how best to lead people in those circumstances. It will enable you to develop your own leadership strategy, taking from leadership role models not at random, but in ways that are most likely to be effective for you.

I have been working in leadership development for many years, both with CEOs and other senior managers and with people who are in far less senior roles. The quality of leadership I have found among the people I have worked with is not a function of seniority. Some very senior people have very poor leadership capabilities, while some of the best leaders I have worked with will never head up major organizations – mostly because they don't want to.

Two of my chosen examples of leadership never headed up large formal organizations. Martin Luther King did hold executive positions in a number of Associations and Committees. But his power did not emanate from his roles. It came from the way he behaved as an individual. Gandhi's influence did not come from a position in a political party. It came from his teachings. If you equate leadership success simply with seniority in formal organizations, you may miss the point. And in so doing, miss your chance to be a great leader.

This is not a book about management. Leadership is something anyone can demonstrate, irrespective of their seniority or position. Management is about being formally in charge of things or people, and can involve techniques or rules about how to do it "properly": how to run meetings, how to appraise performance, and so on. Management is, in my experience, something people do at the times when they are not doing the other parts of their job. Their style to management is manifested when they are doing management. But leadership is what one does all day and every day, because it is about how you are, in your character, and how this comes across in what you say and do. A person's management style can, and sometimes is, at odds with how he or she leads people.

This book is not about climbing ladders. It is about becoming the best leader you can be. And that is one reason why I have chosen as my primary case studies leaders from the broader context of politics. I recognize that, for most of my intended readership it is exploring leadership in their roles as professionals or managers that is most important. And I shall use many examples of leaders in organizations as the book develops. But to set the scene most clearly, the four political figures I have chosen not only have had a great deal written about them, that makes it possible to gain a number of different perspectives on their lives and characters, but they are also better known as icons of their own particular ways of leading. Icons but not extremes. If I chose extremes, they would provide far less practical help. A book written on the basis of what we can learn from Hitler, Che Guevara, Jesus Christ and Moses would be fraught with difficulties for obvious reasons.

The people I have chosen can also generate strong feelings. Many people dislike the politics of Margaret Thatcher; Gandhi and Martin Luther King were both assassinated, evidence enough that not everyone loved them; and Roosevelt has had many detractors both in his lifetime and afterwards. But in their own ways, these four people represent both the iconic and the real. Individually, they also represent extremely well the four very distinct approaches to leadership that this book will explore.

One reason for this is that each of them, in their own way, developed and stuck to an approach to leadership that was thoroughly consistent with their characters. If there is one thing on which most writers on leadership now agree it is that effective leadership grows out of what works for the individual leader. For example, in an in-depth survey of 18 successful business leaders, Ruth Tait says, "Almost all . . . spoke about the need to 'know thyself,' to carefully examine one's own strengths, interests, motivation and to choose a career path based on this understanding, rather than on what others or society thought was statusful and worthwhile."[1]

People are different from each other. It may also be thought that, if there's one thing each of us knows about, it's ourselves. After all, we've lived with ourselves all our lives. Therefore, it would seem, developing a leadership style based on our own characters should be simple.

In my experience, this is not the case. The fact is that many of us just don't know ourselves well. Many of the less successful people I have worked with fail to achieve what they set out to do because they naively try to follow leadership role models that just don't work for them. Fighters try to be teachers; natural pacifists try to fight; free spirits try to be grown ups; and believers in hierarchy pretend to be democrats. It doesn't work because people see through you. Of course, for all of us, there comes a time to fight for what we believe in; we have lessons to pass on to those who can learn from us; hierarchies happen and need to be managed; and everyone should have a voice at some time.

As leaders we need to be adaptable and well rounded. But we also need to have a core strategy, a firm and consistent framework upon which to build our unique leadership styles. As Ruth Tait discovered from her conversations with a cross-section of business leaders, "If there was a consensus, it was on the impossibility of defining a set of necessary and sufficient attributes that define leaders – all agreed that business leaders come in all shapes and sizes, with different styles, approaches, strengths and weaknesses."[2]

This book provides one way of exploring your own character and the leadership style that will match that character. It is not the only way. People are complex and any model like the one this book uses has its limitations. Therefore I do not see this book attempting to replace any others in the field. Rather it is supplementary. It adds a dimension that I, and almost all the people I have worked with, have found enormously helpful.

In my practical work with leaders I do not place a book in people's hands and ask them to read it. Those I work with directly want something more accessible and immediate. Among the tools I use in these situations is a suite of questionnaires I have developed over the past 15 years. They help people quickly arrive at some idea of their core characters and how those characters currently inform their leadership styles and their daily lives.

But like most such tools, they have to be used with care. Much of the value of its output comes from talking it through. They are not like questionnaires in weekly magazines; these are fun but harmless, even if, as is always possible, when you fill them in you cheat and lie. It is because we can and often do try to fool ourselves about who we are that debriefing the questionnaires is the most critical part of the process. That is why the questionnaires are not included here. As you read this book, and as you consider what it can tell you about developing your own unique style of leadership it is important that you are as honest with yourself as you can be. Building a leadership strategy on false foundations is dangerous.

Self-deception, the process of having inaccurate impressions of oneself is not a pathology or mental illness. It is extremely common. Among the many hundreds of people I have worked with on the leadership issues covered in this book, a significant number have had to confront some level of self-deception. Usually, it is simply a matter of degree: someone thinking they are more competitive than they are in practice, for example, or, more commonly, less so. But in quite a few cases, it is a difference of kind, in which persons see themselves in a very different light from the "reality" of how they actually live.

One of the most common forms of self-deception I come across is the serious, responsible, and risk-averse individual who, remembering his heady student days when he partied "every night," still sees himself as this hedonistic youth. These days the rebellion he sees as a key part of his character is manifested in wearing comical socks.

It may be, and sometimes is the case, that this comical sock-wearer still is a rebel at heart. In such rare cases, it does not take long to surface the deep sense of frustration with life that he feels day in, day out. And usually this is the start of a coaching program that will help him out of his living hell. But in the majority of cases, he really is how he comes across: contented with his lot, but having fond memories – and that is all – of an episode that has long passed.

"The theory of self-deception was foreshadowed by the sociologist Erving Goffman in his 1959 book 'The Presentation of Self in Everyday Life', which disputed the romantic notion that behind the masks we show other people is the one true self. No, said Goffman; it's masks all the way down. Many discoveries in the ensuing decades have borne him out."[3]

Some psychologists refer to this kind of self-deception as "character-armour," "the face the self turns to the world."[4] The challenge, if you are to develop a leadership style that will work for you, is to avoid using character-armour on yourself.

That people are able to do so is not only my own experience, but also well researched. What psychologists call "denial," "reversal," "projection," "isolation," "rationalization," and "sublimation" are not the preserve of the mentally ill, but what people are inclined to do to themselves whenever it is convenient to the unconscious.[5]

Perhaps the best way you can check yourself for signs of self-deception as you review how you relate to the leadership styles in this book is simply to keep asking yourself, as I do with the people I work with, "Really? Are you sure? Is that what you really believe? And if so, how does this show in how you actually live your life?"

Remember, a common form of rationalization is to blame your current lifestyles on situations for which you "had no choice." As you read about the leaders in this book, consider what history would have been like if each of them had thought that way.

As you need through the book, you will come across a significant number of questions. These have been brought together in the Appendix, and you may want to work through the questions & exercises in the Appendix as a way of keeping track.

CHAPTER 2

Stories

Stories have meanings

In Chapter 1, I said that circumstances are not the primary driver of leaders' styles. The first reason I gave was that circumstances are never just circumstances. In this chapter, I shall say why.

In Chapter 1, I also referred to the fact that good leaders have high levels of self-awareness; a major factor in what Daniel Goleman calls "emotional intelligence".[1] Part of being aware of oneself seems to be to have the ability to look at one's own life story and deduce from it what has influenced the development of character.

Whenever I work with leaders, I listen to them telling me stories about themselves. They know what events in their lives have been important and have taught them important lessons, many of which they apply to how they lead. For some writers, the ability to define yourself through the story of your life is a crucial part of achieving maturity. "Finding the great story that informs your life is a sacred task."[2]

Maybe "sacred" is pushing it for most of us, but I do agree that the more we can identify what have been the seminal events of our lives, the better we will be able to understand ourselves, and thereby develop the leadership style that suits us best.

Part of the problem is that, once we arrive at the age of 30 or 40 or 50, we have lived for so many days and nights that it may be hard to pick out from all the events that have happened to us the vital ones that have influenced who we are.[3]

As it happens, however, most of us have little difficulty in picking out the important moments from the mundane. Martin Luther King, for example, tells of his journey to collect the Nobel Peace Prize. His plane was delayed. The pilot announced the delay and apologized; the cabin crew kept the passengers catered for. But for King, what was happening on the ground was of greater interest. The ground crew were working away at solving the problem. Unannounced and unnoticed by most, these workers, the "unsung heroes" were the ones who were making things happen, solving the problem. They symbolized for King the unsung heroes that his life was dedicated to helping. Life's "ground crew" were the rightful recipients of the Peace Prize.

Think about similar events in your own life. The chances are that what may otherwise have been insignificant events, soon forgotten, have become important to you because of what those events mean for you. So to some extent, it's not the stories themselves that are important as what the stories mean.

Take a look at the following stories, and consider which, if any, you find familiar. Do any of them seem to match stories from your own life, and, if so, what do they mean for you?

Things were getting out of hand; people were being stupid; I just walked away and never looked back.

Things were getting out of hand; people needed guidance; I took control of the situation and sorted it out.

The odds were stacked against me; I wasn't expected to win. I pulled out all the stops and came out on top. It felt great.

Everything was going so well; I didn't see it coming. I failed, but have learnt so much from that failure.

It all came together so well; there were all the people who are so important to me all gathered together, and it all seemed so perfect.

As the sun began to set, someone said, "I'm looking forward to going home," and I thought, "Home is wherever I am right now."

I realized that the things I used to think were so true were, in fact, misguided. So I threw away what I had believed in before and started again.

One of the best days of my life was when I achieved a goal I had been pursuing for years. I thought "at last", and felt elated.

Nothing could compare to the day we – just the two of us – turned our back on it all and headed for our new adventure.

Nothing could compare to the day we all sat together and celebrated being "one big happy family".

I'm sure that what happened was meant to be; it was "written in the stars".

I was determined not to let it happen; I summoned up huge reserves of determination and turned back the "inevitable" tide.

I realized they had done wrong, but I knew that, without hesitation or reservation, I would forgive them.

I realized they were depending on me, but they needed to make it on their own. I set them free to make their own way.

I realized they were treading on too many toes; they had overstepped the mark and needed to be shown the error of their ways. I showed them.

I realized that I knew more about them than I could possibly have found out directly. It was as though I could read their minds, understand so much about them without a word being spoken.

For each and any of these stories that resonate with you, consider what it has taught you about leadership. Did it tell you that you have to fight on and never give up fighting for what you believe in? Did it teach you that failure is the best way to learn? Did it tell you that people look to you for guidance and authority? Did the lesson show you that people respond best to being free? As you read through the section of this book that explores the four major leadership models, and as you recognize in those models elements of yourself, recollect these stories as moments when those lessons of experience reinforced for you how you like to lead.

Since I have not met you, none of these stories can have been gleaned from any knowledge of your life. Yet, if you are like most of the people I have worked with, at least some of the stories match experiences to which you can relate. There is no mystery in this, of course. What is happening is that I am telling stories that are occurring time and time again and to many different people throughout the world.

One of the things that people who study other cultures discovered is that there are some stories that seem to be told in almost every culture of the world. Known as myths, they are stories that continue to make sense of people's lives as they confront the kinds of challenge we all face, whether we are a CEO or a hunter-gatherer.

"One measure of how deeply these myths express elemental human concerns is the extent to which they are both timeless and universal. Mythologists and anthropologists see the same themes, situations, and stories played out again and again, across the ages and around the globe."[4]

In our modern culture the word "myth" has often come to mean something that is not true. That a story is not, literally, true does not mean it should be dismissed. If that were the case, Hollywood would not exist, and most of what is put out on our television screens would disappear. Despite our technological sophistication, our culture continues to consume stories that are not strictly true. Cinema and television provide us with our own modern myths. We know actors are not really the people they represent, but we are willing to suspend our disbelief because the stories we are watching make some sense to us.

The ability to make sense of the things that happen around us is a particularly important human trait. Not only does it stop us going mad ("nothing makes sense any more!") but it also enables us to make sense of our unique experiences to other people. One of the most important features of the job interview is telling our stories and hoping that the interviewer makes the same sense of them as we do.

Different points of view

In 1993, I led a project for a client organization. Its initial purpose was to find ways of increasing efficiency and effectiveness in major project work – the client was a specialist manufacturer. It was part of the "mythology" within the firm that one particular project, where a process known as "simultaneous engineering" was adopted, had produced very good results, and it was felt by the Manufacturing Director that the lessons learnt from that project should be applied across the business in future.

The problem was that, when interviewed, few of the people involved in the project had drawn similar conclusions from the experience. Indeed, in some cases, the lessons learnt were contradictory between different people.

What this reminded me at the time was that experience is not a set of objectively observable "facts" that lead to inevitable conclusions; it is different for each individual going through the "experience." It was only by bringing the whole team together, and through constructive discussion of the perceived "lessons" that we were able to draw out a set of consistent and practically valuable principles from the project.

In our daily lives, we often come across this kind of situation in which people see things differently. This is one of the greatest challenges to leadership. If everyone saw things the same, the formula for leadership would be simple.

"Beauty is in the eye of the beholder," says the proverb. The same applies to leadership. The main reason for this is that there is a fundamental difference between "facts" and "opinions."[5]

Imagine a management team getting together for a meeting. The facts being discussed will be sales figures, numbers of vacancies to be filled, the texts of written reports, and so on. Amongst the statements of facts will be opinions, such as whether the figures are healthy, how the quality of prospective candidates for vacant posts differs, and what people feel about the sentiments expressed in the reports.

The difference between facts and opinions is well known. What is surprising to some people is, first, how much of the dialogue that takes place in such meetings is opinion. In some research, figures of well over 95 per cent have been cited as the percentage of dialogue that is opinion. Whatever the "real" figure, all those who have researched this topic are agreed that a great deal more opinion than fact is debated.

One reason that people are often surprised by this is that many of our opinions are so clear to us that they feel like facts. Of course, we think, in the current climate these sales figures are good; Mr X is the best candidate; and the author of the report does not know what he is talking about.

The second surprising thing is that, in a very significant sense, opinions say more about the holder of those opinions than they do about the subject matter.

To illustrate this, let us imagine two people talking about their boss, who has just made a major decision. One person says, "That was a really brave decision." The other takes a sharp intake of breath. "Brave?" he says, "That was the most stupid thing he could have done."

Was the decision brave or stupid? I believe this is the wrong question. It assumes that there is a means by which *the truth* can be arrived at. It works on the basis that one of these two opinions is right and the other wrong. And the chances are, most conversations of this kind continue on that basis, with each participant trying to convince the other that he is right and the other wrong. Few such discussions end up with a clear winner.

Good leaders know why this kind of dialogue is ineffective. They know that the second surprising thing about facts and opinions is that opinions are best reframed along these kinds of lines: what each participant is saying is "What the boss has just done is an example of what I define as brave or stupid." In other words, opinions are a better insight into the mindsets of their holders than they are a description of objective reality.

A good leader, faced with an opinion he or she disagrees with does not think, "You are wrong." He or she thinks, "So that's how you see it." Because, from the point of view of someone who sees this kind of decision as stupid rather than brave, it is not wrong to call it so. It is just a different point of view.

And if you want to change someone's point of view, calling it wrong may not be very effective. What you may have to do is to work on the reasons why that person equates this kind of decision with stupidity. And that means influencing how they see the world, not just this decision.

Influencing how people see the world is a complex process. It starts with recognizing that you have to know where the other person is coming from, how they have arrived at the way they see things. So long as fighters see pacifists as cowards who would fight if they had the guts, and pacifists see fighters as mindless bullies bent on destruction, they will always be at odds.

It is one of the most important themes of this book that a good leader should know his or her own preferred leadership model, should be aware of how that differs from those around him or her, and thereby avoid the basic error of dismissing those who are different as wrong. And part of this process depends upon recognizing how those around us are likely to make sense of what we do.

If a boss is a fighter by nature, but has subordinates who are pacifists by temperament, the boss is likely to develop, very quickly, a reputation that he or she will find it hard to shift. People in the public eye know that, very often, it is their reputation more than their actions that is paramount. And that is because actions are not just actions, they are part of stories that have meaning. They can be both brave and stupid at the same time.

On balance, whether the majority sees an action as brave or as stupid depends upon who is most effective in managing the actor's reputation. Margaret Thatcher soon learnt this lesson: "Once a politician is given a public image by the media, it is almost impossible for him to shed it. At every important stage of his career, it steps between him and the public so that people seem to see and hear not the man himself but the invented personality to which he has been reduced."[6]

For "politician" read "leader."

Striving for objectivity

Most of us know that there can be a difference between people's reputation and how they see themselves. This is especially true if, like me, you have had the experience of being misunderstood. What goes through your mind is the thought that, "But I'm not like that. You don't understand." Reputations are simplifications, and can miss the subtlety and complexity that informs people's real lives.

Biographical writers often say that their prime motive in writing about their subjects is to put the record straight and to see the person behind the image. For example, Ralph Abernathy said of his book on his close friend Martin Luther King, "[I want] to let everyone know that this legendary figure was also a human being, and that this humanity did not detract from the legend but only made it more believable for other human beings."[7]

People I work with often complain that they feel as though they are fighting a constant battle to "put the record straight" in much the same way. The problem, as they see it, is that their reputation is at odds with reality. They are, to that extent, misunderstood. There is the real person, whose intentions are good and known to themselves, set against the image that is false. This is not only wrong but unfair.

Sometimes this mismatch between reputation and "reality" works in our favour. Some people I work with confess that their greatest fear is being "found out." They feel that people give them more credit than they deserve.

After all, they are only doing what comes naturally and easily to them. Surely all this praise is misplaced, and when people realize how ordinary they are, the honeymoon will be over.

Whether we are the victims of unfair criticism or the recipients of unfounded praise, the same process is going on in other people's minds. It is simply part of the shorthand of human cognition that we classify and characterize on less than perfect evidence. You don't need to be beaten up too often by a boss to see him or her as a bully. You don't have to be let down very many times to see someone as a cheat or liar.

We are taught that it is wrong to work with such stereotypes. We tend to avoid calling people "bean counters" to their faces (unless we are particularly upset with them); in our appraisals, we have learnt not to refer to people as "spineless wimps." But we also know that it feels natural to sum up our views of others (individuals as well as groups) with such shorthand. It is natural.[8]

That something is a natural human trait does not make it right. But knowing that it is natural makes it easier to understand how to deal with it constructively.

Earlier I referred to the story-telling element of the job interview. Another well-known element is the "gut reaction." How long does it take, when interviewing someone, to make up your mind about them? Most people acknowledge that the gut reaction takes place within a few minutes at the most. There is a good case for suggesting that it takes a few microseconds only![9]

The research shows that, because of the way our brains are wired up, we have an attitude to something or somebody before we know what or who it is. Enabling us to survive in situations of danger or opportunity, this feature of how our minds work explains our gut reactions. What it means in practice is that, despite wanting to believe that we treat each situation with cool objectivity, we have emotional reactions we may not even be aware of. These emotional reactions have a major influence on how we interpret what we see or hear.

When we are interviewing someone, and we listen to their stories, it is possible to see in these stories all the good things. Each part of the story reinforces the positive impression we are forming. On the other hand, we can listen to the stories with increasing disbelief. As the interviewee carries on, we see them digging a bigger and bigger hole. The more they say, the more evidence we have to show that this person is just not right for this job.

What makes us interpret someone's story in one way or another? At least part of the answer lies in this unconscious emotional reaction, over which we have no conscious control. We don't choose to have positive or negative gut reactions. Neither do we choose the way in which that gut reaction colors how we take what we hear as evidence for or against the candidate.

Even those most objective of folks, scientists, often have difficulty actually seeing data that contradicts what they expect or want to see.[10]

We can and do change our minds about people. There are two quite distinct ways of going about this. The first is to seek out further information, trying to find evidence that proves us wrong in our assessment. The other is to rethink the evidence we already have, turning the same stories from tales of villainy to tales of heroism.

Consider the following sentence written about Gandhi: "He had marched on Dandi, picked up a pinch of salt and shaken the British Empire."[11] This is not literally true. Why can picking up a pinch of salt have such an enormous effect, leading ultimately to the collapse of the British Raj and independence for India? It was not because of any physical link. It was what the action meant. Although from a legal standpoint, Gandhi's action was simply a crime, from a symbolic point of view, it was a gesture of resistance.

As leaders, it is not what we do or say that is important, it is what these words and deeds mean. Although in many sense leadership is practical, it is, perhaps more importantly, symbolic.[12]

What about Martin Luther King's speech at Washington in 1963? How did the fact that a black preacher had a dream change anything? "Millions of white Americans, for the first time, had a clear, long look at Negroes engaged in a serious occupation. For the first time millions listened to the informed and thoughtful words of Negro spokesmen, from all walks of life. The stereotype of the Negro suffered a heavy blow. This was evident in some of the comments, which reflected surprise at the dignity, the organization, and even the wearing apparel and friendly spirit of the participants. If the press had expected something akin to a minstrel show, or a brawl, or a comic display of odd clothes and bad manners, they were disappointed."[13]

People began to reframe the image of the black working class. Managing perceptions is powerful. So much so that "the FBI was concerned about the 'rise of a messiah' who could unify, and electrify, the militant black nationalist movement."[14]

The dangers of such symbolic power are clear. One of the lessons of the Second World War is that messianic leaders like Hitler can create havoc if unchecked. In a more mundane world we try to counter the power of reputation, prejudice, and subjectivity by introducing more objective ways of assessing the performance of people in leadership positions. Performance Management systems, 360° appraisals, and measurable targets all seek to provide a more balanced (and some would say sane) approach that minimizes the potentially negative effect of an over-dependence on image.

Such checks and balances can be superb (although many are very poorly designed, developed and used). But it is important for anyone who is a leader to recognize that the facts will always be tempered with the symbolic. For leaders, managing meaning is, and will always be, at least as important as managing data.

We cannot ever know absolutely everything about our leaders, and those we lead can never know absolutely everything about us. The forensic approach of the court of law, balanced and objective though it may be, is not the reality of leadership in today's organizations, and is unlikely ever to be so. And this is why, in this book, I am advocating that, as a leader, you develop the ability to see what you do as symbolic. When you pick up a pinch of salt, what does that mean to the people around you?

What does your leadership behavior mean?

"Madonna changes her lifestyles and hairstyles, but she is always the outrageous Rebel. Offscreen and on, Jack Nicholson is the bad-boy Outlaw. Meg Ryan and Tom Hanks imbue every role they play with the spirit of the wide-eyed Innocent."[15]

Actors and entertainers may bemoan typecasting, but many of them do it all the way to the bank. Within ourselves as leaders, we are complex and often bemoan the simple ways we can get typecast by our peers, bosses and subordinates. Of course we are more complex than any typecasting will acknowledge, but that's life.

But rather than bewail the fact, why not use it? As individuals, Gandhi, Thatcher, Roosevelt and King were more complex than their images. But maybe it was the image they created or had thrust upon them that gave them their unique strengths and the very power that enabled them to be successful. Although it was literally true of them, Gandhi is not primarily remembered as a lawyer, Thatcher as a housewife, Roosevelt as a victim of polio, or King as a plagiarist.

So who are you, as a leader? And what does this tell you about how best to make use of your image or reputation?

This book may help you answer that question. Already, the stories at the beginning of this chapter may provide some hints. Which of them most closely matches your own life story, and thereby, your image?

Another clue may come from how you respond to the modern myths we call cinema and television. Largely lacking a body of oral, traditional mythology, we in our culture satisfy our urge for stories and the mythical characters within them by following the exploits of imaginary people in the many soap operas, situation comedies and other dramas that make up so much of television and radio schedules worldwide.

And despite the fact that we know, when we watch films like *Independence Day*, what is going to happen – the story is simple and timeless – we still watch them.

If you know this film, consider who it is you relate to most strongly – who, for you is the hero? Is it the President, symbolising authority, strength of purpose and responsibility? Or the fighter pilot, who can't wait to get in his plane and take on the enemy face to face? Or the scientist who cycles around saving the environment, and for whom there must be a way of out-smarting the invincible threat. Or the guy at the research facility who has been trying to make the captured alien spaceship work for years, and for whom the invasion is "really exciting" because all the little lights and gizmos have now turned on?

What kind of character is the hero of your own story? The more you can answer that, the closer you are getting to finding the firm foundations on which to build your leadership strategy.

CHAPTER 3

Science

Stories carry different meanings

One of the stories quite a few people tell me starts like this:

> "I grew up in a very poor neighbourhood. We were always short of money, and had to make do with the bare essentials"

Another one I hear occasionally starts:

> "In my early childhood one of my parents ran off and left us . . ."

In each of these cases, what I cannot tell from the story itself is what the teller has learnt from it. This is because poverty in childhood sometimes leads a person to strive for betterment. This kind of person has learnt that you have to stretch yourself, to go for it, and to make sure that, through your own endeavors, you achieve what you could not achieve in childhood. But for others, the same kind of impoverished childhood teaches them that money can't buy you love. These people learn that the best things in life are free, and find contentment in family, community and humility.

Being abandoned by or experiencing the death of a parent can also lead to contrary lessons. For some, the great sense of loss they felt by being abandoned teaches them the need for caring, responsibility, and sticking to the family; it often leaves them with a level of uncertainty or fear of abandonment that drives them to hang onto certainties. For others, the experience is said to have set them free, learning early in life how to fend for themselves and to depend on no-one.

This suggests that life's experiences can teach us different things. It seems to mean that stories do not necessarily carry with them inevitable meanings. The 'moral of the tale' depends upon something in the character of the teller.

This is one reason why I believe that defining your character cannot depend solely on retelling the stories of your early years. It's what you make of them that is important to self-awareness. And what you make of the stories of your youth is likely to depend on something deeper than the experience alone.

Character and strategy

In the previous two chapters I have referred to foundations upon which to build your leadership strategy. The word "foundations" conjures up a very fixed concept. Don't we change as we grow up? And if so, how would these foundations allow the flexibility to adapt to such changes?

I work in leadership development. If I did not believe in people's ability to change behavior, I could not do this job. But there is a difference between trying to change character and developing different behaviors.

If I chose, I could spend more time in the gym, perhaps to build myself up with a view to playing a sport better, say basketball. But there is no regime of physical education that would enable me to grow six feet tall, so I may become better at basketball, but I will never become great at it.

Recently, especially with the completion of the human genome project, scientists have begun to explore aspects of human behavior that, like how tall we are, may not be as easy to change as we may once have believed. What this means is that it may be as hard for me to change my fundamental character as it would be to change my height. Once a conscientious carer, always a conscientious carer, although how this element of character actually influences how someone behaves can, and often does, change.

In this chapter I will look briefly at where we are at the moment in understanding the relationships between genetic inheritance and behavior.

Let me start by saying, quite categorically, that I do not believe there is a deterministic relationship between genes and behavior. Nor does any sane scientist. What we do is not caused by genes, just as it is not caused by our social background. But what we do may be influenced by genes. And just as I suggested in the previous chapter that knowing how our gut feelings can influence our ability to respond objectively to other people, here I am suggesting that the more you know about these kinds of influences the more you can adjust for them – if you really want to.

Think of leadership as being a mix of "character" and "strategy." By "character" I mean the key elements of the kind of person you are. By "strategy" I mean the means by which you go about achieving your goals. Margaret Thatcher's legacy is based largely on what she did for the British economy. But she was not a brilliant economist, and "there were more than a few people on both sides of the House who thought she was a boring, middle-class suburbanite, of very limited intelligence."[1]

A major part of Roosevelt's legacy was the New Deal, but at the time of his first election to the presidency, he did not have a strategy to sort out the mess the country was in: "Whatever he offered a bewildered and frightened American electorate it was not what became the agenda of the New Deal. This was not so much because Roosevelt was afraid that if he did so the electorate might reject it, but because that agenda had not yet crystallized in his mind. Nobody, least of all FDR, had any clear idea what the New Deal would mean."[2]

Gandhi was not a lifelong enemy of the British Raj. For most of his life he supported British rule, taking a proactive part in recruiting for the British cause in three wars. "For the greater part of his life he would continue to show the utmost respect for authority. For fifty years he showed his enduring respect for the duly constituted authority of the British Raj."[3] And Martin Luther King did not invent his strategy: he went to India and brought back Gandhi's passive resistance as the way to meet his ends.

In each example, the key to the success of leadership was the character more than the strategy. That is why this book uses character as its basis. What strategy you adopt should be determined by who you are. You are a person first, a leader second.

Where character comes from

This is a subject in which I have had to change my mind. As a postgraduate I studied social anthropology, and in those days was taught to believe that how people behave is completely explainable through the study of the social environment. Like most of my contemporaries, I carried this belief with me for many years. And like most of my contemporaries I felt deeply threatened by any suggestion that any part of someone's character could be innate.

Many people feel uncomfortable with the idea that some parts of their character are born with them. It makes them feel manipulated by their genes. It also feels wrong because people change. A study by Brent Roberts, a senior psychologist at the University of Illinois cited in *Sunday Times* Oct 9, 2005 argues the case for personality change. Like many people he wants to prove the obvious point that we are not pre-programmed automata fixed in patterns of behavior for life.

Like many arguments between scientists, this one is as old as the hills. "Lions make leopards tame," "Yea, but not change their spots." Shakespeare, as so often, seems to have got it right.

This is a book about practical leadership, not about an academic debate, so I will not try to settle any scientific controversy here. All I want to do is to help direct you to those elements of character that are useful for you to be clear about if you want to develop your strategy in line with who you are. And although you will have learnt things, and changed your views on some matters as a result, there are likely to be some parts of your character that make you the unique person you are and, like our four key case examples, form the foundations for your strategy rather than emerge from your strategy.

And to do this properly means looking at both what you have learnt throughout your life and how instinct may have played its part.

When I stand in front of a group of people talking about leadership, it is often when I first introduce the word "instinct" that I feel the coldest draught from the audience. Animals have instincts; humans have intelligence. How dare I call my audience animals? What science has learnt over the past twenty years is that humans have more instincts, and better developed instincts, than animals. Our instincts for survival, competition, caring for our community, and for language are part of the reason why humans have become so successful. For humans, our instincts are strengths not constraints.

"Defining 'instinct' has baffled so many scientists that some refuse to use the word altogether. It need not be present from birth: some instincts only develop in adult animals. . . . It need not be inflexible. . . . It need not be automatic. . . . And the boundaries between instinctive and learned behaviour are blurred."[4] If there are elements of what makes us tick that are instinctive, however, it is better to know about them than to ignore them.

If I am different from someone else, how much of that difference is due to our different experiences of the world, and how much is innate? This is an important leadership question because it helps me sort out those characteristics in the other person's behavior I can significantly influence from those I will have to live with.

One clue to unravelling this important question comes from studying identical twins. They share the same genes.

"Identical twins think and feel in such similar ways that they sometimes suspect they are linked by telepathy. When separated at birth and reunited as adults, they say they feel they have known each other all their lives. Testing confirms that identical twins, whether separated at birth or not, are eerily alike (though far from identical) in just about any trait one can measure. They are similar in verbal, mathematical, and general intelligence, in their degree of life satisfaction, and in personality traits such as introversion, agreeableness, neuroticism, conscientiousness, and openness to experience. They have similar attitudes to controversial issues such as the death penalty, religion, and modern music. They resemble each other not just in paper-and-pencil tests but in consequential behavior such as gambling, divorcing, committing crimes, getting into accidents, and watching television."[5]

What this means is that, as a leader, if you want to use the "horses for courses" approach, and have identical twins on your team, they are most likely to operate best on the same course. But at another level, you know that one possible result of doing this is that the twins themselves may want to emphasize their differences. If part of their shared character is competitiveness, this may be even more apparent. They will want to compete with each other.

This is to some extent because "what we call personality is to a considerable degree a question of brain chemistry. . . . It is an intimate part of our make-up, and our genes are programmed not only to produce social behavior, but to respond to it as well."[6] Our genetic makeup is fixed. What is not so certain is how our genes will respond to what is going on around us.

"Experience seems actually to switch on certain genes, which in turn switch on others."[7] It's a two-way street. It suggests that some of our genetic makeup is potential. Unless certain things happen, the potential to do things remains untapped. For example, although it seems that all human beings have the potential for language, the "language instinct," where children have grown up away from people or from anyone willing to talk to them, they reach an age after which it is impossible for them to learn to talk.

The perceived threat that, by mapping the human genome scientists would make the awful discovery that we are all robots, following the dictates of our genes, disappears when we recognize that, although genes are "selfish" and, of themselves, biological mechanisms with no consciousness, how they influence our behavior is far from determined. "Genes themselves are implacable little determinists, churning out utterly predictable messages. But because of the way their promoters switch on and off in response to external instruction, genes are very far from being fixed in their actions. Instead, they are devices for extracting information from the environment. Every minute, every second, the pattern of genes being expressed in your brain changes, often in direct or indirect response to events outside the body. Genes are the mechanisms of experience."[8]

So if genes do not determine our behavior, but represent the potential for certain character traits, what kinds of experience activate this potential? What Freud taught us is that "there are such things as 'formative experiences'; that they come very early; and that they are still powerfully present in the adult subconscious."[9] But what Freud got wrong was his insistence that character is formed primarily through the influence of our parents. There is now a mass of evidence to show that the environmental, as opposed to the genetic influence of our parents on our character is minimal.[10] We are like our parents because of our shared genes, not because they brought us up.

Extremely bad parenting can have a lasting impact, of course. But studies show that how children respond to different kinds of parenting varies so much that no one style of parenting is guaranteed to deliver one kind of personality in the child.[11] If you are a very bad parent, you may screw up a child, but if you are a very good parent, you have absolutely no guarantee that the child will develop into a good adult.

One of the stories I hear quite often is:

"My parents were very strict. . . ."

Like the two stories at the beginning of this chapter, this is another that carries with it different lessons. Strict parents teach some people the value of clear guidelines and boundaries, the value of rules and the need for responsibility in life. They teach others that you have to break free as soon as you can; that imposing your own views on others is counter-productive, and that people have to discover what's right and wrong in their own way.

Once again, we have a problem. If neither your experiences in childhood alone, nor your parents' ways of bringing you up can explain your character, where does your character come from?

People who believe that a significant part of the answer really does come from what happens to us in our early years have researched character-formation within peer groups. "Each child soon realizes what he or she is good at and what he or she is bad at – compared the others in the group. He then trains for that role and not for others, acting in character, developing still further the talent he has and neglecting the talent he lacks."[12]

One of the possible reasons why further studies of peer group influence on our characters is potentially fruitful is that the peer group offers a far richer set of possibilities to "realize what you are good at." Relationships between parent and child are highly constrained by their very lack of reciprocity – parents rule, children depend. Even in large families, birth-order sets strong limits to reciprocal relationships. At least in a peer group you have a good chance of taking a leadership role.

As an explanation of the roots of character, however, the influence of your peer group as a child, simply shifts the problem. You realize what you are good at, but where does that talent come from in the first place?

Let's back off here. The scientific debate will go on and on. All I want to do here is to reinforce the key message about where character comes from.

The key message is that, if your leadership strategy is best developed on the foundations of your character, you need a deeper understanding of yourself than you will get by looking back at the text of your life story. *The meanings you give to your story, and not just the story itself, should tell you the kind of person you are.*

Developing character

"As you grow up, you gradually express your own innate intelligence and leave behind the influences stamped on you by others. You select the environments that suit your innate tendencies, rather than adjusting your innate tendencies to the environments you find yourself in."[13] Which is all very well if you can always do so. But life is never that simple, and much of what happens to us in our lives frustrates this kind of selection, or "niche-picking" as the social psychologists call it.

As you look back on your life, and how it illuminates the development of your character, you will recognize a tension between times when you have been able to move towards "environments that suit your innate tendencies" and those in which you have had environments thrust upon you.

Within these environments, you may have acquired "core values" you think you believe in, like the comical sock-wearer in Chapter 1. If you are unable to disentangle those beliefs that you have acquired from those which are true to your core character, you may be experiencing one of the most common causes of stress in the work environment – trying to be someone you are not.[14]

Are parts of your supposed character like a hideous family photograph you keep on the shelf because you ought to, but deep down you would like to dump? As you read through this book, please keep trying to sift out what is really you from the bits and pieces you may have been constrained to pick up for reasons of expediency.

If this proves too difficult, there are hundreds of books you could turn to that may help. None is perfect, but you may find *T A Today*[15] helpful. It is not built around the model I am using in this book, but it is a good way of sifting through your life story and separating the wheat from the chaff.

If you go back to your own stories, think what you have learnt from them, and why you have drawn the conclusions you have. If you grew up in poverty, did this teach you to strive for success or that happiness does not depend on wealth? If your parents were strict, did you learn discipline or that rules are there to be broken?

There seems to be a very good reason why experiences do not carry with them their own meanings. The fact that you put your own stamp on your memories is, at least in part, due to the fact that "The acquisition of a memory is distinct from its retrieval; different genes are needed in different parts of the brain."[16] Remembering what happened is not like putting a photograph into a box and then picking it out again. It is more like putting the photograph into a box and then trying to draw it from memory. Remembering is a creative act, influenced by our genes, and reconstructing the meanings that we are temperamentally inclined to put upon the memories.

You don't just remember, you rewrite the past. And how you rewrite the past tells you a great deal about your character.

"Having a certain set of genes predisposes a person to experience a certain environment. Having 'sporty' genes makes you want to practise at sport; having 'intellectual' genes makes you seek out intellectual activities."[17] Having genes that give you a thrill when you win will make your stories those of success. Having pacifist genes will make your stories those that prove the futility of fighting.

This, of course, is too simple. People do not have a gene for sportiness or a gene for pacifism. But it is certain that the ways in which we have experiences and then recall them is influenced by the interaction of genes, proteins and hormones within our brains. And here, it is the experience that takes the lead.

One reason why some people find it hard to believe in the genetic bases of behavior is that they think of it as a one-way street, with genes at one end of the chain, and what people do at the other. That's not true.

When we experience stress, our bodies secrete a hormone called cortisol. This switches on certain genes in our systems. Genes respond; they don't just determine.[18] The complexity of what happens when we are under stress is enormous. But there are two important factors to bring out.

The first is that such complexity in our systems means that people are not at the mercy of their genes. Accepting that genes play a part in what we do does not mean we cannot make choices. We do.

The second point, however, is that there are some people who are temperamentally more prone to stress than others, who therefore experience situations as stressful that other people find unthreatening. "I've had a stressful day," says either that the day has been stressful, or that the speaker is a person who gets stressed easily. Or both.

If you are easily stressed, then it is likely that you will experience situations as stressful; to that extent being the kind of person you are, your life story is more likely to be a story of stress and worry; you'll simply have more cortisol to deal with than more phlegmatic types. But you can still make choices. If you are sensible, you will make life choices that reduce the chances of being in situations which are likely to cause stress. Knowing this about yourself puts you back in charge – even if you cannot guarantee that you'll never be faced with stressful situations.

If you are the kind of person who suffers stress more than others, don't put yourself in career or domestic situations that will increase your chances of getting heart disease, cancer or memory-loss, three of the common outcomes of high levels of cortisol in your system that result from experiencing stress.

The message is simple. Make life choices that are in tune with the kind of person you are and you will be happier and healthier.

The key message is: match your lifestyle with your character; and that includes matching your leadership style to that character, too. Just as it would be silly for a stressful person to seek out stressful situations, so it is silly for competitive people to try to develop a character and leadership style that denies the values of competitiveness.

Two dimensions of character

Character is complex. Each of us is different. In Chapter 2, I referred to the human tendency to classify and that, despite the dangers of stereotyping, such classifications can be useful.

The model of character I am using in this book carries with it this mixture of risk and usefulness. By sticking to only two dimensions, the model is simpler than many others.

By comparison, consider the 12 dimensional model used by Carol Pearson.[19] Here she articulates "Twelve archetypes to help us find ourselves and transform our world." It's an exciting idea and I think it provides a lot of insights, especially around the way in which our stories bring out some of the key elements of our characters. But I find the idea of shifting between 12 different mindsets, trying to bring out the strengths of each of these elements of character, a bit too daunting. Perhaps that says something about my character.

The other concern I have with models like this is that they don't rest on the kind of science I believe we should not ignore when considering character. In some respects it fails to answer the question, "why 12 and not 10, or 24, or 16?" Many of the psychometric tools available these days have the same "arbitrary classification" problem. As simply classifications and descriptions of behaviors, the boundaries they draw between types may be no better at reflecting what goes on than any other. If none of them do more than describe and classify behaviors, and if they offer no explanation of what may influene your behaviors, how do you choose which classificatory model to work with?

More robust from this point of view is the Myers Briggs Type Indicator™ (MBTI™); I have noted my favorite book on this in the Bibliography at the end of the book. The MBTI™ has the obvious merit of being very popular and widely known in organizations. Although first developed many years ago on the basis of a theory devised in the 1920s by the Swiss psychologist Carl Jung, and well before the recent researches into brain, mind and behavior, it does seem to reflect a great deal about how the human brain develops.

For example, Donaldson[20] has developed a model of the "unfolding" of human minds whose component parts are a very close match to the MBTI™ model, although at no point in her book does she cite Jung or any other writer on the MBTI™. Her conclusions seem to be so close not because she has been influenced by this other school of thought, but because she has come, independently, to very similar conclusions.

I have used the MBTI™ for many years in my work with leaders. As a tool for exploring style it is brilliant. But although it really helps in understanding how people operate, it does not and cannot touch upon why they do the things they do. As a tool for explaining how I am likely most effectively to achieve my goals, it has no equal. But as a tool for explaining what those goals may be it doesn't even get to the starting gate. That's not what it was designed for.

Although I have come across tools that, like the one in this book, do try to get at the heart of what drives us, none that I have found get over the "arbitrary classification" problem.

This model, I believe, has deep roots in the science of genetics and behavior. It looks at two dimensions of character that really do lie at the heart of who we are and what we fundamentally believe in.

At either end of each of the dimensions lies what I referred to earlier as "instincts." All human beings have instincts for survival, competition, caring for our community and for language. Since people are complex, and have thousands of thoughts and feelings, instincts influence us in an enormous variety of ways, many of which we rationalize as considered choices. But few parents *choose* to love their children; they just *do* love them.

In that process of rationalization, however, we may lose sight of the many and various ways in which our instincts actually do underpin an enormous amount of what we do, simply because it feels right. It also makes it difficult to untangle what we have learnt through experience from what comes naturally. That is why, as we explore each of these instincts, we shall see that they affect a broad range of thoughts and feelings that may not obviously be clustered together as responses to the same instinctive drives.

The key message is that some of the most important but least conscious of the ways in which our behaviors are influenced are instinctive. We don't learn them; *they are an inherent part of what it means to be human.*

But one thing that is puzzling about these instincts is that, to some extent, they contradict each other.

Survival

This is, clearly, not an instinct that is unique to humans. What is interesting is that, like the other instincts that have evolved in humans, it has developed into a sophisticated set of drivers.

Survival lives in the emotional world of risk and danger. Were it not for dangers from the environment, there would have been no reason for its evolution. As humans evolved, as a species we became social. Families and clans became the environment in which infants grew up. This proved a mixed blessing for the survival of the individual. On the one hand, the grown-ups were there to protect; on the other, being bigger than infants, they could at times, impose a threat as well as afford protection.

So as individuals, we had to learn what was a threat and what represents safety. Learning can be a chore, but it can also be fun. Our survival instinct evolved alongside our instinct to play, and by playing, learn valuable lessons on survival. Through the rough-and-tumble of play, individuals learnt their place in the "pecking-order," how far you can push the alpha male before receiving a punitive swipe, how far you can jump before you have to be picked up and dusted down.

And who learns the most? The risk-taker. Ironically, our instinct for survival underpins our tendency to take risks. Risk taking is fun. Pushing boundaries is fun. Being punished for misdemeanours is not fun. Being held back from experimentation is not fun. Being free to play and be myself is fun.

This is even more true if you are relatively responsive to levels of a hormone called dopamine in your brain. Receptivity to hormones is, to some degree, dependent upon genes. Although it would be too simple to equate different versions of a single gene with "novelty seeking personalities" it is not inconceivable that it is down to how receptive to dopamine each individual is that makes them more or less of a risk-taker in their character.[21]

The problem with having fun, taking risks, living on the edge and pushing back the boundaries is that, while you are indulging in all this, you are not taking responsibility for others.

In our model, this aspect of character is called the "Adventurer."[22]

Caring for the community

Humans make extraordinary sacrifices for others. Genes may be "selfish," but they have been at least partly responsible for the development of an instinct to take care of others, to nurture, to protect and provide. And we humans have evolved a highly developed sense of this kind of responsibility, leading to charitable works, acts of bravery (or stupidity, if you think that way) in battle – throwing yourself onto a wounded fellow soldier to take the full blast of a grenade, and the acceptance of accountability for thousands of others' lives.

This is the other side of the coin from survival in several senses. Its evolution in the context of a social habitat enables us to understand why this instinct may have developed beyond caring for only direct biological offspring. Looking after a sister's baby looks after the gene pool, even if not so directly. Looking after other strong males may reduce another male's chances of impregnating as many females as possible (a typical drive for the Adventurer), but it does maintain the collective strength of the clan or group.

If receptivity to dopamine may play a part in how strong your Adventurer instinct may be, receptivity to oxytocin could be a significant player in how responsible you feel toward others.[23] One of the effects of oxytocin is to increase faithfulness and commitment. Without these behaviors, it is unlikely that you would be bothered with the welfare of others.

In our model, this aspect of character is called the "Guardian."

Competition

There is no surprise that evolution should have given us an instinct to fight. For long periods of the development of the species, we had to fight for territory, food and mates. In the words of Robert Winston, humans are "super competitive."

As our instinct to compete developed, it brought with it an important rider: at least temporary suppression of any compassion for the loser. It would have been counter-productive for hunters to pause for too long and empathize with the antelope he was about to kill. And even though many societies that practise hunting have a deep, often religious respect for nature, and take pains to preserve the local fauna, the deer still gets it.

In our culture, this instinct finds its outlet in two significant ways. The most obvious is sport. Take away this instinct, and the whole enterprise becomes pointless and stupid. The artificiality of people in strange outfits chasing after an inflated piece of leather with the view to getting into some arbitrary space called a goal, or people using sticks to get a small white ball into a series of holes in the ground (when it would be so much easier to simply place it in each hole) is obscured by this instinct.

The other manifestation the competitive instinct lies in western capitalism, which is inherently competitive. Companies strive to beat the opposition, to capture market share, and to win customers.

As with the non-specific nature of the other instincts, our need to win moves with us, from sporting team to team (witness the transfer system, in which a player quickly changes allegiances to the new team) and from company to company. Such moves immediately convert former "homes" into "enemies" to be beaten.

One reason why we have invented sport is that what we evolved to compete for is no longer scarce. In western culture, food is abundant; the state has taken over responsibility for territorial battles; and roughly the same number of males and females are born in societies where monogamy is the norm.

The scarcity that fuelled the evolution of the instinct to compete has been cleverly replicated in sport by the invention of the "trophy." Whether this be a gold medal or a silver cup, it is the symbolic rather than the market value that drives individuals and teams to win it. Although it would be possible to make and distribute copies of the cup to all participants in a sporting competition, this would somehow "miss the point." There has to be only one winner.

The reason the trophy is valuable lies in the physical nature of the trophy; if I have it you don't have it.

It is likely that the hormone most active in competition is testosterone, although during any competition, hefty doses of adrenaline help fuel the fight.

In our model, this aspect of character is called the "Warrior."

Language

For the Warrior, it is the physical nature of the trophy that is important. If I have something, such as a car, a medal or some food, then by giving it to you, I don't have it any more. But with the evolution of the instinct for language something quite different happened: "A recipe for bread, a blueprint for a building, a technique for growing rice, a formula for a drug, a useful scientific law or computer program can be given away without anything being subtracted from the giver."[24] Ideas, unlike things can be shared without the giver being any worse off. They are what one writer calls "nonrival goods."[25]

It is true, in practice, that "this seemingly magical proliferation of nonrival goods has recently confronted us with new problems concerning intellectual property, as we try to adapt a legal system that was based on owning stuff to the problem of owning information . . ."[26] But this is just one example of the contradiction between the Warrior and what our model refers to as the Sage.

For the Sage the fact that ideas and information are "nonrival" that is important. If the Warrior operated in the world of things, the Sage operates in the world of ideas, made possible by our instinct for language. In this world, ideas are not owned, information is infinitely shareable, and the goal is not winning, but learning.

For the Sage, learning is an end in itself. I have come across many Warriors who are voracious readers, who are hungry for knowledge. But for the Warrior, learning has an ulterior motive: knowledge is power. Using knowledge for gain is, in the spirit of the Sage, to cheapen it.

To recap, in our model, this aspect of the love of learning is what defines the Sage.

How the two dimensions influence character

One way to represent the four key instinctive influences on character is as follows:

Each pole of each dimension contradicts the other. Risk-taking and responsibility do not sit side by side. Ideas and things are different universes. Yet people all share these four instincts for survival, caring for others, competition and language. What makes us different is which end of each dimension is the dominant part of our character.

It is likely, given the evidence from the research I have referred to in this chapter, that the particular instinct from each pair which is dominant for each of us, is to a large extent decided by our genetic make up.

Consider the two stories I referred to at the beginning of this chapter.

> *"I grew up in a very poor neighbourhood. We were always short of money, and had to make do with the bare essentials."*

If I am being told this story by someone who is more Warrior than Sage, I would expect to hear that he or she has learnt that you have to stretch yourself, to go for it, and to make sure that, through your own endeavors, you achieve what you could not achieve in childhood. But if I am talking to a Sage, the chances are he or she would say money can't buy you love; the best things in life are free, and I find contentment in family, community and humility

The other story was:

> *"In my early childhood one of my parents ran off and left us."*

For a person who is more Guardian the story is more likely to have taught them the need for caring, responsibility, and sticking to the family. For the Adventurer, the experience is more likely to set them free, learning early in life how to fend for themselves and to depend on no-one.

Life's experiences, and the lessons we learn from them, often reinforce our tendencies to believe in what we believe. I am not saying that we cannot learn new things, or that a Warrior will always see things exclusively through a Warrior's eyes. But on balance, I believe that, as Margaret Thatcher put it, "history's lessons usually teach us what we want to learn."[27]

At this point of the explanation of the model, people often say to me, "I think I'm a bit of all of these." They are right. The point of the model is not to amputate any part of your character. You are Warrior, Guardian, Adventurer and Sage. We all are.

Here's an analogy. Are you right or left handed? Most people can and do answer this quickly and easily. They know which hand they use to write and for tasks that require either dexterity or strength. Right handers reinforce the dominance of their right hands by developing skills for such tasks mostly by using their right hands for those tasks. A natural tendency to right-handedness gets strengthened through experience. But few right-handers stop using their left hands altogether.

In much the same way, Warriors can use their Sage throughout life and do so. But when having to choose which to use, Warriors are more likely to operate in their Warrior mode. It comes naturally, just as you don't stop to think, each time you pick up a pen, "which hand shall I write with today?"

Using this analogy, one end of each dimension is like your right hand, the other like your left. I don't know if you are right or left handed. I don't know if you are Warrior or Sage, Guardian or Adventurer. Do you?

The international question

So what of culture? Earlier in the chapter I referred to how I came to believe in the exclusive role of a person's culture in forming his or her character, and how I had to admit I was wrong. But given the obvious differences between cultures and how people behave in different cultures, does this mean that some cultures contain more Warriors and others more Sages?

I shall provide some evidence in later chapters, based on data I have collected from working in many different cultures in many different parts of the world that the answer to that question is "no."

The research I have cited suggests that genes exert a strong influence on character. If scientists found out that the genes associated with behavior are unevenly distributed across the globe, this would suggest a genetic basis for cultural difference. But scientists have found the opposite to be true. "The genetic differences between two individuals chosen at random from one race are far greater than the average differences between races."[28]

There are roughly the same number of Warriors in Nepal as there are in Japan, and roughly the same number of Guardians on Hong Kong as in Italy. You may be better understood as an Adventurer in Australia than you may be in Britain. But that is more to do with history than with evolution.

Warrior or sage, guardian or adventurer?

By now you may be very clear about which elements of character are stronger in you, whether you are better described as Warrior or Sage, Guardian or Adventurer. If that is the case, the next five chapters may best serve as a check on how closely the case studies match your own character.

If you are still uncertain where you fit on either of the two dimensions, the case material may help to resolve this for you. In looking more closely at the stories of Margaret Thatcher, Mahatma Gandhi, Franklin D Roosevelt and Martin Luther King Jr., I hope to show how these elements of character inform the reputations of each leader, but also how they played a part in their less public, more personal lives.

I believe that the consistency between these personal and public personae go some of the way to explaining why these otherwise ordinary people have become such legends.

CHAPTER 4

Values

Where your values come from

The values you hold are a key part of how you see yourself. Whether you know the capital of Peru is trivial. Whether you believe in the sanctity of the family is not. In some respects, we are what we believe in.

And what you believe in is likely to be a key influence on what opinions you hold. In Chapter 2, I looked at how opinions form a very significant part of how people talk to each other, and how differing opinions can have a major impact on the reputation of a leader. Of course, opinions are formed partly on the basis of evidence, but that very evidence is itself often a matter of interpretation. I suggested that considering a leader's action as brave or stupid is not so much a matter of gathering further information as of matching what you see a leader doing against what, for you, is "bravery" or "stupidity."

One of the key influences on your opinions is your set of values. Someone who values bravery is more likely to interpret an action as brave rather than as stupid.

In this chapter I shall explore the ways in which values differ between those most commonly held by Warriors and Sages, Guardians and Adventurers. This will take you another step towards clarifying your own character. It will also help you to look into the minds of people whose characters are different from yours.

The fact that Warriors are likely to hold similar values is partly a matter of definition. If you believe what most Warriors believe in, then, to some extent, that makes you a Warrior. But it is also partly a matter of the development of character.

Where does the set of values I believe in come from?

Until recently scientists believed that our value set is learnt from our parents. This has changed. "When you describe somebody as having a certain personality, you are intending to refer to some intrinsic part of their nature that is beyond the influence of other people – the content of their character, to borrow a famous phrase. By definition, you mean something unique to them. It is, however, counter-intuitive after a century of Freudian certainties to find out how little that intrinsic character is influenced by the family they grew up in."[1]

People born to be Guardians will almost always, whatever happens in their lives, believe in Guardian values. Even if they grow up in Adventurer environments, they will learn from the experience that, in the end, all this personal freedom is irresponsible. Adventurers brought up in Guardian cultures will rebel – big time – and celebrate Adventurer values in spite of the teachings of their youth.

Developing self-awareness is often a matter of scratching beneath the surface to find the real person beneath the veneer of acquired "values." We'll talk about this in chapter 6.

Religion, politics and values

Many of the values people hold are associated with their religion, if they have one. It is obvious that the religion a person follows is not innate. The religious beliefs a person holds are highly influenced by the culture they grow up in. Being a Christian or a Hindu has nothing to do with your genes.

"There is a partly heritable aspect of human nature, which might be called religiosity, and it is distinct from other attributes of personality."[2] In other words, there are many different ways of embracing most of the major religions. History shows that you can be a Guardian Christian, a Warrior Christian, a Sage Christian, and even an Adventurer Christian. The same is true of Islam.

To avoid further theological debate on specific religions, let me just say that I believe that being religious or atheist, Christian or Muslim will have a significant impact on how your values will be articulated. But I do not believe it will fundamentally change your character.

The same is true of politics. There are plenty of Socialist Warriors as well as Conservative Warriors. Being an Adventurer is no predictor of your political leanings. Character, as mapped out in the model in this book, goes deeper than even religion and politics.

But it does not go deeper than morality.

Morality and values

Character and morality are inextricably entwined: "The notion of *character* joins the moral picture, and with it the notion of moral identity: the concept of one's own character that is maintained internally and projected to others."[3] This is because the values we hold are, for us, the right values. And they are right not because we can prove them to be so by any scientific method, but because they are morally right.

Some people do try to prove the rightness of what they believe by looking beyond morality. One common mistake (sometimes called the "naturalistic fallacy") is to say that something must be right because it is natural. This is one popular argument against homosexuality. It is also used to prove the rightness of, amongst other things, hierarchies, democracy, war, peace, co-operation, competition, and "family values."

That something is natural does not make it right. And in any case, there are a great many scientists kept in employment solely for the purpose of demonstrating that last year's "natural" is this year's exception. Similarly, history is swamped with stories of wars and repression all based on attempting to restore what the perpetrators saw as the "natural order." This not the place to critique Hitler's "final solution" nor any other such moral crusade.

Let's just say that what you believe is right is so not because of any other factor than that you believe it to be so. And you believe it because that's the kind or person you are. The challenge is to try to get on with people who are not like you, and who, as a consequence do not believe in what you do.

By "values" I do not mean attitudes. During my lifetime, attitudes to homosexuality have changed. In my youth, homosexual acts between men were illegal. Now it is illegal to discriminate against homosexuals. Attitudes change; values tend to remain constant. Some people I work with tell me that the model of leadership in this book does not work because they have changed. In most cases, the changes they refer to are changes in their attitudes, not their underlying values.

The chances are you have changed a number of your attitudes over the years. As you look at the values discussed in this chapter, consider how they differ from those changing attitudes.

Margaret Thatcher, Warrior

What's your image of Margaret Thatcher? The chances are that your political views will influence the image you have of her as a politician. But even if you never met her, I guess you'll also have some views on her personality. In many cases, people I talk to find it hard to separate these two views. One strongly influences the other.

That's not surprising. I have already suggested that, in leadership what comes first is character; strategy develops later. For successful politicians, the way in which strategy grows out of personality is one of their strengths. As one of Margaret Thatcher's biographers says, "those who have watched the political process at close hand are never in doubt that personalities matter."[4]

Biographers often use their writings to try to correct biased reputations. Although not a loyal supporter of Margaret Thatcher, Sergeant tells us, "It may have suited her self-image to appear unbending and at times ideologically committed to a particular cause, but this is not a rounded picture of Mrs. Thatcher as prime minister. She was essentially a practical politician, not an ideologue. She may have given the impression of doggedly following a single course, but she would duck and weave like any other successful politician, and sometimes she regretted what she had done."[5]

In cultures where myths are the primary currency of story-telling, there is no need for narrators to hedge like this. It is a feature of the mythologies of most cultures that the names of the characters are the same as adjectives in their language – adjectives that mean the very characteristics the people in the myths represent. In Greek mythology, for example, the name "Eros" literally means "love." In our culture, some legends spark off this kind of link – the word "Thatcherite," for example, is an attempt to match the legend with the qualities.

In this book, I am going to tell the stories of the four key characters as legends. For that reason I will not dwell on situations in which they acted "out of character," even though each of them did at some time or another. For example, when challenged for the leadership of the Conservative Party in 1990, according to Sir Bernard Ingham, her press secretary, "she was a fighter, and she didn't fight. It was out of character."[6]

My focus will be on Margaret Thatcher the Iron Lady, once referred to by Tass (the Russian newsagency credited with first using that name for her) as The Cold War Warrior[7], and classified by Patrick Cosgrave, one of her advisors at one time "as a warrior."[8]

The legendary Margaret Thatcher demonstrated all the common values of the Warrior. If the biographies are right (including her two-volume autobiography) so did the woman.

These are the Warrior values.

Achievement and accomplishment

Warriors value achieving or accomplishing things, often for the sake of achievement itself. Being Prime Minister for 13 years was nowhere near enough for Margaret Thatcher. When she stepped down in 1990 to avoid defeat in a re-run of the party's leadership election, one of her primary concerns was what she was going to do with her time. Thoughts of retiring and relaxing, resting on her laurels never entered her head. She had to work, because, as she herself writes, "I would have gone mad without work."[9]

I have met many Warriors from different walks of life. They share a tendency to being workaholic. For some, the products and services they work to deliver are hardly exciting or, in some cases, particularly worthwhile. If you want to understand the drive for accomplishment of the Warrior, don't look at what they want to achieve itself; look at the need simply to achieve.

This valuing of doing something (almost anything) surfaced for Margaret Thatcher most strongly when she had to face the prospect of no longer being prime minister. "Throughout my deliberately busy life I have been able to find solace for personal disappointments by forgetting the past and taking up some new venture. Work was my secret elixir."[10]

For Warriors, the drive for achievement and accomplishment comes first; the actual goals come later. Achievement is for achievement's sake.

Winning

Warriors love winning, whatever they engage in. As a politician, Margaret Thatcher spent a lot of time arguing with people. As a Warrior, this was not a problem for her. "Margaret loves argument, and particularly loves winning."[11] On receiving advice on being a little more diplomatic, her response was typically Warrior. She could see the point her advisors were making, but, in her view, "However commendable, this inevitably cramped my attacking style."[12] It is the Warrior who has immortalized the proverb, "the best form of defence is attack."

Winning is thrilling, especially to the Warrior. Successful sportspeople know how winning can make you ignore everything else, including cracked ribs and broken necks. Margaret Thatcher exemplified this in a television interview before an election. Questioned about some of the policies she was advocating, and the discomfort those policies may bring to some people, her reply was, "Elections are not about sensitivities, they're about victories."

Competition

I remember overhearing a conversation at a garden party in which a woman was complaining to a colleague of mine about her children's school. In her view, the competitive nature of the house system and of their approach to physical education was far too competitive. My colleague's reply was, "It should be competitive. The world is competitive." My colleague is a Warrior.

Warriors agree with the "nature red in tooth and claw" approach to the world. For the Warrior, if you don't fight, they'll walk all over you.

Competition is a value because it fits what the world demands. Throughout her memoirs, Margaret Thatcher used competitive language. For example, describing a bitter debate with her cabinet colleagues on budgetary issues, she says, "Round one went to Geoffrey and me."[13]

Fighting for no reason is anti-social. Therefore Warriors often seek out causes to compete for. And Warrior politicians know that they will win more support if their fights are for the common good. Margaret Thatcher "was never, it seemed, happier than when she was involved in a fight which could be portrayed as virtuous."[14]

The point is that there are Warriors competing on all sides. Footballers, for example, compete for the team they happen to be playing for at the time, even if their first match for their new side is against the team they have just transferred from. What Warriors have in common is not the cause or the team but the competition itself. Warriors come as Conservatives and Labor, Republican and Democrat, right and left.

Advancement and promotion

The desire to get on, proving your value by making progress through whatever system you work in or role you take on is important to the Warrior for two reasons. The first is that it provides you with greater power with which to compete. The second is that it is one of the trophies Warriors seek – status.

The drive to gain status through qualifications, a title, or any other means underpins a great deal of the choices Warriors make. Margaret Thatcher exemplified this when the twins were born. "Margaret was delighted with her offspring and has remained in many ways besotted by her children. But she was not one to be over sentimental. Right there and then in her hospital bed she determined to put her name down for the Bar Finals in December, which would force her to complete the course and have the qualification she wanted, twins or no twins."[15]

The Warrior's potentially single-minded focus on advancement and promotion can sometimes overwhelm less committed people. At University, "Margaret remained aloof. They had fun: she didn't. She went through four years at the university with few friends, generating a feeling, shared by many of her contemporaries, that she was only prepared to offer friendship to those people who might be of some use to her on her climb up the ladder."[16]

I have noticed a tendency for some people I work with to feel reluctant to admit to valuing advancement and promotion, even when it is clear through our conversations that, in truth, they do.

The shifting sands of social attitudes to words can sometimes get in the way for people who are trying to understand their true values. If you are getting stuck on advancement and promotion as a core value, try renaming it "ambition." Are you ambitious? Few Warriors I have met have a problem with this, as 'ambition' in our culture has retained its "hooray" factor, even if "advancement and promotion" have collected some "boo" factor.

Incidentally, when I then ask my Warriors what they are ambitious for, it only takes a few minutes to get back to advancement and promotion.

Margaret Thatcher remained immune to this kind of political correctness. For her, "people must look to themselves first. It's our duty to look after ourselves and then to look after our neighbour."[17] In other words, you are better placed to look after your neighbor if you gain for yourself the power to do so.

Fame

The political correctness that makes some Warriors hesitant to admit to valuing advancement and promotion has hit "fame" even harder. But for the Warrior, being renowned and respected is crucial. The Warrior seeks to be known and held in high esteem for whatever he or she decides to focus on. Fame is one of the rewards that have been tarnished by the cult of celebrity, and it's not surprising that some Warriors feel that their self-respect would be damaged if they admitted to wanting the kind of celebrity that is afforded to large numbers of nonentities whose only claim to fame is fame itself.

Again, it is the word that has suffered from a shift in attitude, not the underlying value. I could use the phrase "positive reputation among large numbers of people" instead of fame. It would mean the same, but be so much easier for Warriors to admit to.

Not many Warriors would honestly say, "I wish far fewer people knew about me." Margaret Thatcher was not unhappy that "Soviet propaganda had dubbed her the 'Iron lady' and this image of her became a fixture on the European scene."[18]

When she won her first election in 1959 as MP for Finchley, she describes how she felt: "I was home and dry – and not just with plenty to spare but with a majority of 16,260, almost 3500 more than my predecessor. The cheers, always more controlled from Tory than from Liberal or socialist lips, rose."[19] These two sentences are about more than the cheers for her as a person. They also show her competitiveness in citing how many more votes she got than her predecessor. Note also the put-down for Liberals and socialists. Another victory.

One reason for Warrior's reluctance to admit to wanting fame is the cult of modesty, an attitude that, like others, shifts with time. But modesty does not fit well with the Warrior. If you want to strive, to win, and to achieve, having belief in yourself is a powerful weapon. At the start of her premiership, Margaret Thatcher's self-confidence was clear: "Chatham famously remarked: 'I know that I can save this country and that no-one else can.' It would have been presumptuous of me to have compared myself to Chatham. But if I'm honest, I must admit that my exhilaration came from a similar inner conviction."[20]

Fortune and material wealth

The instinct to compete evolved most strongly when the species was living in dangerous times and when what you needed for survival was potentially scarce. The trophies of sport and the visible signs of success are evidence you have won despite that scarcity.

Warriors value fortune and material wealth because they demonstrate success in challenging ventures. Many Warriors say they deserve the Rolls Royce or Porsche they drive, since they have worked hard to achieve it. Warriors earn their wealth and the physical symbols that their wealth can afford.

In a competitive economy, Warriors make the system work by driving for the success of their own organizations, and by playing a key part in the consumption of goods that the economy produces. Economists know that when people stop buying, the economy suffers.

Margaret Thatcher's wealth was, until her retirement from Parliament, second-hand. Dennis was a successful businessman, also a Warrior. Subsequently she could command very large sums for her lectures. Although she was not renowned for gathering around her the physical trappings of success, and made much of her frugality as a housewife, she did like to entertain with proper silverware (not available when she moved into Number 10), and did like to make a point with the way she kitted out her new home in 1979: "I also had some fine portraits hung of the nation's heroes; through them you could feel the continuity of British history. I recall on one occasion watching President Giscard d'Estaing gazing at two portraits in the dining room – one of the young Nelson and the other of Wellington. He remarked on the irony. I replied that it was no less ironic that I should have to look at portraits of Napoleon on my visits to Paris. In retrospect, I can see that this was not quite a parallel. Napoleon lost."[21]

Defending your territory

The Warrior deals quickly with all threats, real or perceived. The most justified of all competitions, fighting back against an aggressor is absolutely right. "Turning the other cheek" is very hard to do. For Margaret Thatcher, the

Argentine invasion of the Falkland Islands posed few dilemmas. As she later wrote, "war was a terrible evil, but there were worse things, including the extinction of all that one believed in. We could not let aggression succeed."[22]

When she came face to face with the 1990 challenge to her leadership of the Conservative Party, her initial reaction was to defend her position, her territory. Until she came to realize that she could not win, she rejected the advice from her closest colleagues that almost any result less than a the massive victory that just wasn't going to happen would be undignified. "I would fight – and, if necessary, go down fighting – for my beliefs as long as I could. 'Dignity' did not come into it."[23]

The smart Warrior knows when to back off. He who fights and runs away lives to fight another day. But Warriors hate to back down, and see it as a necessary evil, not to be indulged in too often. As Margaret Thatcher wrote, "Retreat as a tactic is sometimes necessary; retreat as a settled policy eats at the soul."[24]

Physical challenge

In myths, Warriors slay dragons. In the real world, they do the same thing. For Margaret Thatcher, the biggest dragon of all was the National Union of Mineworkers that was holding the country to ransom.

Physical challenge represents the Warrior's drive to stretch him or herself, to do something in the world because it is a challenge. It may be running the marathon in a personal best time, or taking on a new project that will stretch you. On winning the 1979 election, Margaret Thatcher wrote, "Perhaps if I could have foreseen the great roller-coaster of events in the next eleven years . . . I would have felt greater apprehension. Perversely, however, the emotion I felt was exhilaration at the challenge."[25]

Margaret Thatcher's energy was legendary. She could get by with just a few hours' sleep a night, and when she first arrived at Downing Street, "She swept through the place like a hurricane, exuding energy and demanding energy from everyone else. Everything had to be done now, not tomorrow or next week. Everything had to be neat and orderly, and anyone who hadn't grasped her drift by the second telling, felt the rough side of her tongue."[26] Rather than shy away from challenges, the Warrior will relish them.

Being a hero

In some respects we are all the heroes of our own life stories. The kind of hero the Warrior values is he or she who never ceases to strive to better him or herself. Living up to your full potential is a moral duty, and those who show courage and ambition are the Warrior's heroes. Among the heroes in

Margaret Thatcher's pantheon were those members of the Royal Ulster Constabulary who, in defending their territory showed (On members of the RUC) "a quiet, matter-of-fact heroism which I have never ceased to admire."[27]

Margaret Thatcher demonstrated her own heroism after the Brighton bomb, ignoring the fact that she was the intended target, dismissing personal trauma, and taking personal charge of ensuring Norman Tebbit received the treatment he needed. As a Warrior, the enmity of others did not daunt her. It merely strengthened her. Before she became prime minister, as Minister of Education she acquired the nickname "Maggie Thatcher, milk snatcher" and was once voted in a national newspaper "The Most Unpopular Woman in Britain." She wrote of this, "I had incurred the maximum of political odium for the minimum of political benefit. . . . I resolved not to make the same mistake again. In future if I were to be hanged, it would be for a sheep, not a lamb."[28]

Primary motivation: to win and achieve

The values of the Warrior form an agenda for life: to win and achieve. As a governing principle, this motivation allows the Warrior to deal with distractions that could weaken resolve. During the Falklands War, Margaret Thatcher was faced with many such distractions. Were she not so unswerving in her Warrior style, she may have let these get in the way. She didn't. She later wrote, "when you are at war you cannot allow the difficulties to dominate your thinking: you have to set out with an iron will to overcome them."[29]

In her time as Prime Minister, and in the years leading up to her premiership, Margaret Thatcher met a great number of politicians, home and abroad. She expressed her greatest admiration for fellow Warriors. And although she sometimes had good things to say about less Warrior-like leaders, she made it clear that, for her, "personal virtue is no substitute for political hard-headedness."[30] For "political hard-headedness" I think you can safely read "determination to win," even at the expense of "personal virtue."

The key driving force of the Warrior, applied assiduously as Margaret Thatcher showed how, enables Warrior leaders to win and achieve. Successful Warriors find a role, not necessarily in politics, which allows them to follow their instincts and apply themselves to the task of achieving ambitious goals.

It is therefore devastating to the Warrior to have that role snatched away from them. Reflecting on how to apply herself after stepping down from the leadership, Margaret Thatcher realized that there were many opportunities open to her. Many of them looked promising on the face of it, but each of these opportunities had something missing, "a sense of purpose."[31]

In summary, the Warrior is most likely to believe in these values:

- Achievement and accomplishment
- Winning
- Competition
- Advancement and promotion
- Fame
- Fortune and material wealth
- Defending your territory
- Physical challenge
- Being a hero

He or she will be motivated to win and achieve.

Martin Luther King, JR., Adventurer

As one of history's most respected figures, and as a committed Christian preacher, it may not seem obvious at first that Martin Luther King was anything like an "Adventurer." In many ways, his image runs counter to the initial impression of the frivolous, carefree Peter Pan of popular imagination.

The Adventurer is not a child. But within the Adventurer lies a sense that the world is a dangerous place in which one's primary purpose is to survive the constant threat from Captain Hook. To be happy, the Adventurer sees danger as a potential source of fun, and gains enjoyment from getting away with the risks taken and the rules broken.

By breaking the rules, the Adventurer also changes things. Although not working single-handedly, Martin Luther King is credited with bringing about enormous change in the lives of black Americans, especially in the southern states. He was not a legislator; he was no kind of politician at all, never associating himself with any organized political movement. He just stuck his neck out and challenged what at the time seemed an unmoveable status quo. For his pains, he was assassinated. He was pretty sure that was going to happen, and had suffered previous attempts on his life. None deterred him.

As we shall see in more detail later, he was no paragon of virtue. In one of his last sermons he said, "I don't know about you, but I can make a testimony. You don't need to go out saying that Martin Luther King is a saint. Oh no. I want you to know this morning that I'm a sinner like all of God's children. But I want to be a good man."[32] This was not the false modesty often professed by men of the cloth. In terms of what most of his fellow Christians believe in, he really was not a saint at all.

These are the values of the Adventurer.

Freedom

Because of its positive connotations, the word "freedom" can be valued by all, not just the Adventurer. When Franklin D. Roosevelt, the archetypal Guardian in this book, enshrined the "four freedoms" in the charter for the United Nations, it was not the personal freedom of the Adventurer he referred to. For the Adventurer, it is freedom from constraint that is the key value.

This means not being tied down; avoiding responsibilities or constraints; and, if necessary to gain that freedom, by bucking the system.

One of the key challenges for the Adventurer leader is that, as he or she gains followers, they look to the leader for a sense of permanence and continuity. For the Adventurer, this is not always welcome. As Martin Luther King said, "The honours and privileges that often come as a result of leadership contribute only one side of the picture. The greater the privileges, the greater the responsibilities and sacrifices."[33]

The Adventurer is in his or her element when challenging a system; he or she is less comfortable with leading reconstructions. The legacy of other leaders reinforces this: Nelson Mandela was a reluctant President; Lech Walensa, so potent as the leader of the Solidarity movement in Poland, backed off from leadership once the movement's major aims had been achieved.

The Adventurer is in his or her element in times of struggle for freedom. King's view was that "there is nothing more majestic than the determined courage of individuals willing to suffer and sacrifice for their freedom and dignity."[34] The rebellious spirit of the Adventurer enables him or her to put up with a great deal in the cause of achieving that longer term liberation from control. Even to the point of temporarily giving up freedom. Just as Nelson Mandela is remembered for his long years of internment, King knew the inside of many jails:

In 1966 he said, "I've been to jail in Alabama, I've been to jail in Florida, I've been to jail in Georgia, I've been to jail in Mississippi, I've been to jail in Virginia, and I'm ready to go to jail in Chicago."[35] It is one of the ironies of the Adventurer that he or she will put up with being fenced in for the sake of, in the long run, not being fenced in.

Challenging convention

It is not only an Adventurer who will, at some time or another, challenge convention or the status quo. But it is a characteristic of the Adventurer that he or she will do so throughout life. It is part of the essence of the character. King saw this in himself from an early age: "I guess I accepted biblical studies uncritically until I was about twelve years old. But this uncritical attitude could not last long, for it was contrary to the very nature of my being. I had always been the questioning and precocious type."[36]

Earlier I said that having a particular religion is no indicator of the underlying character. Martin Luther King was a devout Christian, but, like so many others, he found within the scriptures messages that were congenial to his own approach to life. From his early studies of the Bible, he identified most strongly with lessons that backed him up in his life's work. For example he wrote, "Jeremiah is a shining example of the truth that religion should never sanction the status quo."[37]

King's selective approach to the status quo stretched beyond religious teachings. Those who fought against him frequently accused him of being simply a criminal, so it was appropriate, in King's view, that he should put the record straight in his famous letter from Birmingham jail. His position was simple. People should obey just laws, but are free to break unjust laws. He explained: "a just law is a law that squares with a moral law. It is a law that squares with that which is right, so that any law that uplifts human personality is a just law."[38]

Although to detractors, some of the behaviors of the Adventurer may look nihilistic – rebelling for the sake of rebelling – leaders who are Adventurers challenge convention for the sake of real change. As King said, "A social movement that only moves people is merely a revolt. A movement that changes both people and institutions is a revolution."[39] Many revolutionaries have been Adventurers. Once again, as with the things the Warrior competes for, there is nothing common in the politics of all revolutionaries, apart from the revolution itself. Revolutions come from the right as well as the left of the political spectrum.

The Adventurer is more likely to start something than to join it. Later, the story of the Adventurer businessman, Richard Branson, will reinforce this in the commercial sphere. For King, there was no "movement" to join. It was coincidental that he was on the scene when Rosa Parks refused to give up her seat to a white passenger on that bus in Montgomery. It was not King's intention to assume a leadership position in the Montgomery Improvement Association (MIA) to which he was elected president. As one writer puts it, "The Montgomery bus boycott thrust King into a leadership position that he did not expect and for which he was largely unprepared."[40]

Joining things means conforming to conventions, the conventions of the organization. As King himself said of his election to the presidency of the MIA, "The action had caught me unawares. It happened so quickly that I did not even have time to think it through. It is probable that if I had, I would have declined the nomination."[41] One of the problems of taking this kind of responsibility is that it makes an individual represent others. The Adventurer needs the freedom to represent only him – or herself.

When King became aware that the Vietnam war represented another struggle of oppressed people against a powerful enemy, he was one of the first in the black movement to oppose it. It made him unpopular with many of his friends and allies. "King was attacked within the civil rights movement and beyond for his daring opposition to war. He broke with other leaders in a dramatic but heartfelt gesture of moral independence. This side of King's public identity is rarely lauded, though his uncanny ability to stand alone made him even greater."[42]

For the Adventurer, challenging convention, including the convention of his or her allies, is far more important than political expediency.

Moving on

Many of the iconic Adventurer movies have been the "road" movies. For Adventurers of the 1960's, Jack Kerouac's "On The Road" was an almost sacred text. For the Adventurer, life is one long "walkabout." Once again, Richard Branson shows in business how this can lead to startup after startup.

In the life of the Adventurer, moving on means having few possessions, few places he or she calls home. "When King died, he still lived modestly in Atlanta, with little money for his family, since he gave nearly every cent he earned to his black organization. When he lost his life he was staying in a humble black hotel in Memphis."[43]

This can frustrate less Adventurer-oriented people, even close family. Martin Luther King won the Nobel Peace Prize, which brought with it a lot of money. He decided to donate the entire amount to the movement. "King's decision greatly disappointed Coretta, who argued that they should set aside $20,000 for the education of their four children."[44]

"You only live once"

The Adventurer lives life to the full, in the here and now, and makes fewer investments in the future than others. Although some Christians of King's acquaintance argued that it is in the afterlife, in Heaven, that the meek will get their rewards, King wanted better lives for people on this earth, and now. "It has been my conviction ever since reading Rauschenbusch that any religion that professes concern for the souls of men and is not equally concerned about the slums that damn them, the economic conditions that strangle them, and the social conditions that cripple them is a spiritually moribund religion."[45]

The legacy the Adventurer wants to leave behind is rarely represented by great works, honors, or wealth. Anticipating his early death, "King implored his eulogist not to mention his Nobel Peace Prize, the several hundred awards he had won, or where he attended school. Instead he wanted the spotlight on what he thought were his life's deeper ambitions, its higher achievements."[46] Towards the end of his life he also said, "I won't have any money to leave behind. But I just want to leave a committed life behind."[47]

Martin Luther King frequently hinted to his close friends that he would be killed at an early age. He did not seem to be particularly concerned about this, at least for his own sake. Instead, "This awareness [of the probable sacrifice of his life to an assassin] released him into a powerful and sometimes perilous psychological freedom."[48] For the Adventurer, "you only live once" is not something to worry about; it's something to focus the mind.

Change and variety

Quickly tiring of the familiar and often trying new things and experimenting, the Adventurer is prepared to make the big changes in life – new careers, new homes, even new families. By choosing to become engaged in the civil rights movement, Martin Luther King sacrificed some of the personal freedom a typical Adventurer tries to preserve. In some respects, he sublimated personal change and variety within the way he saw what he was campaigning for: "The problem of transforming the ghetto was . . . a problem of power – a confrontation between the forces of power demanding change and the forces of power dedicated to preserving the status quo. Power, properly understood, is the ability to achieve purpose. It is the strength required to bring about social, political, or economic changes."[49]

Had he lived longer, who knows what new ventures he may have taken on. As it was, he still managed, through his visits to India and Norway, and through his shifts of focus from Montgomery, through Birmingham, Los Angeles, Chicago and elsewhere, to find himself far more variety in his daily life than he would have if he had stayed put in Montgomery and directed things from there.

It is typical of the Adventurer who does seek gainful employment to leave behind him – or herself a career history that speaks volumes about restlessness.

Fast living

Realizing that life is short, Adventurers make sure that every minute is spent to the full; they live a hectic and demanding life; they have difficulty in saying "no."

Martin Luther King moved quickly. Even when he gained the attention of President Kennedy and his brother Robert, he frequently found them slow to respond. When internal squabbles threatened the pace of the movement, King responded, "This isn't any time for organizational conflicts, this isn't any time for ego battles over who's going to be the leader. We are all the leaders here in this struggle. . . ."[50]

Some people may not understand how the impatience of the Adventurer can fuel his or her preparedness to break rules. Martin Luther King did this frequently, setting the pattern early by plagiarising others' work to get his university doctorate finished.[51] As with all people who become legends, King's cheating has its apologists: "The fault lies not simply with King, although he bears a lion's share of the blame, but with a world that demanded that he and others perform under such conditions."[52]

Fun, excitement, adventure and playfulness

The instinct to play that underpins the Adventurer life has its own rewards. Play is fun. You don't learn from others how to play; it comes naturally. But while Guardians relegate play to a subservient role, especially when it gets in the way of being responsible, the Adventurer plays at and with life.

A devoted husband and father, and devout Christian, Martin Luther King could not stop his Adventurer playfulness: "After spending his last night delivering one of the most brilliant speeches in his career . . . King allegedly rendezvoused with two women at different points of the night and in the early morning fought with a third female 'friend' before being gunned down later that evening at the Lorraine Motel."[53]

It was not simply that King became corrupted by power, and, like other powerful men became attractive to, and thereby attracted to women. "King's habits of sexual adventure had been well established by the time he was married."[54]

King was right to say he was no saint. In that sense of the word, few Adventurers are saints.

Self-reliance

"I sat in the midst of the deepest quiet I have ever felt, with two dozen others in the room. There comes a time in the atmosphere of leadership when a man surrounded by loyal friends and allies realizes he has come face to face with himself and with ruthless reality. I was alone in that crowded room."[55] Martin Luther King was remembering a critical moment in the civil rights movement, when things were going badly. Surrounded though he was by loyal supporters, he felt alone.

Adventurers value self-reliance. As King said of a later moment, when he risked losing the support of his fellow activists by coming out against the Vietnam war, "I came to the conclusion that there is an existential moment in your life when you must decide to speak for yourself; nobody else can speak for you."[56] If you live a life of challenging convention, you run the risk of alienating people who do not agree with you.

Once again, although King felt the moment, he was also being true to what all Adventurers have to live with, and he summarizes this well when he says, "I have always felt that ultimately along the way of life an individual must stand up and be counted and be willing to face the consequences whatever they are."[57]

Adventurers often turn their backs on their families. Often seen as a sign of selfishness, sometimes, however, it is the best way to avoid involving loved ones in the risks the Adventurer will always take. In the early days of the civil rights movement, Martin Luther King's house was bombed. Luckily, the house was empty at the time. But the threats of further reprisals kept on coming.

Having put down the phone after yet another threat to his and his family's life, King had to face the prospect of backing out to save their lives. Sitting alone with a cup of coffee, he agonized. He felt himself drawn to the safe option. "But if I eased out now I would be plagued by my own conscience, reminding me that I lacked the moral courage to stand by a cause to the end. No one can understand my conflict who has not looked into the eyes of those he loves, knowing that he has no alternative but to take a dangerous stand that leaves them tormented."[58]

Having a playmate

The potential loneliness that results from continuously walking away from others can lead to a constant search for a soul mate or playmate. This is a relationship, usually outside the family, with someone with whom you never have to pretend, never have to try to be what you are not, and with whom you are totally free to play and have fun while sharing the deepest emotional intimacies.

Some Adventurers end up marrying their playmates. Others seek this relationship elsewhere. The playfulness and closeness of this kind of relationship is a rich vein for novelists and film makers to tap into, *Thelma and Louise* being a prime example.

I think Martin Luther King wanted Coretta to be his playmate. But he spent his last night in the company of other women, and died a long way away from her.

Primary motivation: for freedom and adventure

All people value freedom to some extent; all people have a sense of adventure. What differentiates the Adventurer is his or her drive to seek these goals above other goals, such as a stable home life, a good career, and respectability.

This does not make the Adventurer amoral. On the contrary, in turning his or her back on conventional rules or dogmas, the Adventurer, in his or her self-reliance, can develop a very strong moral sense. But it will be based on internalized values not the rules of others. Martin Luther King exemplifies this: "On some positions, Cowardice asks the question, 'Is it safe?' Expediency asks the question, 'Is it politic?' And Vanity comes along and asks the question, 'Is it popular?' But Conscience asks the question, 'Is it right?' And there comes a time when one must take a position that is neither safe, nor politic, nor popular, but he must do it because Conscience tells him it is right."[59]

Using his or her internal guide (not always described as "conscience") the Adventurer lives a life of dodging the pitfalls of convention, and (ideally doing no harm to anyone else) doing whatever is needed to keep him or herself free. If, in the process, he or she realizes that things will have to change to achieve that, then he or she will do what is needed to make that change happen. Sometimes what has to change is simple. But, as Martin Luther King realized, some are enormous. When it dawned on him how many individual people were not free as a direct result of the way in which the United States operated as an entire system, he said "we as a nation must undergo a radical revolution of values."[60]

He saw it as his personal adventure to try to bring this change about.

In summary, the Adventurer is most likely to believe in these values:

- Freedom
- Challenging convention
- Moving on
- "You only live once"
- Change and variety
- Fast living
- Fun, excitement, adventure and playfulness

- Self-reliance
- Having a playmate

He or she will be motivated by freedom and adventure.

Franklin D. Roosevelt – Guardian

Franklin Delano Roosevelt, or FDR as he is usually referred to, was elected President of the USA four times. In his day, it was not unconstitutional for a President to go beyond two terms, but "custom denied Presidents more than two terms."[61] During that long presidency, FDR experienced and dealt with the 1930s depression and economic recovery through the New Deal. He also led the USA through most of the Second World War. He died before the Allied victory in 1945. But before his death he had helped lay the foundations for the United Nations.

He made an indelible mark on the political scene in America. "The modern power, reach and scope of the federal government, nationally and internationally . . . sprang from the roots which Roosevelt planted during the New Deal and the Second World War."[62] Unlike many changes brought in by strong leaders, FDR's legacy remains today. He faced strident opposition throughout his presidency, but that opposition melted away once the benefits of what he legislated for were felt.

In the campaign for the presidency in 1940, that led to FDR's unprecedented third term, "it was suddenly understood that some of the welfare measures were untouchable: even the Republicans did not attack social security any more. They preferred to have it forgotten that they had ever opposed it."[63]

Viewed from the perspective of the time, FDR was seen as radically progressive, an approach often associated with the challenges to convention of the Adventurer. But his motivation and his reforms "were designed not so much to stimulate significant change as avert it."[64] As totalitarianism gained strength in Germany, Italy, Russia and Spain, the economic failures of the capitalist economy made the ways advocated by Hitler and others in Europe and Japan increasingly attractive to people who wanted radical change. FDR's aim was to stop the US going down that route.

He succeeded. And in doing so clearly demonstrated and lived the values of the Guardian. These are the Guardian values.

Having a family

The instinct driven by the "selfish gene" – to pass on your genetic inheritance to the next generation – makes humans automatically prone to look after and favor their own biological offspring. But the complexities of living in clans or tribes, and the evolutionary benefits of taking care of others within the whole community lie at the heart of the "family values" of the Guardian.

Roosevelt married, was, apart from one possible indiscretion,[65] faithful to Eleanor, and had children whom he adored. There is no evidence that, like so many Guardians, FDR ever questioned the supremacy of the family as the way for people to live their lives.

But for the Guardian, "family" does not equate simply to biological or genetic kin. The Guardians of this world tend to "adopt" a larger family: the club, society, organization, or, as FDR did, the nation.[66] For many of the voters who supported him in unprecedented numbers, FDR was the Guardian come to protect them. And to FDR, being the nation's Guardian was no chore.

He was a strict but fair Guardian, respecting his family, and teaching his adopted children: "Franklin said, in a thoughtful moment, when he had had some experience as President, that he had to be more a teacher than anything else. And every day in some way he did try to do a little teaching."[67] Like any Guardian, he shouldered responsibility, but, "It was a President's duty, as Franklin saw it, to tell the people what confronted them."[68]

One of the organizations FDR set up as part of the New Deal, The Civilian Conservation Corps (CCC), typifies the family orientation of his reforming model. The CCC "provided for setting up camps for young men whose families were destitute, who could therefore not go on with their education, and who could find no jobs. These young men were paid, but not a full wage, because they were being furnished a living under exceptional circumstances and also being started in education."[69]

Being home

The Guardian values the home. He or she has a strong sense of belonging, centred around the family, and of closeness with loved ones. A place of safety, security, and family association is important. The image of the home as the centre of it all was constantly part of FDR's presidency, and his family home in Hyde Park, upstate New York, welcomed many politicians over the years to a relaxed family atmosphere. "The old mansion overflowed with company and good cheer."[70]

Roosevelt was one of the first politicians to recognize the power of radio to keep in touch with the nation. It is no accident that he called his broadcasts "fireside chats,"[71] an inspired symbolic representation of the warm, safe, homely environment that was the aspiration of the millions in America suffering from the consequences of the depression. The fireside was where they wanted to be, and from where the Guardian dispensed his teaching.

Putting down roots

Establishing a solid base is important to the Guardian. This can be represented by the home or homes. Although Hyde Park was the presidential
family home, FDR also needed to be the symbolic Guardian for those in the
South who saw New York as far away and irrelevant to them.

When FDR contracted polio his political career was threatened. To help
him recover, he invested in a therapy centre in Warm Springs, Meriwether
County, Georgia. It became his "second home,"[72] and was often referred to
as "the second White House." Now he had roots in both of the key areas
where political power drew its strength.

The White House in Washington, however, was where FDR had to establish his presidential roots. "Roosevelt had a love affair with power. The
White House for him was almost a family seat and like the other Roosevelt
he regarded the whole country almost as a family property."[73]

Guardians do not just put down roots in homes. Early in his political
career, he established for himself that he had to be his own man, putting
down his political roots, and being nobody's dependent. His first major
political appointment was as Governor of New York state. It was expected at
the time that he would seek advice from more experienced politicians, and
learn at their feet. But he said at the time, "I've got to be governor of the
State of New York and I've got to be it myself."[74]

Putting down roots means the Guardian is here to stay. This is the base
from which to help other people.

Economic security

All of which requires a degree of economic security from which to work.
For the Guardian, it is not the trappings of wealth that are important, but the
stability of the economic base from which to go out and do one's work.
Although he was born into a wealthy family, FDR felt the need from an
early age to make commitments to earning that would enable him to be the
provider. He had trained at Harvard as a lawyer, but became a businessman,
as vice-president of the Fidelity and Deposit Company of Maryland. "The
salary was . . . more certain than a lawyer's fees. It would keep his expensive family going."[75]

But it was not only his own family's economic security that was important to him, but the economic security of all the nation's families. In his
view, the depression was a clear indication that the current economic system
was failing people, denying them their right to economic security. He had to
teach people a new way. "Belief in 'free enterprise' was something close to

a religion for the American people. They identified it with the pioneer spirit and traditional virtues. 'Rugged individualism' was held responsible for developing the nation into a world power in less than half a century. So, in spite of the miseries arising out of the failures of the free enterprise system to prevent depressions, the belief still persisted that every individual could make his own way in the world and if he failed, it was his own fault."[76]

This was, for FDR, irresponsible dogma, and it was up to him to find ways of protecting people from this creed of self-reliance.

Protecting and providing

When FDR came to power the economy was in a dreadful state. Spiralling downwards, with unemployment increasing daily, banks crashing, and agriculture and industry going to the wall, many people were terrified. Legislation and financial relief were needed, but FDR saw that, without providing hope, people could become so dependent and lacking in the motivation to help themselves so that nothing would fundamentally change. He saw the power of language in reshaping attitudes and told the American people, "The only things we have to fear is fear itself."[77]

Leaders know that, without people following, they are powerless. FDR knew that his role was not simply to provide aid, but also to provide motivation.

But clearly, motivation without something concrete to deliver is not enough. When he took office in 1933 he embarked on a programme called the "Hundred Days." "The highest priority was the economic distress borne by so many families. Franklin asked for funds to be granted – not merely lent – for relief. This was the acceptance of the responsibility for the welfare of individuals that he had promised."[78]

It is central to the Guardian to take responsibility "not as a matter of charity but as a matter of social duty."[79] And because the nation was FDR's family, he fundamentally disagreed with the previous president, Hoover, on the issue of providing aid and assistance. "Hoover had been reluctant to accept this as a governmental duty. Franklin insisted that it must be done vigorously and that it *was* the business of the federal government."[80]

Until the New Deal, it was the responsibility of each state to deal with matters such as these. By dealing with the economic crisis so effectively, FDR laid the foundations of the modern federal state.

It was not an easy ride. Some of the legislation passed in the Hundred Days was soon deemed unconstitutional by the Supreme Court. As any leader knows, not everyone wants to follow, especially those around you who want to have your job. As a consequence, FDR had to change direction in his second term. The legislation passed in this phase of his presidency was known as the second New Deal. It was an "about-face in policy . . . but there was no change in Franklin's major purpose: to get the economy going again and to free its citizens from want."[81]

Strategy is subservient to purpose; and purpose is a defining part of character.

This aspect of FDR's character was a consistent part of the man. As a student he wrote a thesis about his family and their role in society. His key argument was "there was no excuse for them if they did not do their duty by the community."[82] Throughout his life, as with the life of any Guardian, a sense of duty prevailed.

Respect

The default for a Guardian is to respect those in authority. Clearly, Guardians can discover, as anyone can, that people in charge do not deserve that respect. And they know that they themselves need to earn respect from others. But rules, authority and discipline are part of the fabric of the Guardian's world.

Roosevelt, like so many people, began to show his Guardian character at an early age. As a boy, "He liked to be free, as any boy would; and there were often more interesting activities than the duties he was asked to carry out. But the discipline was so easy and so reasonable that he accepted it without much protest. . . . He grew up well within the rules of the family and gave promise of turning out as [his parents] wanted him to."[83]

He continued this response to authority into Groton, the school he attended from the age of 14 until going up to Harvard, where he "accepted the discipline without protest."[84] Although as children and adolescents, Guardians may occasionally challenge convention, on balance, they respect their seniors and follow the rules.

But their sense of responsibility often manifests itself in a recognition that, in due course and through the appropriate channels, they must take on the mantle of seniority themselves. At Harvard FDR did not shine particularly at anything, academic or sporty. "But Franklin was, as always, anxious to get to the very top, and his failure to get there was a nagging dissatisfaction."[85]

Typically, the Guardian seeks power. But this is rarely for the sake of power alone. Becoming the CEO, the goal of many a Guardian in business, provides the power and authority to enable him or her to bring about the kind of organization they believe in. For a politician, it is similarly appropriate to aim for the highest office to achieve that same power and authority. Even when FDR took on his first job as a lawyer in 1907, he said to his colleagues "that he planned to run for public office soon and that he wanted to be president."[86] This was twenty five years before he achieved the presidency (which, in fact, he did not believe he would get until 1936, four more years on). Not for Guardians the impatience of the Adventurer.

Like most Guardians, FDR liked being in charge, and visibly so, whether in politics or on his boat. "He liked being skipper: his vice-president in the 1930s, John Garner, always called him 'Cap'n'."[87] Having respect for others in authority is matched by the Guardian by seeking due respect from others within the community.

Membership of the community

FDR grew up in privileged circumstances. The Roosevelts were rich and, within the American society of the time, the equivalent of aristocracy. With privilege, for the Guardian, comes responsibility. "This sense of *noblesse oblige* was one reason why Roosevelt entered politics."[88] For the Guardian, a sense of belonging to the community does not imply total equality. Someone has to be in charge, and those best to run things should accept that authority and carry out their duty to the full: "As president he ran public affairs like a benign boss . . . integrating the community again."[89]

For Guardians, responding powerfully to the instinct to nurture within a community context, the community is more important than the individual. FDR said that the task of government is "The struggle for the liberty of the community rather than the liberty of the individual."[90] Community first, self second.

Maturity and responsibility

Fitting in means putting aside selfish desires, taking a mature and responsible attitude to life. This was always part of FDR's character. As a student, FDR displayed much of the behavior expected of students, even then in the very early years of the 1900s. Students play. But this does not make them Adventurers. Guardians like to play and have fun, but beneath the surface lies the strong foundation of responsibility.

While at Harvard, FDR met his future wife and lifelong supporter, Eleanor, who "soon discerned that, beneath this surface hedonism, the playboy Harvard graduate, dilettante and editor of *Crimson*, was a serious and dependable young man."[91] His mature and responsible character was not simply the result of being born to the role of the "country squire." Others born to similar privileges did not do what FDR felt was the right way to respond to such privilege, and "he displayed a country squire's scorn for the rich who lacked social responsibility."[92]

Because maturity and responsibility are values held by Guardians, they are not simply what "I" should do, but what others should do as well. FDR's political strategy informed this sense. For example, the plan for agricultural revival in the New Deal was not simply legislation; it was aimed at changing selfish attitudes. As Rexford Tugwell, FDR's assistant secretary of agriculture said at the time of the New Deal: "Under the plan it will pay farmers, for the first time, to be social-minded, to do something for all instead of himself alone. We thus succeeded, we think, in harnessing a selfish motive for the social good."[93]

FDR is such a good example of the Guardian in political action because he demonstrated how character and strategy work together to bring about the achievements that are commensurate with the values of the character itself. He was successful because he was consistently true to the values of the Guardian, and, not long after taking on the presidency, improvements were obvious to those he had told that fear itself is all they had to fear. "[T]he nation's morale was recovering through clever use of press conferences, radio broadcasts and the sheer force of personality by which FDR stamped his authority on the nation."[94]

Developing a legacy

The sense of belonging to the family and community drives Guardians to want to leave something behind – a legacy. FDR's "intention was to start something that would never end."[95] It is "natural" for fathers to want their children to be catered for after they have gone; for FDR, the family was the nation, and his legacy was for all people.

Conservation was always close to FDR's heart,[96] and he put principle into practice initially at home, "So about 1912 he started planting thousands of trees at Hyde Park."[97] The tree symbolizes well the legacy, having roots, a long life, and solidity. But as an active politician, FDR needed to leave more than trees behind, and throughout his presidency, he planted a great many constitutional "trees." "The unprecedented burst of 15 major laws in three months which began the New Deal continued with the second New Deal."[98]

The period of his presidency saw the rise of totalitarianism in Europe and Japan. The Great War was not the war to end all wars, and the failure of the League of Nations after 1918 worried FDR. It is not out of character, therefore that, as American involvement in the Second World War became inevitable, he was already planning how to leave a legacy of peace. "War was a certainty. Franklin was determined to make sure that the settlement following it was a lasting and just one. He envisioned a world organization for securing peace. And planning for that organization, even if it could only be established years in the future, could be started immediately."[99]

That organization was the United Nations, and through FDR's efforts, the United States this time played a key role within this international organization, helping to ensure that, unlike the League of Nations, it would continue its work well beyond his own lifetime.

Primary motivation: to take responsibility for others

Although FDR recovered from the worst symptoms, the polio that struck him in 1929 left him unable to walk. Many people assumed that this would end his political career; no-one, surely, who was so disabled would be able to project the strong image needed to gain the political support necessary to reach the top.

Very severe setbacks such as that which befell FDR can seem to alter character. But as his story shows, character can often fight back. "Though still light-hearted, Roosevelt became more serious and determined to live out his destiny."[100] Others may have seen the illness as a message saying "turn away, go back to Hyde Park, and let others take care of you." But as we saw in Chapter 2, life's experiences mean different things to different people. His rule-governed upbringing did not make FDR rebel; his polio did not make him quit.

He had always wanted the presidency, but he had wanted it so that he could fulfil his duty, to take responsibility. He, and no-one else, had to do this. And it was not the pursuit of any particular policy or strategy that drove him. It was his sense that his destiny was to lead. As he said to one of his advisors as he prepared for one of his presidential campaigns, "There's one issue in this campaign. It's myself and people must be either for me or against me."[101]

The Guardian may not have all the answers to the questions, but he or she knows it is his or her job to deliver when those questions have been answered.

In summary, the Guardian is most likely to believe in these values:

- Having a family
- Being home
- Putting down roots
- Protecting and providing
- Respect
- Membership of the community
- Maturity and responsibility
- Developing a legacy

He or she is likely to be motivated to take responsibility for others.

Mahatma Gandhi – Sage

It may be that Mahatma Gandhi is remembered not so much for what he achieved as for how he went about it. After the Second World War, independence for India from the British Raj may have been an inevitability. The empire was in shrinkage, and India was not alone in establishing self-government.

Understanding Gandhi and his legacy means recognizing that he did not set out from the start to topple the Raj. Before he became involved in that "mission," he led a long and active life outside of the Indian political arena, spending many of his early adult years in South Africa, first as a lawyer, and then taking on an increasingly politicized set of attitudes.

During those years in South Africa there were few signs of the role he would play in India's history. He had gone to South Africa originally to help in a legal case, but settled there to set up a law practice. Perhaps the first signs of his being a little out of the ordinary for a bourgeois lawyer was when he set up a commune, named Phoenix, as a model for the kind of ideal community he would advocate more and more as he grew older.

But in 1905 he was "Rich, influential, with thirty or forty people doing his bidding at Phoenix, in his law office and in his house. Gandhi was living the settled life of a patriarch. Outwardly he gave the impression of a man who has found himself and has no intention of changing. Inwardly he was seething with discontent."[102]

Gandhi's story reminds us that it takes some people a while to realize self-awareness. Certainly his early aspirations to go to London for education, and his behavior while in London speak of an ambitiousness more akin to the Warrior than the Sage. And when he returned to India from his student life, he gave little indication of how he would develop. "Jealous, suspicious, overbearing, he was behaving like the typical Indian youth who returns from London to display his contempt for his native village."[103]

Yet the signs had been there all along. As a child he got into scrapes like any other, and went along with the misdemeanours of his brothers. But when caught stealing with them, he showed already a key part of the Sage character. "All the boys were rounded up and cross-examined. All except one denied they had anything to do with the affair. The exception was Mohandas, then about six years old, who quite simply and without fear explained exactly what had happened."[104]

As with that other archetypal Sage, Socrates, the truth was more important than self-preservation. Truth belongs to the Sage world of language, thought, concepts, and the spirit. Self-preservation belongs in the material world, which, for the Sage, is transient and insignificant.

These are the values of the Sage.

Wisdom

Wisdom is a concept that often gets badly used. Some people confuse it with knowledge. But knowing a great deal does not make you wise. Others, especially those who offer advice with the words, "I think you would be wise to . . ." confuse it with expediency. Yet others see it as a means to an end, a set of rules for success in life. It is none of these. It is exemplified by the attitudes to the material world that Gandhi grew into but never abandoned once he had acquired them: "He feared and distrusted possessions, knowing that in the strict sense no-one possesses anything at all. When people spoke to him about the vast possessions of the maharajahs . . . he would shake his head in bewilderment, wondering why anyone should take pride in such things. He knew only too well where the power and wealth of the maharajahs came from, and in due course he was able to destroy them as easily as a man breaks some dry faggots across his knee."[105]

By the time Gandhi left South Africa, one key element of this wisdom had begun to emerge: his rejection of material wealth. "Just before Gandhi left South Africa he was showered with gifts . . . [that] vanished into the vaults of the African Banking Corporation for the use of the Natal Indian Congress when no other funds were available. . . . A legal document was drawn up to ensure that the jewels were administered properly."[106]

It takes time to achieve wisdom. It may be that nobody ever really achieves it completely. But Gandhi learnt that to get there means reducing to a minimum the interference of the material world. The fact that he often got his way by fasting, denying physical sustenance for days on end, was a powerful symbol of the value of wisdom as contrasted to the worldly weapons of the Warrior.

Learning and understanding

For the Sage, learning is its own reward; it is not predicated on the principle that "knowledge is power." For Gandhi it was not equated to formal education either, as later in his life he criticized schools and colleges for dabbling in knowledge rather than developing wisdom.

Although Gandhi learnt a lot from people he respected, he learnt more and more from his own experience. Sometimes what he learnt changed his attitudes. As an adolescent he hero-worshipped a fellow villager, Sheikh Mehtab who represented "guile, physical strength, domination, and in the eyes of the young Mohandas these were enviable qualities, to be imitated or at the very least regarded with respect. . . . In course of time the spell . . . began to evaporate."[107]

The Sage not only values learning and understanding for him or herself, it is a value to instil in others. The word "mahatma" means teacher, and teaching is what Gandhi did throughout his life – without ever wanting or trying to do so professionally. But what he taught, as a true Sage, was morality, not knowledge.

It was in South Africa that he started on this road. The Sage in him could not abide the expediency of the commercial people he was asked to represent as a lawyer. No matter how much they explained to him that, in real life, in the commercial world, you have to be economical with the truth if you want to make a profit, he could not accept the underlying principles of commercial competition.

"Gandhi now decided that the time had come to vindicate morality. The Muslim merchants in Pretoria were thoroughly untruthful in their business, and he therefore called a meeting and addressed them on the subject of truth, contending that there was no validity in their claim that it was impossible to speak the truth and still remain solvent. . . . With that speech the familiar Gandhi, always insisting on the truth, begins to emerge."[108] With his or her lack of interest in material wealth, this focus on truth is more important to the Sage than any principles of economics.

Search for truth

"Truth hates secrecy. The more you act openly, the greater are your chances of remaining truthful. There is no hatred, there is no place for fear or despair in the dictionary of the man who bases his life on truth and non-violence."[109] These words of Gandhi highlight one of the consequences of the values of the Sage: that to be open to the truth at all times means being open and exposed.

The Sage is vulnerable. Always open to the possibility of being in the wrong, he or she remains open and prepared to accept whatever happens to him or her. When the truth is confronted with hostility, there is no place for fighting back. It was this realization by Gandhi that led him to develop the strategy of passive resistance that he called "Satyagraha."

The first three Commandments he published for those who would follow the way of passive resistance say, "(1) A Satyagrahi, that is a civil resister, will harbor no anger. (2) He will suffer the anger of an opponent. (3) In doing so he will put up with assaults from the opponent, never retaliate, but he will not submit, out of fear of punishment or the like, to any order given in anger."[110]

This is the main reason for the Sage being diametrically opposed to the Warrior. For the Warrior, a truth is something that, where necessary, needs to be defended; by force if necessary. For the Sage, the truth is something to be lived, and to be taught by example, but not to be a reason for violence, even under extreme provocation such as the Amritsar massacre.[111]

Before becoming engaged in the struggle for Indian independence, Gandhi found himself involved in a number of "political" campaigns. One of these was on behalf of poor peasants working in the indigo fields in Bihar. To help their cause, Gandhi drafted in a team of investigators, whose job was to talk to the peasants, and seek the truth.

But, as the team found out, the search for truth is not simply an intellectual pursuit of answers to academic questions. It is a way of life: "Though they all regarded themselves as educated men, he insisted that they should regard themselves as clerks, accurately reporting the statements of the peasants. Furthermore, they must live the simple, dedicated life as befitted men eagerly searching for the truth."[112]

Humility

The commitment to truth and to non-violence that characterizes the Sage is linked to an essential humility. In 1921, despite his best efforts to teach non-violence, he found himself on trial for his involvement in disturbances caused by less patient supporters. Although Gandhi was not a participant in the violence that took place, he accepted full responsibility, and said in his trial statement, "I do not ask for mercy. I do not plead any extenuating act. I am here, therefore, to invite and cheerfully submit to the highest penalty that can be inflicted upon me, for what in law is a deliberate crime and what appears to me to be the highest duty of a citizen."[113]

Gandhi often blamed himself for the misdemeanours of others. His first recorded fast was to punish himself for some sexual indiscretions perpetrated by youths in his Phoenix commune in South Africa. But by taking on so much of others' responsibility, Gandhi posed himself a problem. The more he punished himself, the more he, by implication, encouraged others to acts of self denial and sacrifice. As he wrote, "I do not know what evil there is in me. I have a strain of cruelty in me, as others say, such that people force themselves to do things, even to attempt impossible things, in order to please me. . . . I put far too heavy burdens on people."[114]

As a consequence, Gandhi occasionally found himself perplexed. A close friend and teacher of Gandhi was a man called Gokhale, who castigated Gandhi during one of his visits to the Mahatma. Gandhi "was utterly contrite, without quite knowing what sin he had committed, for it seems never to have occurred to him that Gokhale was warning him against the sin of spiritual pride, the pride that wilfully commands others to obey and incessantly interferes with their lives."[115]

One of the ironies of the Sage's experience of life is that the denial of the importance of the material world implies a denial of the physical presence of others. Some sages in history have "solved" this problem by living as hermits. Those who remain within the community, especially when they have acquired dedicated followers, sometimes have to come to terms with the frailties of the flesh. Gandhi's frailty was a truth he sometimes kept from himself: "Though he proclaimed his humility, he was intolerant of criticism, and was more dictatorial and more self-indulgent than he knew."[116]

Celebrating others

Loving your neighbor, even when he or she is set on being your enemy is part of the Sage value-set. Having been away from South Africa for a while, Gandhi was set upon when he returned. Narrowly escaping with his life, he later declined to prosecute his attackers: "I beg to state that I do not wish any notice to be taken of the behaviour of some people towards me last Wednesday, which I have no doubt was due to misapprehension on their part."[117]

Sometimes people do things or believe in things we don't do or believe in. When their actions of beliefs have a negative impact on our lives, we want to change them. What Gandhi brought to the indigo workers was a way of changing the millowners that did not involve direct confrontation. "Every day there were meetings under a *babul* tree near the Sabarmati river, with Gandhi addressing the workers and calling for discipline, determination, and the acceptance of suffering. Perfect discipline prevailed at these meetings, and no-one was permitted to make any disparaging remarks about the millowners, who were represented as honourable but mistaken men genuinely attempting to do their best for the workers."[118]

The Sage starts from the assumption that people they disagree with are not ill-intentioned. They are, through no fault of their own, misguided. Winning them over means helping them realize the truth, not fighting them.

Mental and spiritual development

For the Sage, the material world offers little of true value. In his Confession of Faith, 1909, Gandhi says, "Increase of material comfort, it may be generally laid down, does not in any way whatsoever conduce to moral growth."[119] To understand how Gandhi developed his approach to Indian independence, it is important to recognize that, due to his belief in the essential goodness of people, he did not have a grudge against the British rulers themselves. The problem was not British rule, but the way in which they brought with them technology that brought a materialism he felt to be alien to his idea of the ideal way of life for himself and his compatriots.

"Railways, machinery and corresponding increase of indulgent habits are the true badges of slavery of the Indian people as they are of Europeans. I, therefore, have no quarrel with the rulers. I have every quarrel with their methods."[120] The Sage tries to live as much as possible in the world of mind and/or spirit. Developing this ability not to depend on material goods is the discipline of the Sage.

Seeking spiritual inspiration

"What Gandhi had in mind from the beginning was something essentially positive, an outgoing of spiritual power and purification through suffering."[121] The Sage believes that, if you keep asking yourself questions about the value of what you strive for, it always comes back to something beyond the physical. If you think you want a fast car, what will that get you? If the answer is prestige, then what will prestige get you? This philosophical "reductio ad absurdum" leads to mental or spiritual value. Everything else, for the Sage, is merely a means to one end: inner harmony.

Inner harmony

In my work with all kinds of leaders, Warriors, Guardians, Adventurers and Sages, one thing keeps coming up. At the end of the questionnaire, I ask what people are most looking forward to in the next two to five years. Among the options I offer is *"a greater sense of contentment with myself or life."* Most of the data I have collected is from relatively successful people in business, most of whom have further to go in their careers. They could choose *"greater recognition, through salary, bonus, etc,"* or *"promotion."* But a very significant number state a preference for contentment. They are not all Sages, but something is not right.

Getting back to basics, the Sage pursues a vision of simplicity and harmony. Gandhi's vision was of "a peaceful and idyllic village community in India. Always there was the vision of the Indian village with its buffaloes and cows, the peasants working in the fields, the women suckling their babies in the shade of the *neem* trees, the ancient religious ceremonies."[122]

Self-awareness means, in part, being able to check out your ideal vision against your whole value set. This rural paradise was, for Gandhi, the truth. For many others, it may have cosmetic appeal, but it would not produce the goods. Inner harmony means living a life in line with your values. Unless you are really a Sage, your true vision is likely to be very different from

Gandhi's. Inner harmony means being at peace with the world, and this is not achieved through fortune or material wealth; it is achieved by minimizing your dependence on the physical world for what you really need.

Love of the arts

In their search for truth, most Sages look to the arts. The myths of other cultures are stories containing "universal truths." The novels, plays and cinema of our culture tell the same stories over and over. The arts do not provide information, but they do inform our sensibilities about what's important in life.

In many cases, artists advocate spiritual values as superior to the material world. One of the best examples is Thoreau who wrote, "Most of the luxuries, and many of the so-called comforts of life, are not only not indispensable, but positive hindrances to the elevation of mankind. Man is rich in proportion to the number of things he can do without."[123]

In this value alone Gandhi differed from most Sages. He had no interest in the arts.

Primary motivation: to learn and understand

If it were not for the fact that Gandhi had been responsible for bringing about such significant change in his lifetime, it may be difficult to see how a Sage leader ever gets anything done. The process of trying to understand, and through understanding influence others is not always effective, of course. When Hitler was leading Germany through war and mass extermination, Gandhi took the extraordinary step of writing to him, addressing him as "Dear Friend." "That I address you as a friend is no formality. I own no foes. My business in life for the past thirty-three years has been to enlist the friendship of the whole of humanity by befriending mankind, irrespective of race, colour or creed."[124]

There is no record of a reply. And we know the letter did not stop Hitler in his tracks. The Sage can, for this kind of reason, appear naïve and ineffective. But they believe that what will make wars less likely is not increasing physical power or cynical diplomacy, but mutual understanding.

In summary, the Sage is most likely to believe in these values:

- Wisdom
- Learning and understanding
- Search for truth
- Humility

- Celebrating others
- Mental and spiritual development
- Seeking spiritual inspiration
- Inner harmony
- Love of the arts

He or she is likely to be motivated to learn and understand.

CHAPTER 5

Conflict

How values can influence conflict

Many of the situations of leadership development I am invited to become involved in revolve around scenes of conflict. By conflict I do not mean open warfare or major hostilities. It is often low level conflict. People do not trust each other; one group does not respect another; or an individual feels completely out of place.

There are many sources of such conflict. In my experience, the one that is often overlooked, and is therefore much more difficult to resolve, is a clash of the kinds of values I have described in the previous chapter. I am not saying that all organizational conflict is like this. Warriors can fight each other, often do, and respect each other's "strength of character" to "fight their corner."

In this chapter I shall focus on those kinds of conflict that can be linked to these different sets of values. There are several reasons for doing this.

Firstly, people are not always clear about their values. Many people I work with have rarely, if ever, taken time out to question what is really important to them. Just as your own skeleton lies hidden beneath layers of tissue and muscle, so some people's values form the basis of their character but remain unnoticed. People often take what they believe in for granted. Surely everyone believes the same?

Secondly, people are often reluctant to talk openly about their values. It is a private matter that is of no concern to the organization or to any interfering consultants who want to poke their noses into things that are none of their business. I am sometimes told that what a person does in his or her organization is a legitimate subject for discussion, but discussing character is intrusive and should not be allowed.

Thirdly, it is sometimes very helpful for conflict resolution to separate out deeply held values from attitudes. Organizations that promote "corporate values" often overlook the point that a person's values are not changed simply because he or she says they follow those corporate "values." But what people can, and often will do, is to adopt a set of attitudes in line with what the organization is promoting. Attitudes are negotiable in a way that values are not.

Finally, and in consequence of these points, people often seek causes of conflict elsewhere. One example is to blame different cultures for conflict. Clashes of culture can create conflict. But I have come across situations in which a much more significant factor has been clashes of character.

In one memorable case, I was working with a team in Hong Kong, who had recently been placed under the leadership of a South African. They found it hard to get on. The new leader had been trying to solve the problem by becoming more sensitive to the local culture, but this was not making much difference. He is a Warrior, while the team members are predominantly Sage.

Culture did have a role to play here, but not as he anticipated. There are as many Warriors in Hong Kong as elsewhere. But, as we will explore in more depth in chapter 15, the local team had unconsciously recruited people like themselves – Sages. In so doing, they did create a team culture that followed Sage values. But it was not the culture that drove this. It was the character of those who were in charge of recruiting. There was a clash of cultures between the new leader and his team. But, until they could all appreciate the secondary nature of this culture clash, and recognize the underlying clash of character, the conflicts between them remained unresolved.

How values affect what you see

In Chapter 1, I said that leadership is not a simple response to circumstances, because circumstances are not just circumstances. Thatcher found herself faced with what she saw as a sick economy in need of some tough remedies, but got into conflict with people who felt that protecting workers from unscrupulous employers was what was needed. Gandhi found himself confronted with the British Raj, but he got into conflict with people who believed that the British had provided stability and beneficial technological development. Roosevelt felt that the Depression demanded an end to the system that had failed millions of Americans, but got into conflict with those who deeply believed in the preservation of the "rugged individualism" that had made America great. And King's insistence on the removal of segregation was out of step with those who firmly believed that blacks and whites should live their lives according to their different needs.

Partly as a consequence of what these four leaders have achieved, many attitudes have changed. That is one of their most important legacies. In

Britain, as I write, New Labor has been elected three times in succession (no Labor government achieved this before) on a political platform that some would describe as more Thatcherite than Thatcher. Partly thanks to Gandhi, democratic self-government is now the norm, and empires the exception. Social security remains a core part of US policy. And segregation on racial grounds is now illegal throughout the western world.

But it may have been different if Thatcher had not seen a war to be won; if Gandhi had not seen "badges of slavery of the Indian people," if Roosevelt had not seen a nation in need of protection and provision; and if King had not seen injustice in action. To a significant extent, it comes naturally to the Warrior to see challenges, the Guardian to see people in need, the Sage to see a denial of truth, and to the Adventurer to see conventions to be challenged.

That other people living in the same circumstances as these leaders did not see the circumstances in the same way is not wholly to do with their characters, of course. But to get other people to see things as you do, to adopt attitudes you want them to adopt, you need to know how to get beneath attitudes and understand what influences the ways they see circumstances. In other words, it helps to look at your values not only through your own eyes, but also through the eyes of people who see things differently.

Sometimes this is the starting point for effective conflict resolution.

Typical sources of conflict

If you look at the values associated with each of the four leadership models, and how they influence attitudes, you will see that many of the values are diametrically opposed. In the following section, I look at contrasting values.

Not every Warrior will feel exactly the same about the Warrior values, nor about the Sage values that oppose them. But in the following stories I present them in a simplified form to highlight the kinds of attitudes I have come across that underpin some of the conflicts I have encountered in my work with real people.

Warriors and Sages believe in different values, as do Guardians and Adventurers. In my experience, these values are rarely discussed within organizations, even where the organization espouses "core values." Since many of these value statements define attitudes and not values, this is not surprising. Nor is it surprising that those values that are published as "our values" are often things everyone who works in an organization would buy into, like teamwork, respect for individuals, and honesty.

Where Warriors and Sages differ, and where Guardians and Adventurers differ is in the underlying values that drive attitudes. Many of the

Warrior/Sage and Guardian/Adventurer conflicts I have come across stem from assumptions by both parties that the other believes in the same values as themselves. Their shortcomings, therefore, appear to lie in each party's failure to live up to those assumed values.

For this reason, some Warriors do not trust or respect their Sage colleagues, and vice versa. Similarly, some Guardians deeply suspect the motives of some Adventurers (and vice versa, again). But it is often hard, in an organizational context, for people to be sufficiently blunt to state this lack of trust openly.

It is different in families. Family members are here to stay, and have to be dealt with, "warts and all." But this does not stop family members from trying to change each other. It is often quite the reverse. It is within the family that value-driven conflicts are the stuff of an individual's experience. You may recognize some of the following scenarios. They are a very condensed set from an almost infinite number of family conflicts.

Warrior and Sage

Matthias's story

Matthias is a great disappointment to some of his family. A gifted scholar, he sailed through his academic exams, and was, according to those who taught him, destined for greatness. There were hints of a Nobel Prize in the fullness of time.

But, soon after taking on a research role in a EU-sponsored laboratory, Matthias seemed, according to his family, to lose interest. He did his work diligently, but seemed to lack the ambition to make something of himself. Headhunters contacted him about highly paid research jobs in commercial laboratories, but Matthias always turned them down.

His parents argued that, by being a "big fish in a little pond," Matthias was missing the opportunity to become famous for his work, and that it was Matthias's duty to apply himself to "more important" things than his little research project. Even if he could not bring himself to move on, they said, surely he could seek promotion within the laboratory, and get some recognition for his work.

When they visited Matthias in his little cottage in the Hartz Mountains, his parents were appalled at the "squalor." He drove a battered and unreliable old car, and his house was a "pigsty," lacking many of the amenities that they deemed a necessary part of modern living. They berated him for letting them down, for being such a disappointment. Throughout his glittering academic career, they had been able to hold their heads high among their friends and colleagues. Now, they were the parents of "that poor boy" who seemed to have lost his way.

There had been hints of this, to be sure, during Matthias's childhood. Considered a "wimp" by his classmates, Matthias had never enjoyed the rough and tumble of the playground or the playing field, preferring to bury himself in his books. From his parents' point of view, the resulting shyness was preventing him from facing up to the challenges of life, and letting both himself and them down.

When Matthias explained to his parents that he was happy, they retorted that he could be much happier if he set his sights a little higher. That, in turn, would make them happier. The argument came to a head when, as so often happens, his parents accused Matthias of being selfish and lazy.

Juanita's story

Juanita's mother has mixed feelings about her daughter's visits. She loves to see her, but feels intimidated by her presence. Moreover, she is torn between loyalty to her husband, who finds Juanita intolerable, and the love she feels for her daughter.

Juanita has "made good," and her visits back home always cause a stir. Neighbors twitch their curtains as her enormous car squeezes into the narrow streets where they live. Juanita is proud to park outside her parents' house, and sees the neighbor's interest as something her parents should take pride in too. She is their successful child.

Her father shows little interest in looking at the photographs she has brought. They show Juanita and her colleagues at a luxury hotel, mixing business with pleasure, and celebrating another great year. Juanita particularly wants them to see the picture of her receiving the employee of the year award, but her father mutters about the people she must have trampled on to get to the top.

Despite her best efforts, Juanita cannot seem to make her success an implicit criticism of her father's lack of it. And when she explains the healthy competition that makes everyone up their game, her father bemoans the "dog eat dog" world that Juanita and people like her have created. He suspects the creeping influence of the "gringo culture" she seems to have so happily embraced at the expense of their traditional loyalty to the family.

Her father has always had a suspicion that Juanita has a ruthless streak. As a child, Juanita was always desperate to win at everything, and, despite constant pleas from her mother to "play nicely" Juanita seemed to stop at nothing to get her own way. And now, here she was, once again, showing off her trophies and little victories. Why can't she learn not to be so pushy in life?

Temperatures rose as Juanita asked why her parents couldn't be proud of her, instead of always criticizing. "Don't you want me to make something of myself?" she asked. The argument came to a head when, as so often happens, her parents accused Juanita of being selfish and greedy.

Guardian and Adventurer

Jane's story

By the time Jane reached her mid-forties, her family began to realize that she was never going to grow up, although none of them admitted that they had given up hope. The habit her mother had acquired over the years of telling Jane what she ought to do and what not to do was not going to be broken, much to Jane's constant frustration.

Although everyone agreed that Jane was a warm, kind and considerate person at heart, the family could not understand why she couldn't settle down and take a bit of responsibility. While her siblings and cousins knuckled down to sensible jobs and providing grandchildren, Jane seemed to prefer animals to people, and flitted from job to job.

As the years rolled by, Jane visited her childhood home less and less. Each time she came, she was presented with a busy schedule of visits to aunts and cousins; after all, "blood is thicker than water," and, as her mother reminded her, she never knew when she would need their help in some crisis or other.

For crises there were. Having "callously" walked out on her first husband – a childhood sweetheart the family adored – Jane had found herself in a number of very "unsuitable" relationships, and had got into all sorts of scrapes. And just as she seemed incapable of making the effort with her husband, Jane crossed swords with boss after boss, treating them with a complete lack of respect, and, thereby, failing to establish the glittering career she clearly had the talent for.

When Jane's mother came for a visit, everything was prepared for a comfortable stay. As always, Jane made up the spare room to be welcoming. She cooked her mother's favorite meals, and had a bagful of the kinds of little gifts her mother adored. But it was not long before they were at each other's throats. It would have been better, according to her mother, if Jane had spent the little money she had to spare on making herself and the house a little more presentable.

Jane explained that she would dress to suit herself and not follow convention, and that the house was simply a place to move on from when the mood took her. The argument came to a head when, as so often happens, her mother accused Jane of being selfish and irresponsible.

Mark's story

When his brother appeared on the doorstep, Mark had a deep sense of dread. It usually spelt trouble, although, as always, the greeting was cheerful and light. His brother rarely visited, having always said that he found Mark's lifestyle stifling and rigid – "life in the 'burbs' " he calls it.

Mark had never been attracted to the reckless abandon with which his brother and his friends lived their lives. Never learning from experience, they all seemed to lurch from one disaster to another. Life is unpredictable enough, Mark thought, without asking for trouble. He did what he could to help when asked, but would have preferred it if, like him, they had made some provision for the "rainy days" that became a monsoon at times.

It was very early in life that Mark had realized that the world owes nobody a living. He quickly developed a sense that it would be up to him to take care of his parents when they became old and infirm, and that, if he were to be able to fulfil his ambition to have a happy family, he would need to shoulder the responsibilities that went with it.

Life threw problems at Mark, but he was resilient and dogged. Each time he took a deep breath and got on with it. Consequently, when his parents retired, he had been able to help set them up in their dream condo in Florida. His children had been coached and guided through school, and were all headed for the careers they had set their sights on, and he had made provision for his own retirement, still some years in the future.

What upset Mark was his brother's dismissive attitude to all this. Mark expressed disappointment that his brother's arrival had not been announced, and that it had meant he, Mark, would be unable to go to his local Little League meeting, letting everyone down. And all he got in reply was contempt. "Live a little," said his brother.

"I do," replied Mark, "And, unlike some, not at other people's expense." The argument came to a head when, as so often happens, his brother accused Mark of being boring and conformist.

Matthias, Juanita, Jane and Mark are neither unusual nor extreme examples of people whose characters and values are at odds with others in the family. In most real life conflicts like these, no-one ever wins. But in most real-life stories, the warring factions learn to live with each other, or to find compromises. The family provides a "safe" haven in which to allow yourself to be you, and remain relatively unchanged by these conflicts.

In some respects, this is the "natural" experience of most people throughout recent evolutionary time. In the kind of small-scale societies that typify human existence before the relatively recent explosion of technology-driven urban life, conflicts had to be dealt with one way or another, and rules and methods developed to suit the respective cultures of each society. In general, total exclusion from the family, clan or tribe was the exception. People with whom one had conflict were here to stay.

It is not so easy in the work environment. Here, different rules apply, not least of which is the possibility that one of the parties will leave or be removed. It is partly because of this "get-out clause" that I find some people I have worked with less competent in conflict resolution. In their minds, either they or the enemy needs to go, and this means that a solution to the conflict is less pressing.

Another rule is that people have to work for the organization's survival, especially in the private sector, where any weakness within the organization's fabric threatens to make it vulnerable to the competition. I may be able to live with the fact that my brother or sister is fundamentally misguided in how he or she lives her life, but, as a leader within an organization, should I seek to weed out those who I believe are a threat to our organization's culture, or even to its very survival?

To tolerate or not to tolerate?

Attitudes in our society have tended towards greater tolerance. It is now not only right and proper to tolerate others' sexuality, religion, or race, it is illegal to discriminate on such grounds. People are learning the benefits of diversity within teams based on cognitive styles. Visionaries and detail-people learn how to get the most out of each other to form strong partnerships, while rationalists partner to mutual benefit with those with well-developed people skills.

But for some people, tolerating other people's character is much harder. If I believe people should be responsible and mature, it is a betrayal of myself and my beliefs if I sit by and let those who flout the rules get away with it. But if I believe in the freedom of the individual above all else, it would be a betrayal of that belief and of myself if I did not challenge any convention I came across that I felt limited that freedom.

Later in the book, I shall return to the leadership challenge represented here. Leaders have to decide whether to establish a clear set of moral rules based on their values, or whether to accommodate those whose values are diametrically opposed to their own.

The influence of organizations

As a species, humans have evolved strategies to deal with the complexities and ambiguities of life. Most people have the ability to compete where it feels right, and to co-operate where that will work best. Most people know how to take care of others who need it, and how to throw themselves into the moment and enjoy the deep joy of feeling totally free from responsibilities. And in their daily lives, most people will not even notice the potential internal conflicts between the Warrior and Sage, or the Guardian and Adventurer.

But something odd happens when we enter an organization or institution. The world of work is a world of purpose. Within an organization, it makes sense to ask, "What are you **for**?" In our ordinary lives, this question does not. We just are.

There has been little time in human evolutionary history for us to get used to this. In the four million years or so during which the species has been evolving, our psychological make up has been adapting to circumstances in which the locus of experience is within the tribe or clan, and in which people did not "go out to work." Having a "job" is, in historical terms, very different. In the small scale societies that typify human experience over the majority of human existence, "unemployment figures" make no sense.

In the western world of technology and commerce, however, most people get up in the morning, leave their homes, and enter a different realm of purpose and identity. This is where people's instincts for survival, to compete, to take responsibility, and to learn seek opportunities for expression.

It is in the workplace that some of our Warrior need to compete will be satisfied. Our Guardian will find comfort in the authority vested in those in charge (whether ourselves or others). Our Sage will delight in co-operative activities seeking new knowledge. And our Adventurer will be switched on when we have something to do that is novel and exploratory.

But people's needs are not all the same. Warriors learn how to "play nicely," but if they are denied the chance to take on challenges and be rewarded for their success in meeting these challenges, they will feel dissatisfied in their work. Sages can throw themselves into competitive activities, but, unless they see a worthwhile purpose behind being asked to stretch themselves day in day out, they will begin to wonder what is the point of clocking on every morning. Guardians will be happy to challenge convention and go out on a limb now and then, but will begin to despair if such activities do not lead to clear plans and directions. And Adventurers will recognize the value of systems and processes up to a point, but will, eventually, feel an overwhelming need to break free.

It is often at times when people feel these stresses that they utter the plea, "We need leadership."

But what people mean by this is not the same. What Warriors and Sages, Guardians, and Adventurers want from leaders is very different. That's what Part 2 of this book explores in more detail.

Piling on yet more challenge to the Sage is not, in his or her eyes, leadership. Setting down ever clearer rules, roles and responsibilities is not what Adventurers call leadership. Preventing people from getting stuck into an exciting battle with the competition is not good leadership for the Warrior. And saying to people, "Do whatever you want," is abdication from leadership in the view of the Guardian.

It may be tempting to infer from all this that the ideal leader is infinitely adaptable, balancing Warrior with Sage, Guardian with Adventurer. That is not what experience and research tell us. Margaret Thatcher is not remembered for compromise, but for strength. Mahatma Gandhi is not revered for taking up arms against the enemy, but precisely because he consistently advocated peace. Martin Luther King's legacy is robust because he never did shy away from challenging the conventional wisdom of his peers. And Roosevelt followed his beliefs and values consistently and steadfastly throughout his life.

Trying to be all things to all people is not interpreted as adaptability in a leader. It is vacillation and inconsistency. Leaders succeed because people learn what to expect from them, and then see what is being expected delivered unwaveringly, consistently and comprehensively.

And in all cases, leaders who do this build their leadership strategies on what they believe in: their values, which, in turn, shape their characters.

In leadership, character comes first, strategy emerges from it.

At this point, therefore, take time to consider whether these last two chapters have helped resolve for you whether you are more Warrior than Sage, or more Guardian than Adventurer.

Internal conflict

As humans we have all inherited the instincts that form the four elements of character I am describing in this book. What makes us different is the degree to which each of these instincts influence who we are. You have the ability and motivation to fight, to learn, to take care of others and to have fun.

What makes people different is how they deal with the contradictions between the value sets. Some of the time you can deal with the contradictions by segmenting yourself. You can be Guardian at work and Adventurer at the weekend. You can be Warrior in your job and Sage at home.

This works reasonably well. But it has its problems and limitations.

The first is that there come times when we have to make choices. When a career opportunity comes along that conflicts with the needs of the family, what do you do? When the pressures of your current job become an almost intolerable strain on you personally, but there is no alternative that will meet your financial commitments, what do you do? When a rival threatens to take credit for work you have done, what do you do? When you fall out of love with the father or mother of your children, what do you do?

In situations like this, being a bit Warrior and a bit Sage, or a bit Guardian and a bit Adventurer doesn't help. When the chips are down, you have to make up your mind. And you have to live with the consequences of your decision. Being honest with yourself, and thereby being true to yourself in the decisions you make and live with means knowing more about yourself than that you are "a bit of both."

Being a "weekend" Adventurer, or a "weekday" Warrior means it is likely that in one or the other role you are literally "acting out of character," or pretending. Many Warrior fathers or mothers pretend to be Sages at the weekend. But they spend their time teaching their children how to compete. Many "'weekday Warriors" try to battle it out at work with the best of them. They can be amongst the unhappiest people I have worked with.

It is unlikely that you will succeed in being the best leader you can be if you try to be all things to all people. What you may see as adaptability may appear to others as being wishy-washy, inconsistent and insincere.

Look back at the values, and the conflicts between the values and ask yourself, when the chips are down, when I have to stand up and be counted, where am I?

CHAPTER 6

Home base

Change and development

Traditional approaches to development and growth have often been based on the assumption that our personalities change over time. Some people believe that, as we go through the journey of life, we change.

As children we are expected to almost exclusively to be Adventurer. As we grow, with floods of testosterone taking charge of our bodies, we are expected to take on the Warrior. We mature into the Guardian, encouraged to do so by the higher levels of oxytocin in our systems which are the result of regular sexual activity and (in women) childbirth and breastfeeding. Finally, we are expected to acquire the wisdom and insights of the Sage, and become revered elders.

The anthropological record shows that this is a journey that is common to many societies. Many of these societies developed, and some retain, rites of passage marking the key transition points on that journey. Those who fail to adopt the behaviors of the appropriate role may be encouraged to "grow up."

This idea places pressure on us to conform to the expected values and behaviors of the stage we have reached in our lives. But for Adventurers, parenthood and seniority at work do not always bring the contentment they are expected to deliver. Archetypal Guardians often devote a fair amount of their childhood to trying to take charge of anything they can. Grandfathers can remain fiercely competitive, ruing their physical frailties as they reduce the frequency of "winning" (many such ageing Warriors become almost obsessive dominoes players). And childhood Sages sneak off from gym and games to bury themselves in a book, earning the reputation for being wimps.

Many of those rites of passage in traditional societies were characterized by fear and brutality. Some members of the cultures may have had to be strongly persuaded to move into lifestyles that they were not happy about.

Some people do go through life changing events. The most obvious example is when you go through an experience that is highly stressful.

Stress produces cortisol, which, in turn, switches on genes that switch on other genes, and so on. Genes are not the starting point of behavior: they don't cause who we are. Through the interaction of genes, receptors, hormones and experience, we interact with the world as we experience it.[1]

In general, the complex system that is our genetic make up, our receptivity to hormonal influence, and all the other parts of our individual make-up tend to return to equilibrium whatever we do. Your first parachute jump may be a memorable experience that provides new perspectives. But it is unlikely to change your character. Being ill-treated and under constant threat of death may do.

In much the same way, people tend to oscillate back to "equilibrium" in their characters. "As we get older we stay the same, only more so." Part of the challenge of self-awareness is to find that Home Base away from which external influences may have drawn you, or from which you may have wandered.

Let me once again distinguish between character on the one hand, and attitudes and behavior on the other. As children we are taught how to behave, and we acquire attitudes from parents, family, and peer groups. We grow up within a particular culture, and, if we belong to a religion, it is likely that it will be the religion of our family.

During adolescence many people gain freedoms they never had before, and students are notorious for their Adventurer attitudes. If we marry and have children, we acquire responsibilities that limit risk-taking. But these are like life's clothes that we put on and take off according to our changing situations. Beneath this attitudinal clothing lie those elements of character that make us who we are: intelligence and core personality or character. "By adulthood, intelligence is like personality: mostly inherited, partly influenced by factors unique to the individual and very little affected by the family you grew up in."[2]

As we go through life, we are told to modify some aspects of our behavior. Warriors may constantly be told to be less competitive and to learn how to lose gracefully. Guardians may be told to "get a life." Sages will be accused of being wimps, and to toughen up. Adventurers will almost certainly be told, time and time again, to grow up.

To gain acceptance by people who are close, most of us will respond to these messages and adjust. We want to fit in. But as time passes and we learn more and more about ourselves, we feel more or less comfortable in the clothes we have put on.

I have met so many people who feel uncomfortable in this way. Some of them are Warriors who have tried to suppress their competitive spirit but find themselves picking fights over trivial things. Some are Guardians who are stressed by the cavalier attitudes of their colleagues. Others are Sages who cannot get to grips with the relentless pursuit of profit over people. And others are Adventurers who think they are biding their time until they can break free from their responsibilities and set off on the adventure they know, deep down, will never happen.

These people share two things in common. The first is that they are all more or less unhappy and frustrated. The second is that they have allowed other people to write the agendas for their lives.

Who is writing the agenda for your life? If it is not you, and you are therefore living outside your "Home Base," the chances are that, as a leader, you are swimming against the tide, and will find it impossible to maximize your leadership potential.

Home base

Imagine a spectrum, with Warrior at one end and Sage at the other. Somewhere along that spectrum is one aspect of your Home Base:

The dot represents the degree to which you associate with Warrior values or Sage values. At the far left is "pure" Warrior; at the other, "pure" Sage. In practice, nobody is either 'pure' Warrior or "pure" Sage. But in the previous chapter I paired up the Warrior and Sage values, suggesting each contradicted the other.

We make choices. In many cases, these choices are not "a bit of this and a bit of that." They are either/or choices. Consider these situations:

You are at a career crossroads. You have two job offers. Job number 1 is better paid, and is a significant challenge, so much so that it is likely that you will have to work very hard to make it a success. Job number 2 you will certainly be able to do well, as you have proven in the past that you are capable of doing this kind of thing excellently. Although it pays significantly less, it delivers much more direct benefit to the community.

The Warrior chooses job number 1. The challenge is an inherent part of job satisfaction, while the benefit to the community will accrue from the additional wealth created by any such enterprise. The pay is an additional extra. The Sage chooses job number 2, recognizing that a career that makes a direct and positive contribution to the well-being of others is the right choice for him or her.

Your organization operates a mentoring system. You have two possible mentors to work with. Mentor number 1 is a renowned high-flyer who is going places. He or she has made rapid progress up the organization, and, although he or she may have trod on a few toes to get there, many people recognize that "you can't make an omelette without breaking eggs." He or she has agreed to mentor you if you want it, but has warned that you will have to keep up a hectic pace, and that you will have to learn as you go, as he or she has little time for idle chatter. Mentor number 2 is a well-established and wise person who has expressed an interest in helping your development. He or she has warned that it takes time to grow into good leadership, but that he or she will guide you all the way. The fact that he or she has, as some people say, plateau-ed, means he or she will have much more time to devote to your development.

The Warrior chooses mentor number 1, not wanting to be associated with someone who has stopped fighting. The thrill of keeping up the pace with mentor number 1 is part of the attraction, and no-one wants to turn down the chance of being associated with a winner. The Sage chooses mentor number 2, feeling wary of becoming tainted by the questionable ethics of mentor number 1, and recognizing the lasting benefits of learning from the wise.

You find yourself mixed up in a political battle. Your opponent is known to be dangerous and a born fighter. Moreover, he or she has many people on his or her side. But you think they are doing something very wrong.

Knowing the fighting skills of the opponent, the Warrior takes on the challenge, planning a campaign that will outsmart him or her, and produce the right outcome. It may be a bloody affair, and may take time and skill, but, far from being a deterrent, this only makes the battle the more exciting. Battle will only be engaged when the forces for good have been properly marshalled. The Sage talks to the opponent, putting all the cards on the table, and inviting the opponent to see the error of his or her ways. Even though by so doing, the opponent has every chance to use the information shared against you, the Sage believes in working together toward a solution.

You have experienced a spectacular failure in a job. The Warrior immediately looks for another job just like it so that, this time, he or she can get it right. Not wanting to be defeated, he or she believes that it is only by getting straight back in the saddle that you can overcome defeat. The Sage realizes his or her shortcomings, and learns that some jobs are just not for him or her. Valuing humility over pride, the Sage re-evaluates his or her strengths and weaknesses and turns away to find a job that is more in line with what he or she can do well.

These are the kinds of situations that test our character, and that allow us to explore the inner conflict between our Warrior and our Sage because the choices we make are value choices.

The Warrior chooses the challenging job, the high-flying mentor, to fight for what is right, and to go back and prove him or herself in the next job because that is what Warriors believe in. The Sage chooses the job that does good for others, the wise mentor, the path of peace, and to turn away from failure because that is what Sages believe in.

This is why, in these situations, the Warrior may interpret the Sage's choices as cowardly, naïve, or lacking in ambition. And why the Sage may see the Warrior's choices as shallow, self-interested and aggressive.

Faced with an either/or choice in each of the Warrior/Sage values, people are more or less consistent in which of the pair they choose. It is this degree of consistency that leads to this aspect of your Home Base.

In this example:

The person has been 100 percent consistent in choosing Warrior over Sage values. This does not mean he or she has no Sage at all. It just means that, in each and every case where he or she had to choose between the opposing pairs of values, he or she always chose Warrior over Sage. There is, for this person, little doubt about what's important to him or her.

In my experience of working with people using this model, those whose Home Base lies at or near one end of this spectrum are not unbalanced or extreme in their behaviors. They are, however, clear and consistent. The people who I find are struggling are those who plot on this spectrum somewhere in the middle:

This is not adaptability; it is uncertainty. Uncertain leaders rarely make good leaders.

The other spectrum is that between Guardian and Adventurer. It is completely independent from the Warrior/Sage.

The conflict between each end of this spectrum provides us, once again, with choices. Consider these situations.

You job has become boring. But you have a mortgage, children to support, and very little chance of getting another job that will bring in anywhere near enough money to support your family to the standard they have become accustomed to.

The Guardian recognizes that there are more important things in life than his or her level of boredom. His or her primary duty is to provide, so he or she sticks with the job, and compensates for boredom at work by spending quality time with the children and enriching their lives. The Adventurer resigns. He or she knows that something will turn up, and hopes that the children will realize one day that any hardships they may go through are better than sacrificing your personal freedom for the sake of just a job.

A lot of your time at work is spent on unproductive red tape. The Guardian builds consensus among others who feel the same, and works toward a means of reducing red tape by persuading the powers that be to consider changing the system for the better. The Adventurer breaks the rules of the system, and waits. He or she may get into trouble, but by disobeying the rules of the system, he or she may prove by his or her actions that the system is unnecessary, and destroy it.

You are offered the chance to start something new. The problem with the opportunity is that it is very high risk. It is a completely new direction for the organization, and the chances of it working are slim. You will be working with little support from the senior people, and if it goes wrong, there is no guarantee that there will be anything for you to go back to. Because of the risks, the organization wants you to keep the project under wraps, and you will have few, if any, people working with you. You will be on your own.

The Guardian weighs up the probabilities of success. On the one hand, if it works, it will benefit the organization. On the other, it will be a lonely and risky venture that could rebound very badly. He or she listens to the advice that this is a "poisoned chalice" and says "thank you but no thanks." The Adventurer throws caution to the wind and goes for it.

You have worked hard and are offered a promotion. The new role carries with it considerable responsibility for budgets, people, and the direction of strategy. The salary increase is considerable, and your new title will reflect your new-found seniority. In your capacity as manager, you will have little, if any, time to do the kind of job you have been doing. It is a significant shift away from doing to managing.

The Guardian accepts the promotion as the next step in his or her career, and feels appropriately rewarded for his or her hard work. The Adventurer declines if the promotion means he or she no longer has the chance to do what he or she loves to do. He or she knows that he or she may find the responsibilities of management oppressive if it involves only maintaining the status quo.

The Guardian chooses to stay with the steady job, to look for evolutionary change to unproductive systems, to decline the poisoned chalice, and the promotion because these choices are in line with what he or she believes in. Similarly, the Adventurer's values are what influence his or her choice to quit the boring job, to break the rules, to go for the adventure, and to stay free from the burden of responsibility.

The Guardian may see the Adventurer's choices as irresponsible, destructive and reckless. The Adventurer may see the Guardian's choices as dull, obsequious, and unadventurous.

Once again, where you sit on the Guardian/Adventurer spectrum depends on how consistent you are, not how "adaptable."

By combining how you make more or less consistent choices in these two dimensions you can map your Home Base on a two-dimensional grid, like this:

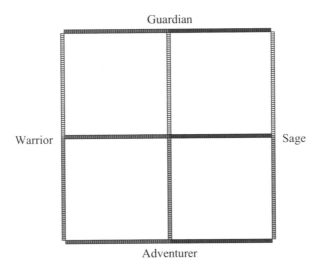

This gives four distinct kinds of Home Base: Guardian/Warrior, Guardian/Sage, Sage/Adventurer, and Adventurer/Warrior. The characteristics of people who "live" in these four kinds of Home Base make them very different kinds of people from those whose Home Bases are different.

At this point, I would like to restate an important point. Not all Guardian/Warriors are the same. There are many other aspects of personality that this model does not measure. For those familiar with MBTI™, an ESTJ Guardian/ Warrior will behave very differently from an INFP Guardian/ Warrior, even though they may believe in the same values.

Even within the same Home Base, people will differ in the degree to which their values influence their behaviors. In describing those four archetypal leaders' values, I have deliberately overlooked, so far, the values that are not directly related to their legends.

Clearly, Margaret Thatcher is Warrior and Guardian, but she is remembered for her Warrior. In terms of this model, she is Warrior/Guardian, not Guardian/Warrior. "She lived for work, and particularly the work of politics. 'Home,' she once confessed, 'is what you come home to when you haven't anything better to do.' "[3] She also wrote in her autobiography: "While the home must always be the centre of one's life, it should not be the boundary of one's ambitions."[4]

Gandhi's sense of responsibility makes him a Sage/Guardian; his respect for authority is clear from another extract from his *Commandments for a Satyarahi*:a: "A civil resister will joyfully obey all the orders issued by the leader of the corps, whether they please him or not. He will carry out orders in the first instance even though they appear to him to be insulting, inimical or foolish, and then appeal to higher authority."[5]

FDR was a fighter as well as Guardian. He showed few of the qualities of the Sage: "The idea that he was remotely interested in becoming an intellectual shows how little Butler [President of Columbia University] understood him."[6] And many of those of the Warrior: "'there is nothing I love so much as a good fight,' he told the New York Times."[7]

There is also no surprise that Martin Luther King was Adventurer/Sage. He adopted Gandhi's strategy of passive resistance as the right way to achieve his goals: "Admittedly, non-violence in the truest sense is not a strategy that one uses simply because it is expedient at the moment; non-violence is ultimately a way of life that men live by because of the sheer morality of its claim."[8]

What makes these examples so powerful, however, is the clarity with which they used their primary set of values as drivers of their strategies.

Four kinds of home base

There is no such thing as a "typical" Guardian/Warrior, nor of members of any of the other three primary Home Bases. How people behave depends upon many other factors. But some of the insights people can get from becoming aware of their Home Bases, especially where they interact with people from different Home Bases, may be helpful. Take the following four cases. In each, the person I am describing and what they gained from their individual analyses is real. I have changed their names and the names of their organizations to preserve their confidentiality.

Victor, Sage/Adventurer

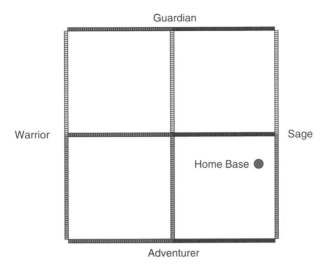

Victor is in his mid-fifties, and works for a large European financial institution. His family is wealthy, and he is well-connected. At the time we worked together, he had been offered the opportunity to change his role within the organization. For five years he had been head of the organization's human resources department, but had decided that he needed a change.

His most important values are:

- Seeking spiritual inspiration
- Fun, adventure and playfulness
- Change and variety
- Love of the arts

None of these are commonly represented as the core values of his organization, which can be characterized as 'Guardian/Warrior'. Victor's challenge is how to develop and maintain a leadership style that is both in line with what he believes in, and is true to himself on the one hand, and which will not be so counter-cultural to his organization that he fails to be as appreciated and respected as his collagues.

In the eyes of some of his colleagues and direct reports, Victor lacked credibility. He believes in the essential goodness of people, and gave them enormous degrees of freedom to develop to their own strengths. He watched a great deal of political battles that took place in his organization with bemused detachment, preferring not to get embroiled in what he saw as posturing.

Despite his years of experience and the success of many of the initiatives he started, Victor is viewed with suspicion by some others. Some see him as weak and unwilling to stand up for himself. Others interpret his lack of direct involvement in the internal politics as deviousness. Under pressure from many people around him, Victor spent many years doubting himself, and often woke up in the mornings convinced that he had to change.

His problem, however, was that he had tried to change several times in the past. Each time, he had found himself trying to pursue strategies others found so easy. Try as he may, his heart was not in the fighting, jockeying for position, or relentlessly leaning on his people for results. Almost inevitably, he blamed himself for what he saw as his own shortcomings, and found himself oscillating between his attempts at being Warrior/Guardian and feeling stressed on the one hand, and drifting back into his natural style, and feeling inadequate on the other.

Like so many others, Victor's real issue was a sense that what came naturally to him was not "right." This led him to be hesitant and apologetic when he was in Adventurer/Sage mode, and to be half-hearted when in Warrior/Guardian mode. Consequently he became less effective, and ever more stressed.

Now that he has explored both this model and his place within it, Victor can finally settle down to the development of his natural style, and deliver to it with confidence. This has not made others around him suddenly change their minds about him; some still interpret his style as weak and lacking in authority over his staff. But now Victor is in a position to develop his style with confidence, and remove the self-doubt that previously caused the hesitancy that others saw as proof of their analysis of him.

In his new role, Victor has the chance to build his leadership style in line with what he fundamentally believes in. Others may not believe in his values, but they will be unable, as before, to undermine him quite so easily.

Roger, Guardian/Sage

Roger is in his late forties. A well-educated and experienced manager, he works for an international bank. Having steadily climbed his way up to relative seniority, he found himself working in a management team headed up by a younger, dynamic and energetic man who was determined to make this area of the business an outstanding success. Roger's new boss was Gerry, the Guardian/Warrior I shall describe in the next section.

Roger's core values are:

- Wisdom
- Having a family

- Inner harmony
- Learning and understanding
- Fast living

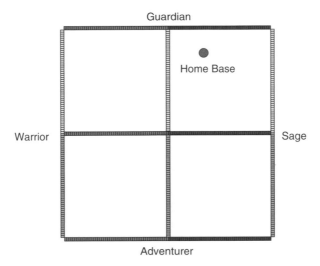

"Fast living" is an odd core value for a Guardian/Sage, but Roger had become something of a professional ex-pat, and had nowhere in particular to call home. He had acquired a great deal of international experience, and this had been one of the main reasons for his value to Gerry's team.

Gerry's arrival on the scene meant that what had become something of a backwater in the company was going to become one of the most exciting and dynamic environments in which to work. Gerry had great ambitions for the team, and was setting the team the most challenging goals they had ever experienced. For Roger, Gerry's arrival was a mixed blessing.

On the one hand, Roger could see the benefit of having such as dynamo in charge. On the other, Gerry's relentless agenda was a threat. Roger could see that the painstaking work he had put into achieving a good work/life balance was in danger of being undermined. Roger was proud of his loyalty, but knew that his loyalties were going to be divided if he did not take care.

During the first six months I knew Roger, and in the early days of Gerry's leadership, Roger found himself stepping up a gear or two. He volunteered to take on a number of initiatives, got involved in several others, and threw himself into the job of helping to grow the business in line with Gerry's bold vision. What he did not notice, however, was that, at the same time, he was losing the personal touch that had characterized his natural leadership style. Roger was trying to become Gerry.

Roger took a step back once we had discovered his Guardian/Sage preferences. He said that, on reflection, one of his key drivers is "trying to learn what I can do for others." But under the new regime, he had to admit that he was actually trying to find out what others could do for him. He was in breach of one of his lifelong principles which was, in his words, "to use your time wisely."

The problem for Roger was that while he was in such close and constant contact with Gerry, he found it difficult not to be seduced into operating as though he were another Gerry. The problem was resolved partly through careful consideration of what was best for Roger, and partly by good fortune.

Gerry's success in growing the team's business was rewarded by his being given an empire three times as large. Now there were four businesses to run across the globe. All four businesses needed to be brought up to the same level of activity, and needed integrating into a cohesive unit. Much of the business was to be done in the Far East, where Roger had a good deal of experience. Gerry needed someone to head up the far eastern operations; Roger needed somewhere he could lead in his own way.

Since culturally, the Guardian/Sage model is more familiar in the Far East, this was Roger's best chance of blending his leadership style with Gerry's desire to get the best out of the growing business opportunities. Both agreed and Roger set out with his family to re-establish his own way of leading.

Gerry, Guardian/Warrior

We met Gerry in the previous section. His meteoric rise to success had been fuelled by a burning ambition. He told me "I want to run a billion-dollar business."

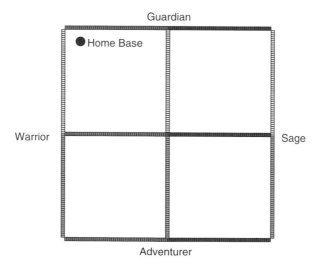

Still less than forty years old at the time, he was well on his way. He was one of the best deal-makers in the business, and had a contagious energy and drive. On taking over the business, he quickly started to set extraordinary targets, despite the fact that the markets were in apparent decline and competitors were laying people off in anticipation of a major downturn. Gerry saw the competitors' actions as an opportunity to walk into undefended territory.

Although Gerry had managerial experience, this was the largest business he had run. He inherited a wide range of people with very mixed skills and personalities. He set about promoting those he admired for their ambition and determination, and gathered round him a strong team of people who were prepared to step up to the challenges. He also saw a lot of dead wood.

Not everyone in his team was similarly enthused by these ambitious targets. But Gerry knew that, if he were to have any chance of galvanizing his people, he would have to set the pace himself. This was not difficult, as he has an almost inexhaustible supply of energy. Leading from the front, Gerry involved himself in almost every deal, providing excellent negotiating skills and seeing opportunities everywhere.

Everyone knew that Gerry had problems in the balance between personal life and work, and some also feared that the example he was setting meant a similar threat to their own work/life balance. His direct reports rated his self-awareness as low. They also said that they believed that he was more interested in his own career than in them, that he could be arrogant, could adopt a bullying style under stress, and had demonstrated significant insensitivity to people. When Gerry and I discussed some of this, he responded, "It's closure, not control."

Gerry's initial reaction to discovering his Guardian/Warrior preferences was that he was not surprised at all. The key learning for him was that there are in this world, and within his team, people who were both different, but also, in their own ways, highly effective. A lot of Gerry's "dead wood" was alive and brimming with potential. It was as we were talking about Juan that the penny dropped.

Juan was, in Gerry's eyes, failing: a nice guy, but lacking the killer instinct. Gerry was seriously considering "letting Juan go." But at the eleventh hour, Gerry realized that Juan represented what the team desperately needed: an excellent manager of people. And then there was Derek, who was slow to clinch deals but who had an uncanny knack of building lasting relationships built on implicit trust. And Mario who could settle any dispute, no matter how vitriolic it had become. And Roger, who was perfect for the far east.

Gerry knew intuitively that people are different, and that each has his or her own strengths. But up to this point, he had seen these strengths as compensating factors, as silver medals in his race rather than gold medals in their own disciplines. Unconsciously, Gerry relegated these strengths to the second division, and despite his efforts to treat them no differently from the "winners," could not avoid making them feel undervalued.

The power of this model for Gerry was its ability to reframe how he thought about those who were not Guardian/Warriors like him. Once he could honestly appraise them as successful Guardian/Sages and so on, rather than failed Guardian/Warriors with compensating but second-class strengths, he could and did pull back from creating around him a tribe of Gerry-clones, and give himself the chance to create the diversity his business needed for the long haul.

Your home base

There's a wonderful irony when, in my work with highly paid investment banker Warriors, they tell me that fortune and material wealth are not important to them. The Porsche must be an investment for the sake of the children's future, then. And the Rolex watch, the Armani suits, the Mont Blanc pen, and all the other trophies that prove their success.

Some values are so deeply embedded that they become invisible. The least honest of my Warrior clients even say that they are in the business only to save up enough money to afford to go off and become unpaid voluntary workers in the Third World. The number of such Warriors I have worked with over the years who have actually done full-time voluntary work can be counted on the fingers of one hand. They must still be saving up.

The point of this is that it is hard for some people to come to terms with who they really are. Those pressures to conform, indeed, the whole of our experience of socialization into the norms and culture in which we grow up build layers of attitudes upon our deeper foundations. Sometimes these layers can obscure what we truly believe in.

It is not just Warriors who can fool themselves. I have known Adventurers who swear that their families are the most important thing in their lives, but who rarely prioritize home over other options. I have met Guardians who tell me that their deepest desire is to go round the world backpacking – once they have paid off the mortgage.

Sometimes it is hard to sift out the wheat from the chaff.

How stories can help

In chapter 2, I said that we often interpret the experiences of our lives in ways that are in line with our characters. Strict parenting gives Guardians a strong moral sense, but makes Adventurers determined to be liberal parents.

Poverty in childhood makes Warriors even more determined to make a success of their lives, but teaches Sages the value of humility.

Sometimes, however, people I work with seem to contradict this. They say they believe in one set of values, yet the stories they tell, and the lessons they say they have learnt from those stories are at odds with those values. For example, some people I have met say they are Sage in their values, but all the stories they tell about how they come to be the people they are, are stories of beating the opposition, winning against the odds, and showing people the error of their ways. These are Warrior stories, and are in line with the values of winning, competing, and achieving.

There are a number of reasons why this kind of apparent contradiction may come about. One is that people are complex and should not be expected to be either one thing or another. I can go along with this so long as you do not use it as a cop-out. It goes back to the "I'm a bit of both" way of avoiding the rigorous process of achieving self-awareness. Everyone is a bit of both, but simply leaving it at that is not enhancing self-awareness, it's avoiding it.

A second reason for this apparent contradiction between values and formative stories is that the lessons of the stories may have been those that have been imposed by other people. Warrior parents of Sage children can be tempted to bring out the competitive spirit in little Johnny by constantly banging on about that egg-and-spoon race he won back in junior school. Said enough times by people we love and want to believe, we can find ourselves writing our life stories through their eyes, not our own.

A third reason for this apparent contradiction is that it is the stories that tell the truth. For a variety of reasons some people espouse values that they never follow. They say they believe in one set of values, but apart from the words, nothing in what they do, or in how they look at the formative events of their lives supports this.

In my work in leadership development I almost always use my leadership model in conjunction with other psychometric tools, including the MBTI™. When I run analyses, one statistic stands out as significant.

One aspect of MBTI™ separates out people with a preference for Thinking from people with a preference for Feeling. The Thinking function is that part of people's cognitive make-up that deals with logic. Essential to Thinking is that it operates in the abstract. Through abstraction, we can learn the rules of arithmetic: that one plus one equals two. It is not a matter of debate, it just is. So we use the Thinking function to deal with problems in the abstract, finding solutions that would apply in all similar circumstances.

The Feeling function is neither cool nor analytical. Part of its activity is empathy. When we watch a detective film, for example, we use our

Thinking function to follow the plot and try to work out whodunit, while we operate in Feeling more when we feel ourselves drawn to the character of the detective, or empathize with a victim. Thinking helps us to work out what something is; Feeling helps us to work out what it means for us.

Some people have a preference for Thinking. This does not mean that they cannot empathize or operate in the realm of meanings. It means that, faced with a problem, they will naturally focus attention on the problem itself in the first instance. Other people have a preference for Feeling. This does not mean that they cannot think logically or objectively; it means that, faced with a problem, they will naturally focus on the person who has the problem in the first instance. In general, for Thinkers, it is the problem that needs attention first; for Feelers it is what the problem means to the person facing it that is most important.

In my statistical analysis, people with a preference for Thinking are significantly more likely to have contradictions between their formative stories and their espoused values. This does not mean that everyone with a preference for Thinking will express this split. Not does it mean that all Feelers have stories totally in tune with their espoused values. But where there is a significant gap between values and stories, it is more common that this person does have a preference for Thinking.

Some people are so comfortable with the cognitive process of abstraction that they can happily objectify themselves. Treating themselves almost as case studies, they have a tendency to deduce their values from external evidence, such as what people ought to believe in, rather than look inside themselves to feel their values. Such people almost always have a preference for Thinking, and are more likely to operate with principles rather than with values.

Principles are rules for behavior; values are beliefs that can and often do inform behavior. Principles are adopted from outside; values are inherent in our character. People with a preference for Thinking, being more liable to treat themselves in the abstract are more likely, therefore, to express a set of principles they feel they ought to follow, and assume that these are their values.

As you consider the values described in chapter 4, and compare them with the stories you may have reflected on in chapter 2, ask yourself the following questions.

Are the values I most approved of really my values or are they a set of principles? Are the lessons I say I learnt from the experiences of my past my lessons of those taught to me by others? And if there is a mismatch between my values and my stories, where does this come from?

Why bother?

Developing effective leadership depends upon building on firm foundations. Those leaders I have worked with who do a good job are almost always people who both know themselves, and who are true to what they know. Many of those who struggle have been on leadership development courses where they have been convinced by case material and solid research data that the key to leadership success lies in behaving in one way or another, and they have valiantly tried to apply the principles they have learnt. Good intentions, but rarely effective.

You are unlikely to be a successful leader if you try to be someone you are not, no matter how much evidence is available to show that other people have succeeded with such strategies. If you are a Guardian/Sage, don't try to lead primarily by challenging convention. If you are an Adventurer/Sage, don't try to lead from the front unless it is the only option. If you are a Warrior/Adventurer, don't set yourself up as the wise counsellor; develop the skill, but don't make it the cornerstone of your leadership strategy. And if you are a Guardian/Warrior, don't try to become one of the "lads" unless you are doing something away from the office, and are deliberately showing a different side of yourself.

In the later chapters of the book we'll look at many different ways of leading. A good leader will be able to be flexible, and adopt styles outside of his or her Home Base where necessary. But these will be additional skills, added to a firm foundation of skills that grow naturally out of your Home Base.

What you need to develop is a mode of leadership that people can see as consistent and comfortable for you, and which is your default mode. Like Margaret Thatcher, Martin Luther King, Mahatma Gandhi, or Franklin D. Roosevelt, you will develop a clear and consistent style that people can rely on.

That style should align strongly with your Home Base, with your values. If you pretend to be the kind of leader you are not, you will be putting on a series of masks. Even if you don't see through these masks, others will.

CHAPTER 7

Where you are now

People do not always operate within their Home Base. Some of the people I work with are at a stage of their lives where how they are behaving is not completely in line with their stated values. There are a number of reasons why this may be, and some of them will have a direct influence on their attitudes to leadership.

In this chapter I look at some ways in which people I have worked with are doing just that. They have deliberately or unintentionally "drifted" away from their Home Base, and this has had a variety of impacts on how they lead others. And because there are many different ways in which you can be operating away from your Home Base, I shall introduce quite a number of these case studies, each illustrating one of the more common kinds of "drift."

One of the most common reasons for a shift "south" (from Guardian towards Adventurer) is the adventurousness of youth. In the previous chapter I said that the journey through life from Adventurer through Warrior and Guardian to Sage is largely an illusion. Adolescents do rebel and take themselves off on adventures. But Guardians who go through this stage do not become Adventurers, they simply enjoy the holiday from responsibility. Few truly regret moving back "north" when the time is right, even though the freedom and fun leave lasting positive memories.

Sue, the career adventurer

Sue is Warrior/Guardian. In her Home Base, the fact that she is not 100 percent Warrior is down to the moderating influence of her parents. Her values are consistently Warrior, but she feels that more of the stories that formed her are Sage than Warrior. She was taught throughout her childhood not to be so aggressive, and remembers the praise she received when she made mistakes and learnt from them, accepted that she is not in control of everything, and learnt to develop empathy for people around her. But she is in no doubt that it is the Warrior that is her major driver.

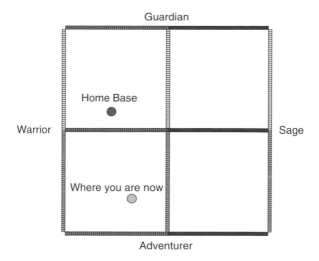

She is less certain about the Guardian, having some Adventurer values. These have made Sue more willing than some of her colleagues to take risks. Despite her number one value being **economic security**, when the business wanted someone to move from London to New York for an undefined period, she was the first to volunteer. Two other key values for Sue are **competition** and **achievement and accomplishment**, while her primary motivation is **to win and achieve**.

She also values **putting down roots**, and sees the New York assignment as an extended adventure that will enhance her career and give her a better chance to be successful in the organization. It is the kind of challenge that the Warrior loves.

Knowing that her assignment is aimed at starting up new ways of operating in the New York office, Sue has adopted the Adventurer/Warrior approach. She has little managerial authority, and is leading by sharing the challenge with her new colleagues, and exploring with them ways of making the new ways work in their local environment. She is relishing the freedom and the sense of adventure, and is happy, while the assignment continues, not having direct responsibility for people or budgets. Being away from Head Office is not a problem for Sue, as she knows that her drive, enthusiasm and determination will make the assignment successful, and she will return in triumph.

So for Sue, the distance she has moved from her Home Base is not an issue. It is a temporary shift, and she remains in control.

But not all such dramatic shifts are so constructive.

Bill, the "last laugh" battler

Bill is in his early sixties, but as energetic as a teenager. He is stubborn and, in many people's view, self-opinionated. He has a quick intelligence, and has learnt the arts of political compromise. For years he climbed the ladder within a major European financial institution, and took the most senior back office job as his final promotion within the organization. In this job he set about doing what he felt was right, and became a thorn in the side of many people who found him difficult to work with. Bill was always right.

When the organization took a major shareholding in one of its subsidiaries, Bill was offered the role of CEO. The subsidiary was much smaller, and was seen to be poorly administered, with little chance of its ever amounting to much of a business. For some people, the role of CEO was clearly a poisoned chalice. For Bill, it was a chance to make a point.

He was not going to slip into obscurity, but was going to make the subsidiary a dynamic and successful business in its own right. A management buy-out was always one of the options in his vision. But even if that were a step too far, he was determined to show his detractors that he could run a front-line business despite any obstacles they, the major shareholders, could put in his path.

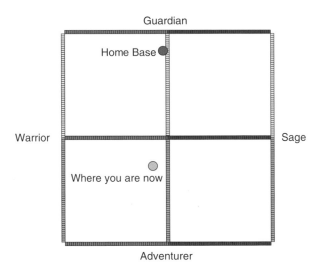

Bill's Home Base is Guardian/Warrior. His Warrior is less clear, as he does have some Sage values, and his experiences over the years have reinforced the benefit of not treating every battle as a war. What shocked Bill when we started working together was the distance from Home Base his current lifestyle represented. He was living in Adventurer/ Warrior territory. But unlike Sue, he had not planned this, and, as a result, was not in control of the consequences.

The Guardian in Bill convinced him that everything he was doing in his new role was for the benefit of the people in the subsidiary organization. His success would be to their benefit. But to achieve such success he had to be radical, to challenge convention, and make serious changes. At the time of his arrival, the subsidiary was as bureaucratic and sluggish as the parent organization, and he would not get far if he had to go cap in hand and beg every time he wanted to do something differently.

To some of the less adventurous of his new employees, Bill started to behave like a spoilt child. The subsidiary looked like a toy he was playing with. He appeared to take no notice of the insecurity he was causing for those who were less than thrilled by how he seemed to be taunting the parent company.

What made things worse was that Bill is a poor communicator (an INTJ in MBTI™ terms). Like many people with the same cognitive style, Bill often forgets to tell people what he is thinking, and even when he does talk his ideas through, he is less than rigorous in explaining how he got to his conclusions. He also has "twenty five ideas before breakfast," and frustrates people around him by constantly appearing to change his mind. For Bill, it is simply coming up with new thoughts; to others, he appears to start something up and then drop it overnight.

The reputation Bill unwittingly created for himself was one of reckless irresponsibility. He appeared to be interested only in proving himself right; the transformation of the subsidiary became a one-man campaign of self-interest. Despite saying that he valued consultation and dialogue, time and again he brought about changes that only he could understand. In his impatience to get things done he lost the one thing a leader should always try to hang onto: the trust of his people.

Whereas Sue was operating out of her Home Base as part of a planned strategy, Bill was doing so without noticing. In my experience, being as far from Home Base as Bill was is always risky. It is enormously risky if you do not even know you are doing it. Bill needed to rethink seriously his strategy for change, and bring it back much closer to his Home Base. From there, he could regain control of the situation, and bring his people onboard alongside him, instead of turning them away.

We'll come back to Bill's story later in the book.

Hans, the Warrior who gave up

When I work with people with this leadership framework, one of the first things I look out for is any significant shifts between Home Base and where the person is now. For some people like Bill, this is a signal that a strategy may be adrift. For others, it is one potential indicator of stress.

Long term stress is associated with high levels of cortisol in the system, and can lead to heart disease, cancer, and memory loss. Unfortunately, levels of stress are another thing you can try to pretend to yourself about. When I talk to people about any significant shift from Home Base, many of them are reluctant to accept that there is a problem at all. For people like Sue, there may be no problem. But for others, what they say they are in control of is often symptomatic of an issue they don't want to confront. This can be very stressful.

Hans is a Warrior. The only Sage value he chose over Warrior values is **inner harmony**. This may be a deeply held value for him, but it may also be that, at the time we started working together, inner harmony was a very distant but desirable objective. All his other major drivers are Warrior drivers.

Amongst his highest values are:

- Advancement and promotion
- Fame
- Competition
- Being a hero

Hans is a proud man with a track record of success.

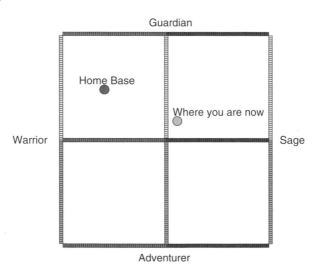

But he does not live the Warrior life right now. His focus is on self-improvement, learning and leading by teaching. These are all good developmental strategies for Warriors, and initially Hans spoke to me in positive terms about his new-found Sage qualities. Many Warriors arrive at a stage in their lives where they recognize the value of broadening their skills. As people achieve more senior status, leading from the front has to be balanced with diplomacy, tact and a degree of humility.

Good Warriors recognize that these additional skills are in support of the primary Warrior values and competences. Others seek to change themselves. The development of additional skills and competences that are part of the armoury of people from Home Bases other than our own is hugely powerful. The attempt to change yourself fundamentally is both difficult (some would say impossible), potentially stressful, and probably pointless. Warriors are naturally gifted at Warrior leadership; they are strangers in the land of the Sage, and are likely always to "speak with a Warrior accent."

In Hans' case, the move to greater self-development was linked with a strong desire not to be tied down, and a withdrawal from the fight. Hans was unhappy. His drift eastwards on the model was not, as it soon became clear, primarily an attempt to achieve a more balanced lifestyle; it was running away from a war he had decided he could not win.

The root cause of Hans' problem was related to his work. When I asked him about stress, he said that he was surprised how stressed he felt, given that he was definitely not overworked. What Hans discovered is that it is not always the volume of work that creates stress; it may be how the work impacts how we feel about ourselves, and our sense of self-worth.

In the next chapter, when we look at the job role, we will pick up Hans' story again. What his case has already shown is that not all differences between where you are now and your Home Base are positive. The compromises they often represent can be rationalized away if you want. But unless you have a clear plan to take yourself back to Home Base, as Sue did, please treat such rationalization with a very large pinch of salt.

Victor's struggle for credibility

In the previous chapter we met Victor, the Sage/Adventurer plagued with self-doubt.

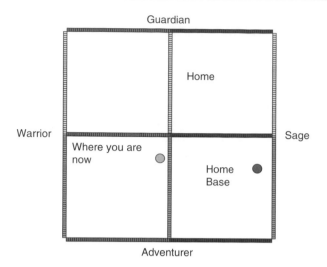

Victor has moved west, but not north. There are a number of reasons why, in how he is living his life at this point, he has not tried to move north-west, not least of which is that moving both north and west at the same time is doubly difficult. But for Victor, not moving north is crucial in his personal life.

Like many Adventurers, Victor is playful, and may not be as faithful to his wife as Guardians may wish people to be. But his playfulness is one of the key factors in how he chooses his friends. Victor gets on best with other Adventurers. "When it comes to attitudes that are heritable, people react more quickly and emotionally, are less likely to change their minds, and are more attracted to like-minded people."[1]

People talk of the "chemistry" that seems to exist in some relationships. Although it may also be the case that "opposites attract," in my experience of working with this framework, lasting relationships seem to depend upon proximity of people's Home Bases. This is not surprising. In relationships, tall people can live happily with short people, introverts with extraverts, and tidy people can even learn to live with disorganized ones. But over time, people who believe in fundamentally different values are going to struggle to maintain good relationships with one another.

Adventurer/Sages can develop the utmost respect for Guardian/Warriors, but they are less likely to want to become their soul mates. Whereas in the arts much of the interest lies in watching the relationships between people with very different characters interact with each other, in real life, people tend to gravitate to like-minded others.

So most of Victor's friends are Adventurers too. They understand and do not berate him for his infidelities. They share his delight in challenging convention. And they know why he is reluctant to get deeply embroiled in the politics of the organization, even though that is the normal way to get on. In short, unlike some of his colleagues, Victor's friends do not give him a hard time for being Victor.

Moving north would mean betraying his friends. Victor does not want to do that. They keep him sane. But at work, and at home, Victor is constantly encouraged to toughen up, to be more ambitious, and to assert himself more. So Victor has moved west. He needs a plan to get back home.

Brian, the wannabe Sage

The final reason for a mismatch between Home Base and where you are now I will look at is a common one. It is rooted in the "wannabe" syndrome. In these cases, Home Base is not true.

Brian went to college with Gerry, our Guardian/Warrior from the previous chapter. After college, the two went their separate ways, but their friendship left a mark. Some years later, they met up again, and Gerry offered Brian a job. They met again when Brian took on a consulting assignment with Gerry's team. Brian had gone into consulting, while Gerry had focused on the investment bank.

Brain's Home Base plotted as Sage/Guardian. Gerry is solidly Guardian/Warrior. But they are not as different as Brian first believed. Where Brian is now on the model is much closer to his true Home Base than was originally thought. Rethinking his Home Base, Brian is Guardian/Warrior, just like Gerry his hero.

One of the key factors in how people tend to define themselves is by contrast. Parents know how easy it is for their children to exaggerate certain personality traits to differentiate themselves from siblings with whom, in reality, they have a great deal in common. Minor personality differences are reinforced and strengthened until "the quiet one" by contrast becomes "the quiet one" in life. Traits that start life as slight contrasts to siblings or close friends become self-perpetuating elements of identity. But they don't always become solid elements of character.

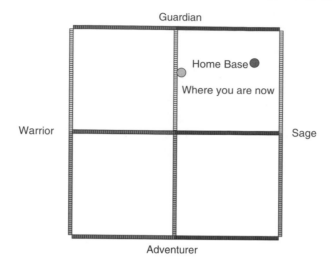

Something like this may have been one influence on Brian's initial self-assessment as Sage. Compared with Gerry, Brian is much more Sage. But as it emerged in looking closely at where Brian is now, compared with the population of true Sages, Brian is Warrior. Brian plays to win, seeks challenges, wants success, and hates both losers and having to work to other people's agendas. He agrees that his primary motivation is to win and achieve, yet he chose, in selecting amongst competing values, all Sage values over Warrior ones.

Brian's current job, by providing him with challenges, opportunities to beat the competition, and so on, is satisfying, and not the stressful environment it would be to a real Sage. In Brian's case, the difference between Home Base and where he is now is not stressful, because his Home Base is a fantasy.

Where you are now

Consider your current lifestyle and attitudes. What are you trying to become? What do you spend your time on? What switches you on, and what turns you off? What would make you happier, and what do you try to avoid? Who are your role models, and who do you have little time for?

Now compare what you have come up with to your values, and to the stories of your life. Are all these consistent with each other? If so, you are likely to be happy with yourself, even if you may not be happy with your lot. If you are striving for something you do not yet have, so long as you are clear that the goals are clear, achievable, and, most importantly, what you really want in life, then think of yourself on the journey you need to go on.

But if you do find inconsistencies, then this may be the time to question where these inconsistencies come from. Are you striving for something someone else told you that you ought to go for? And if you are living a life currently that is out of step with what you really believe in, why are you doing this? If you have made compromises, how long will you have to live with them?

Finally if, like Sue, you are going through a stage in your life that has taken you away from your Home Base, but which is under your control, and you know the way back home, just pause and ask yourself if what you are looking at is a clear route home, or one of those rationalizations that are so artful in obscuring from you issues you really do know you should confront, but have told yourself is really not a problem. Not today, anyway.

CHAPTER 8

Job role

If you, like many people, have ever been in a job where things don't seem to be quite right, you may have decided that the time had come to move on. When I talk to people about jobs they have left, it is not always clear to them what was wrong with the situation. In many cases, people blame the boss; some people like to support the notion that "people don't leave jobs, they leave bosses."

If something about your job is not right for you, it is not surprising that the boss will be the focus for much of your dissatisfaction, as he or she represents the authority or force that keeps you in a place that you have become disenchanted with. The imbalance in a power relationship between a boss and subordinate magnifies the focus on the way the boss represents the experience that you no longer enjoy.

But every boss is just another person, and not all bosses, in my experience, are as bad as they seem to become in the eyes of those who want out. The problem is that, unless you can make a more accurate assessment of the components of your experience of a job that has let you down, you may find yourself in the same unhappy situation again. In my experience, a relationship with a boss is a catalyst for increasing frustration, not a cause.

So a question I often ask in these situations is. "Apart from your boss, what else may have been wrong for you in your job?"

Although a job has many components, the following three seem to be most influential in how you experience the job, and how you interpret what is going on around you. The three I shall look at in this chapter are:

- The organizational culture
- The demands and rewards of doing the job
- The relationships you have with others at work

Organizational culture

This is another topic on which many people have written already.[1] None, however, have used the leadership framework of this book. Neither is this book specifically about organizational culture as such. But the successful leaders Tait writes about agree that it is important to "Select corporate environments that suit your personality type, approach and values, where you will enjoy your work and be good at it."[2]

I think it is dangerous to try to define **the** culture of an organization, since how each person experiences an organization will be different. For example, a dedicated Warrior may see his or her organization as lacking in drive and ambition, while a Sage working in the same place may worry about the aggression he or she sees all around him or her. Culture is, to some extent, in the eye of the beholder.

So to follow the advice to "select corporate environments that suit your personality type, approach and values" you will be better to draw your own conclusions about the culture of your organization, or of any organization you are thinking of joining.

Whatever anyone else may say about the culture, it is how you experience it that counts.

This is especially true where you may decide that the best way to assess the culture would be to match up the organization's values with those listed here under the Warrior, Guardian, Sage, and Adventurer headings. As I suggested earlier, it may be that what is published by an organization may be better described as attitudes than values. It may also be the case that published values are what the organization aspires to more than how it actually operates.

In Chapter 15, I shall revisit the issues of leadership and organizational culture in more depth. At this stage, as we explore your current situation rather than the strategy you may want to adopt, it may be most helpful to make a "gut feel" assessment of where, in the model, your organization "fits." This will give you an idea how the organization's culture influences your leadership style right now.

If you think that you and your organization share the same Home Base, it is likely that how you operate is culturally positive, which should feel positive. But if you and the organization do not share the same Home Base, it may be worthwhile taking a step back and asking yourself a few questions.

Are you sure that you have assessed both your Home Base and the organization's Home Base accurately? How aware were you before you did this exercise that you and the organization are "out of step" with each other? Has being out of step with the organization's culture caused you any problems in the past? How are you currently managing to operate successfully in what is essentially an alien culture? Can you continue to survive and thrive in an organization that is not in tune with your Home Base? If so, what plans do you have in place to minimize the potentially negative impact of operating out of your Home Base on a daily basis? If not, what should you do about it?

The demands and rewards of the job

The experience of doing a job provides opportunities – to succeed, to learn, to try out new things, or to take care of people. It also provides satisfactions – when you win a deal, take charge of a crisis, learn something about yourself, or break a few rules. You have responsibilities, some of which you enjoy more than others. You have good days, and you have bad days. Different people assess what's good or bad about a day in different ways.

It is in how you experience a job that you recognize where your job takes you – to Guardian/Warrior, to Sage/Adventurer, and so on. In my experience, the people who are happiest in their work are those whose job role allows them to be themselves. In other words, their job role and their Home Base sit closely together. Some people, however, operate day by day in job roles that take them way out of their Home Base. This usually causes problems, as the following case studies show.

Hans, the warrior who gave up

We met Hans in the previous chapter. Looking at his job role helps us to understand why he was giving up.

As the model shows, Hans has drifted even further east in his job role than in his lifestyle overall. In his case, much of this drift is due to his perception that he is not being allowed to be a Warrior. His assessment of the organization is that achievement and attainment of goals are neither particularly valued nor rewarded, removing from him the motivation to operate like a Warrior. He no longer sees the job as giving him the opportunity to be successful, gets little satisfaction when he does achieve a goal, and does not feel challenged or stretched.

He does not even want more recognition from the organization for what he does day by day, and although taking the job in the first place seemed like a good idea at the time, now he's not so sure.

Hans sees his organization as Sage/Guardian, although this assessment is not shared by all his colleagues. To him, however, it has failed to be the kind of place that he wanted it to be, and, feeling out of place, he has decided to move on. As a Warrior, however, his decision is an unhappy one. It is a kind of surrender, although he prefers to call the situation, "a battle not worth fighting." In the past, he has always left a job in triumph. Now he feels let down, and is leaving the job disillusioned and defeated.

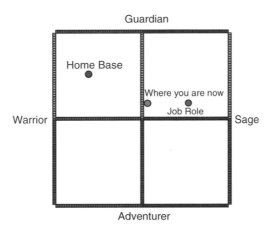

Before taking on a new role, Hans will take more care to ensure that his natural style is welcomed and rewarded in his new organization.

Victor changes jobs

One thing most people recognize in Victor is his charm. Being so clearly Sage rather than Warrior, his lack of "ambition" may have made him appear vulnerable when head-on battles had to be fought, but he had a knack of winning people over to his ways of thinking. Because it was clear that Victor's motives were not about empire-building for himself, people listened to his points of view with more open minds than is common in his organization. Victor was successful because he knew how to talk and listen to people.

So when the post of Head of HR became available, he was one of the most senior people available whose personal characteristics made him seem a natural choice. Victor could also see that the organization needed some radical changes in the area of people management, something that had, over the years, become stagnant. Poor people management was a major issue, and morale was low.

With typical Sage/Adventurer gusto, Victor set about bringing in radical change.

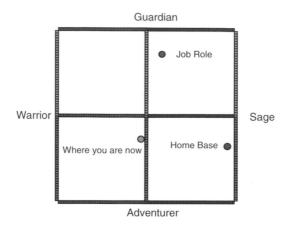

By the time we went through our leadership analysis together, Victor was highly frustrated. The first two or three years in his role were exciting and rewarding. But as the changes bedded down, the role became less about introducing change, and more about managing the new status quo. Now the job role was a long way from Victor's Home Base.

Not only was Victor expected to take a stable and responsible approach to his role as the most senior "people-person," but, more importantly, the role allowed very little scope for the Adventurer in him. It stopped being fun. Every time there was any issue related to people, his senior colleagues expected Victor to take responsibility and sort it out. In a highly regulated environment, where employment law took precedence over "common sense," Victor became a highly visible administrator, with little room for freedom of manoeuvre, and very little independence. There were battles to be fought, too.

Victor's Job Role was over 30percent points at odds with his Home Base. Because of this very significant stretch, Victor had already decided to move on by the time we went through his analysis. Our work together helped him confirm what he already knew: that his levels of stress brought about by the job he was doing were untenable.

Victor is now heading up a new initiative with a new team, working in an area the organization has little experience with. Although it may not be the perfect fit for Victor, the chance to start something new, and the independence the very novelty of the situation provides means that, for a few years at least, Victor can go back to his Home Base and lead from there.

Bryony, a Guardian with no family

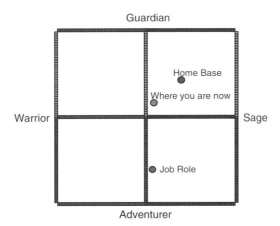

Bryony's Home Base and Job Role are about the same distance apart as Victor's, but in her case, the two are reversed. It was the problems that this kind of split brings about that led me to be asked to coach Bryony. At that time, no-one knew what the problem was. All everyone, Bryony included, knew was that her career was going downhill, and something needed to be done.

As a diagnostic tool, the model can quickly identify the sources of issues such as those Bryony was facing. It works even better in conjunction with other tools, such as the MBTI™, which provides insights into cognitive styles rather than values.

Bryony wants to take responsibility for people. She is Guardian/Sage. But as an undeveloped ISTJ, she has not concentrated sufficiently on her interpersonal skills to make people comfortable working with her. Her cognitive style leads her to be an independent problem – solver by nature. Logical, precise, conscientious, and data-oriented, Bryony can sometimes appear cold and unapproachable. She has not developed the ability to deal with ambiguity and uncertainty, so she can come across as dogmatic and dismissive of people she sees as sloppy in their thinking and style of working.

Bryony and her manager had thought that what she needed was a more independent role, where she did not need to have too many people working directly with her. The project she took on gave her a great deal of freedom, and enabled her to get on without having to manage too many relationships. On the surface, this seemed an ideal solution. But it was not working.

Both Bryony and her manager had good intentions. Recognizing the problems Bryony's manner was causing, they felt that minimizing contact with people she could "rub up the wrong way" would resolve the problems. It was not the answer. No-one can work without any contact with others at all, and when she did interact on her project with people both within and outside the organization, her impatience seemed to be an even bigger issue.

Two things were going wrong here. Firstly, neither Bryony nor her manager could see that isolation from other people was forcing her into Adventurer territory, giving her freedom and independence, but denying her a sense of belonging, and the chance to create a "family" around her. Secondly, the role took away the opportunities Bryony needed to practise her interpersonal skills. They got worse, partly because unhappy people, like Bryony, make poor learners.

To become the Guardian/Sage leader she wanted to be, Bryony had to convince her manager to bring her back into the mainstream, and help her develop her interpersonal skills. Bryony's story teaches us that strategies for leadership development that are out of step with your Home Base can be destructive.

Ali, the sleepwalker

Sometimes you need a jolt to the system to wake you up. Ali got one when we worked together and he came face to face with what he had been trying not to see for years. Ali was in the wrong job, and probably in the wrong organization.

Ali is a Guardian/Sage working his way, slowly, up the corporate ladder of an investment bank. A dutiful family man, he would get up each morning and go into a work environment where he felt stressed and inadequate. His wife often asked him why he didn't consider resigning and finding a job where he could be happy. Ali would always reply that he had responsibilities, and that things would get better when people accepted him, when he learnt how to work more effectively in the system, and when the time was right.

Ali worked conscientiously, but there was no passion in him for the work he was doing. His annual bonus was regularly smaller than his colleagues' bonuses, but that was fair: they brought in more than he did. One day, he said, "I'll learn how to be as good at doing deals as they are." He was, in fact, resigned to a life of mediocrity.

His dream, he said, was to work with children, teaching, helping them to grow. His wife urged him to follow his dream; he would be excellent in such a role. But Ali just soldiered on. As we looked at his Home Base and Job Role, I asked him who was stopping him following his dream. The next day, Ali started to plan the rest of his life, looking for a role that would enable him to follow his dream and become an excellent teacher, and, as a consequence, a better father and husband.

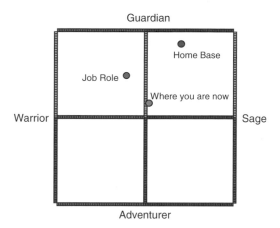

Your job role

These case studies, which are only a small selection from hundreds of people's stories I have heard, highlight the importance of matching your job role to your Home Base. Values are not just things we believe in, they create needs. An Adventurer needs freedom and independence. A Guardian needs to take responsibility within a community of which he or she feels a part. A Warrior needs the chance to meet challenges and to excel. A Sage needs to be doing something inherently valuable in his or her daily work.

If your needs are not being met by your job, you will probably feel unfulfilled, you could be suffering low level but constant stress, and may not be performing to your maximum potential. How well is your current job role meeting your needs? Where in the model is your Job Role compared with your Home Base?

If you are a Warrior, does it provide you with the chance to win? If you are a Sage, is it a true learning environment. If you are Guardian, does it provide a community you feel you belong to? If you are Adventurer, does it give you the freedom you need?

If your Home Base and Job Role are far apart, what should you be doing about it? You may want to turn to the Appendix again to note any answers you want to record, and to plot your Job Role against your Home Base.

The relationships you have with others at work

In chapter 5, I explored the kinds of inherent conflict of values that can get in the way of good relationships. But although having a different Home Base from others can cause conflict, it doesn't have to.

In my experience, you reduce the chances of conflict by moving into the other person's space, if only while you are directly interacting with them. This is how it works.

The first step is to recognize that people's values are not like their attitudes. You can change their attitudes, but not their values. Consequently, building good relationships depends upon you not trying to change other people's values. Not only can you not do it, but also trying to increases the chance of conflict rather than reduce it.

Secondly, although you may not agree with the other's values, you have to respect them. No matter how clear it may be to you that your own values are right (and by implication, theirs are not right), you cannot prove the rightness or otherwise of values.

Thirdly, treating others' values with respect is neither betraying your own values, nor putting yourself at risk of "becoming one of them." I have met many people who have got stuck on this one, fearing that their integrity will be compromised if they do not keep the "aliens" at arm's length. Remember, just as you can't change their values, they can't change yours. Respect is not surrender.

Fourthly, don't expect them to move into your space, unless they have the same insights into these different value sets as you do. They may not realize, as you do, the background to the differences between Warriors and Sages, Guardians and Adventurers. You need to make the effort.

Lastly, moving into their space is not being dishonest, deceptive, or putting on a mask to hide your true nature. Remember, Sages have some Warrior in them, and Adventurers have Guardian instincts. When you move into someone else's space, you are simply allowing those parts of your character that are not the core of who you are to have a role in how you operate. A Sage who competes does not become a Warrior; he or she is a person who has switched into their Warrior for the purpose of fighting a battle.

But do bear in mind that by switching into a different mode, you will be using a part of your character that is less natural to you. Moving into a different Home Base is not play-acting. But as you will be relying on parts of your character that are less significant to you may need to take more care in how you come across. If you are right-handed, think of it as doing something with your left hand; it is possible, but it needs more careful monitoring.

In the later chapters, I shall look more closely at specific ways you may manage relationships with people who have different Home Bases from you. For now, it may be worth taking a few moments to consider some of the key relationships you have at work. You may also want to think about relationships outside of work, too.

Consider up to about half a dozen of the key relationships that are important to you. Although you may have to make guesses, where do you think their Home Bases may be? Does this exercise bring out any relationship issues you may have already been aware of? Does it highlight differences you may have not been aware of?

CHAPTER 9

Leadership model

Before we move on to exploring how you may develop your own strategy for leadership, let us look at your current attitudes to the subject. As part of the diagnostic process I use in leadership development, I ask people to reflect on how they see themselves leading right now, and at their "ideal" model of leadership.

Once again, you can tell a great deal about the issues you are dealing with if the comparison between your Home Base and your model of leadership are very different.

Freddy, exposed by organizational changes

Freddy is one of the best people-managers I have met. Many of his direct reports told me that he is the best manager they have ever had. It came as a bit of a shock to both Freddy and me when he found out that he was being penalized one year (his bonus was being severely cut) because he had received poor feedback from some of his people about his leadership.

It was time for us to use the model to see what it told us.

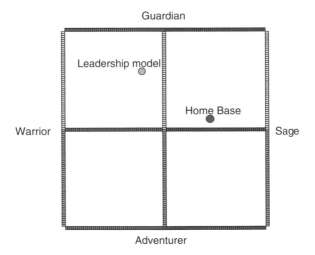

Freddy is extremely bright. His contribution to his organization was highly technical. He and his team did numbers, and they did them brilliantly. Freddy recruited highly intelligent people and was a superb teacher. I believe, from conversations I have had with members of his team, that, in practice, Freddy's leadership of them was best characterized as being very close to his Home Base. He is a natural teacher, gives people a great deal of freedom to learn and grow, and brings out the best in people by letting them find their own path to success.

So what was puzzling was how Freddy, according to his responses to the questionnaire, saw leadership as so clearly Guardian/Warrior.

At the time we went through the exercise, the business was in turmoil. In previous years, although operating in a volatile market, the general trend was steady growth. But Enron and Worldcom changed all that. And soon after those scandals hit the headlines, legislation in the United States made the bulk of the kind of deal Freddy's business was doing no longer legal. It was action stations to re-orient the business to stay afloat.

As part of the senior management team, Freddy was jointly responsible for developing and implementing a new strategy. He was also jointly responsible for some drastic "downsizing." And not being in charge of one of the front line areas of the business, Freddy and his team were more exposed than most to the threat of being "downsized' themselves.

What Freddy's colleagues all agreed was that this was a time for strong leadership. Drastic action was called for; leadership meant being tough, decisive, and prepared to take some very difficult decisions. Freddy responded as best he could. But in so doing, found himself firmly in Guardian/Warrior territory, a place he was ill-prepared to work within.

As Freddy delivered tough messages to his team, one thing they all saw and hated was an apparent change in him. Gone was the teacher; in came the tough guy, wielding the axe, and allowing very little discussion. Freddy's discomfort led to them becoming disillusioned with him. And although many remained firmly loyal to the Freddy they had grown to love and respect, there were enough frightened people to make this year's feedback from his team bad enough for it to impact very poorly on his bonus.

But Freddy was not only acting out of character with his own team, he was also having to come to terms with his reputation among some of his peers, most of whom are Guardian/Warriors by nature. While business was good, Freddy's quirkiness was fine with them. In crisis, it became a threat. This was especially the case for Helen, who was being groomed to take over from the current boss who had already planned to retire before the crisis occurred. Helen had always had doubts about Freddy. Those doubts were largely the kinds of doubts Warrior/Guardians (as she is) often have about Sages who are bordering on Adventurer.

It was clear that Freddy's leadership model was more of a knee-jerk reaction to the situation at the time. What Freddy had to decide was whether, in the circumstances, it was better to continue to try to operate in Guardian/ Warrior mode, or to revert to what he was best at.

As a diagnostic tool, the model works well. Of itself, it cannot take away from Freddy and others who use it the ultimate responsibility to make choices. But, as Freddy agreed, those choices become much easier to make if the confusion surrounding dilemmas like Freddy's can be made so much clearer.

Victor begins to settle to his new role

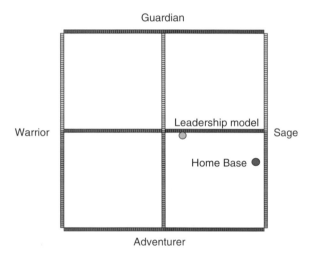

Although he still has some re-adjusting to do, Victor is using his new role to bring his leadership style closer to home. He knows that, in general, the organization prefers a more Guardian style of leadership, but now Victor is leading a team in a remote and distributed set of locations, he has the freedom to develop relationships with his team based more on his own style.

Since many of his team are new to the organization, they will not have been exposed to the "norm," and, I believe, will value the honesty of Victor's approach.

Bill leads from the front

We met Bill, the CEO, in Chapter 7, as he appeared to be using his role as a toy. I know that Bill's intentions are significantly more honorable than they appear to many of his people; he really does want to develop a legacy. His vision is of a strong leadership team to inherit a strong business on his retirement, which is not far off now. But, as we saw in Chapter 7, he is not succeeding in getting his message across with conviction.

Working to a tight schedule as he feels he is, Bill is making a classic mistake: that of telling people they will be empowered, but only when he feels he has got everything right first. This is mixing his leadership messages.

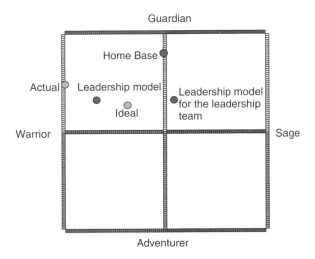

In this version of the model, I have gone to a deeper level of analysis. First, I have split out two different elements of Bill's leadership model: what he says is an "ideal" model of leadership ("Ideal" in the diagram), and how he sees himself leading now ("Actual" in the diagram). Second, I have aggregated the ideal leadership model of the top ten managers in the organization to see where, on average, they see leadership.

On balance, the top team has a model of leadership that is Guardian/Sage, but with a fair smattering of Warrior. Although they value leaders who do lead from the front, and who fight for what they believe in, they also want to be more engaged in strategic dialogue than they feel they are, and believe leaders should create a much more developmental climate then Bill has done.

The fact that Bill's "ideal model" of leadership is relatively close to the team's model suggests that he recognizes their aspirations and would, if he could, meet them. But how he is actually leading is though unadulterated Warrior, with some Guardian.

He wants to step back, and develop his legacy. But he must learn how to re-engage the Sage part of his Home Base if he is both to be true to himself, and to win back the trust he needs from his people to enable that legacy to be developed.

Your leadership model

The remainder of the book is about developing a leadership style based solidly on your Home Base. But for now, it is worth considering how far that may be from how you are leading right now, and from how you currently feel leadership "ought to" be done.

Your "ideal model"

You may have in mind a role model you have admired as a leader. Or you may have read books that you have liked that advocate particular attributes of a good leader. Courses you have attended may have helped build your ideal model. Consider the ideal model. Is it Warrior, Guardian, Sage or Adventurer? Does he or she lead from the front and fight for what is right? Does he or she say "the buck stops with me," and take firm control of every situation? Is he or she a guide or mentor, who gets things done through dialogue? Or is he or she a radical mould-breaker who challenges convention and redefines the rules of the business?

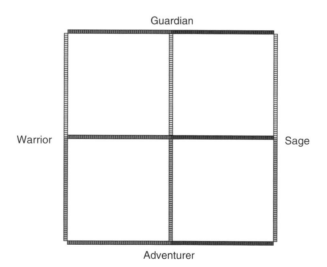

It may well be that your ideal model is a bit of all of these and more. Indeed, many leaders I have met and worked with do manage to combine elements of all of these characteristics. But in general, it has been the core of character that has been what people have admired most. Like Margaret Thatcher, Franklin D. Roosevelt, Mahatma Gandhi and Martin Luther King, they have built on one major element of character, and then developed skills associated with the others as back up.

How you lead now

How would you describe your leadership style now? Are you a go-getter, a steady rock, a wise coach, or a rebel? Do you lead mostly by challenging, directing, coaching, or empowering? Where on the model is your leadership style in practice?

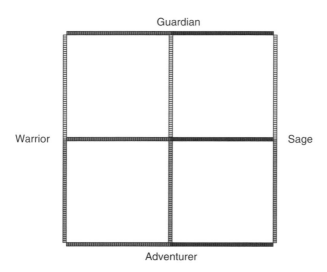

For some people I have worked with this has caused some problems. Many of them carry with them a self-image that may be at odds from how they are seen by others. In leadership, perhaps more than in any other aspect of people's lives, it is how you come across to others that is important. People follow what they see you do, not what you believe inside your head. And as we said in Chapter 2, what you do is open to interpretation. Your act of firmness and courage may be seen by others as aggression.

This is one of Bill's problems. He has yet to come to terms with the potential mis-match between what you intend to convey, and how people may interpret what you do. Leadership is about the stories people tell. Try, as you consider your own leadership style, to see your reputation as a leader through the eyes of those you lead, and not your own.

Many organizations are making this an easier task by introducing 360 degrees feedback. Well-developed instruments can provide important feedback to leaders. If you receive feedback from others, what is their view of how you lead? Is it consistent with your intentions? As you consider the key aspects of your reputation as defined through this feedback, are you seen as Warrior, Guardian, Sage, or Adventurer? And if, on balance, it is a bit of all of these, is this because you are truly successful at being all things to all people, or are you working with a reputation of inconsistency; is your leadership style an inconsistent mixture of all kinds of leadership attributes with no clear cohesion?

Once again, only you can answer this. And once again, you will only benefit from answering it if you are completely honest with yourself.

Your leadership model and your home base

The case studies in this chapter explore just some of the ways in which a significant difference between a person's Home Base and their Leadership Model can cause problems. Many of the leaders I have worked with plot their Home Base and Leadership Model pretty close together. In my experience, this is one of the key influences on their success.

You may have noticed that, when the values of the four different kinds of people were listed, there was no mention of values such as "honesty," "integrity," or "truthfulness." This is because these are not unique to Warriors or Guardians, Sages or Adventurers. They are values that are important to all types.

Everyone can, at times, find themselves doing things that go against these values. Warriors can sometimes tell lies for the sake of a win; Guardians can mislead if the outcome of that action is protection of the weak; Sages can find themselves lusting after material rewards; and Adventurers sometimes compromise for the sake of a quiet life. But most people who manage to survive in organizations realize that such breaches need to be the exception rather than the rule.

On balance, people who achieve long-term success as leaders understand that the people who follow them expect that they can be trusted not to lie to them, that they say and do the same things, and that they are not hiding behind masks.

Being true to yourself, whether that is Warrior truth, Guardian truth or whatever, means that you send out consistent messages. Some people may not like those messages: all four of our political examples experienced attempts on their lives by assassins or would-be assassins. But few were in any doubt about what each stood for.

Consider any difference between your Home Base and your Leadership Model. If there is a significant difference, why has this come about? And what impact might this have on how you are seen by others, on your effectiveness, and on your inner sense of integrity?

CHAPTER 10

Developing strategy

The previous nine chapters have been diagnostic; the remainder of the book is about development. What Chapters 1 to 9 may have helped you do is to make a clear assessment of:

- What is really important to you – your core values
- How you are living your life now, and how this lifestyle differs from your Home Base
- Your job role, and the extent to which it fulfils your needs for self-respect
- How you have thought about, and practised leadership to date

In my experience, many people in leadership roles have collected a toolkit of leadership techniques, all of which have their merits, but many of which are hard for them to apply effectively. Warriors who try to suppress their innate tendency to lead from the front may become frustrated with the back seat they try to sit in, and feel they are failing to add value. But if they have been taught to empower people, and not to get too involved, they try valiantly to put into practice something that they cannot truly believe in, and consequently help no-one, even themselves.

Similarly, Adventurers who try to "grow up" and become serious, responsible father-figures can become excessively authoritarian as they over-compensate for the fact that they are operating outside of their Home Base. Sages can become quixotic and Guardians can become untrustworthy and rash.

I have a great deal of respect for much of what is taught and has been written about leadership, especially in recent years. But what has worried me is the way in which, time and again, "proven" leadership methods are promoted as "the answer," without recognition that any approach to leadership, for it to be an effective tool, has to be harmonious with a leader's character.

Leaders are born, not made. But what makes you a good leader is learning how to lead in the way you were born to lead.

The principle I am working with is that character comes first, leadership strategy second. Before you take on any leadership technique, ask yourself how well it fits with your character.

The foundations of leadership strategy

One of the reasons I have suggested that the political leaders in Chapter 4 were so successful is that they developed strategies that were in line with their characters. Although their strategies were complex, the foundations upon which they were built were completely harmonious with the kinds of people they were. And in each case, character drove strategy, not the other way round.

In Chapter 3, I suggested that the lessons that history and our own experience teach us are often those that reinforce our beliefs. The strategies that each of our political examples developed grew out of the ways in which people with their characters are most likely to interpret things.

Margaret Thatcher and the development of a Warrior strategy

When Warriors "go for it," they need to be certain. As Lord Powell, Charles Powell, her private secretary from 1984, said of Margaret Thatcher, "You have a politician of such deep conviction that whatever cause she espoused she was convinced of its rightness. She didn't have the traditional weakness of seeing both sides of the question. There was one right view and it was hers."[1] What others may see as a search for consensus may be seen by Warriors as "traditional weakness."

This difference is brought out in how Margaret Thatcher developed her attitude to arguments in her cabinet. For her, as a Warrior, people who did not share her courage and determination were "wets." Rather than trying to accommodate herself to the cabinet and to the process of weighing up the pros and cons of various points of view, she developed a confrontational approach to policy making: "Public dissent from the 'wets' was phrased in what was obviously intended to be a highly sophisticated code, in which each phrase had a half-hidden meaning and philosophical abstractions were woven together to condemn practical policies by innuendo. This cloaked and indirect approach has never been my style and I felt contempt for it. I thrive on honest argument."[2]

Many Warriors develop strategies that put them directly in charge. Like Margaret Thatcher, they feel that it is dangerous not only to accommodate too many points of view, it can also be a weakness to accommodate too many people, in coalitions, for example. She disliked them. "It was not just that . . . I did not like coalitions. In practical terms, such talk [of coalitions] reduced the credibility of pledges I was making in my own area. For who could tell what inter-party horse-trading might do to them?"[3] She learnt that, to maintain the strength of her leadership, she needed to avoid what she saw as the dilution of her approach through the kinds of compromise that can come from involving others.

Warriors like to fight, but they also like to win. In the early stages of her premiership, Margaret Thatcher began to suffer the consequences of her habit of "leading with her chin." This was her habit of "putting all her cards on the table very early on in any discussion. This means that if the rest of the table goes against her, she is in the awkward position of either having to back down or fight."[4] Strong though she was in cabinet, she often found herself in a minority over some issue or another.

She learnt that winning is often easier if you size up the opposition first. As she wrote later, "experience had taught me never to put forward ideas at too early a stage."[5] Experience taught her other things, too.

For example, she not unnaturally felt very upset by the outcome of the 1956 Suez affair, from which she drew a number of lessons, amongst which were that "we should not get into a military operation unless we were determined and able to finish it. . . . And finally, he who hesitates is lost."[6] When the Falklands crisis struck, her strategy was fully in line with these lessons. Had she not been a Warrior, maybe the lessons she would have learnt from Suez would have been different. In that case, maybe, also, Britain would not have gone to war over the Falklands.

For the Warrior, popularity is not important if it conflicts with the need to fight for what you believe in. Commenting on her support for the American attack on Libya, she writes, "However unpopular, no-one could doubt that our action had been strong and decisive. I had set my course and stuck to it."[7]

Developing a Warrior strategy, then, is all about making sure you know what you believe in, and then putting aside self-doubts, blandishments from those who want to see the other point of view, and having the courage and determination to go for it, no matter how unpopular it may make you.

In brief, a Warrior strategy is: **lead from the front and win**.

Franklin D. Roosevelt and the development of a Guardian strategy

When, in 1907, Franklin D. Roosevelt declared his intention to become President,[8] the Depression was still over 20 years in the future; nobody at that time could have predicted it. It was in FDR's character to want to take charge, but it was not the pursuit of a particular strategy that drove him to become a politician. As he once said when questioned about his philosophy, "Philosophy? I'm a Christian and a Democrat – that's all."[9]

FDR grew up in a society that had been built partly on values that were not in line with his character. "Belief in 'free enterprise' was something close to a religion for the American people. They identified it with the pioneer spirit and traditional virtues. "Rugged individualism" was held responsible for developing the nation into a world power in less than half a century. So, in spite of the miseries arising out of the failures of the free enterprise system to prevent depressions, the belief still persisted that every individual could make his own way in the world and if he failed, it was his own fault."[10]

The Guardian in FDR saw this individualism as selfishness. But to change deeply embedded attitudes such as these, he needed to have authority. And in democratic America, this kind of authority lay in political power. Like many people who are successful, circumstances helped him on the way. The Depression was proof to him, and those who began to believe in him, that it was only through social responsibility that those in need would be protected and provided for.

"Yet organization alone could not make Roosevelt president. He needed a policy to end the depression. In search of this he displayed a country squire's scorn for the rich who lacked social responsibility."[11] FDR's strategy grew out of his values and the character these values created in him.

Through his political speeches and his "fireside chats," he, as a Guardian will, told people how they should behave. "He told the bankers that they must stop using their depositors' funds for speculation. . . . He told businessmen that they must treat workers as potential customers. . . . He told workers they had a duty to their families and the community along with the rights they were so indignantly demanding. And his preachment to the whole nation was that everyone was responsible for everyone else, that all must work together, trying more to help that to get the best of bargains."[12]

FDR's strategy developed slowly but inexorably. Step by step he looked inside himself and what he believed in, and from his values and character came a way forward for America that came to be known as the New Deal. Because he believed in the value of the community over the individual, and wanting to develop a legacy that would last FDR showed that "Not a philosophy but a temperament shaped the New Deal."[13]

In brief, a Guardian strategy is: **create a community and build a future**.

Mahatma Gandhi and the development of a Sage strategy

Although Gandhi is best remembered for his role in helping India gain independence, for many years of his life he had no intention to pursue this goal. He never fought as a soldier, but in three wars, he supported British military action by providing medical assistance and people. He had nothing against the British Raj.

In his early years, Gandhi was a fairly typical middle class lawyer. But his confrontation with the Muslim law community in South Africa began to influence the development of his strategy, and take his first steps to the pursuit of truth and simplicity. Pivotal in this development was his short visit to a Trappist settlement in South Africa, late in the 1890s: "He spent only a single day at Mariann Hill, but the brief visit left an ineradicable impression. In his own time, and in his own way, he would found a similar community."[14]

"Mahatma" means teacher, a name Gandhi accepted with humility but good grace. It was appropriate since he drew to him people who wanted to learn from his example. And the example he set was one of forgiveness and peace, not of confrontation. To bring about change, for Gandhi, was simply to refuse to accept – to resist with peace, not fighting. In his own words, "A Satyagrahi, that is, a civil resister, will harbour no anger. He will suffer the anger of an opponent. In doing so he will put up with assaults from the opponent, never retaliate, but he will not submit, out of fear of punishment or the like, to any order given in anger."[15]

In contrast to the personal proactivity of the Warrior or Guardian strategies, the Sage's impact is felt through the activities of other people. The fame or renown upon which Warriors and Guardians rely for the visibility their strategies need is alien to a Sage. Gandhi tried, unsuccessfully in the end, to keep a low profile for himself. "At the height of his fame and influence he enjoyed cleaning out latrines. When he was very old, he wandered almost alone into territory where men were murdering one another, offering himself as a simple sacrifice. But simplicity escaped him, and when he was shot down, he was no longer a man but a legend."[16]

Gandhi's story clearly illustrates a very significant element in the development of a Sage strategy, and that is that the Sage does not try to change **things**. By teaching others, he or she changes **people**. In turn, they may, if they choose to do so, bring about change in the outside world. For the Sage, it is not what happens in the physical world that matters. Inner harmony is about how people are, not about how the world is.

In brief, a Sage strategy is: **develop people and foster personal growth**.

Martin Luther King and the development of an Adventurer strategy

Although Martin Luther King adopted his policy of passive resistance from Gandhi, he did not develop a Sage strategy. He borrowed a technique, not a strategy. "It was in this Gandhian emphasis on love and non-violence that I discovered the method of social reform that I had been seeking."[17] The word "method" is revealing, as is King's impatience with some of the practitioners of pacifism who "had an unwarranted optimism concerning man and leaned unconsciously towards self-righteousness."[18]

As a Sage, Gandhi preached the importance of inner harmony. King wanted to change the world. "Our revolution was genuine because it was born from the same womb that always gives birth to massive social upheavals – the womb of intolerable conditions and unendurable situations."[19] As a Sage, Gandhi accepted, or merely resisted passively, the status quo. As an Adventurer, King challenged it.

The status quo King wanted to change was one in which the major problem was the lack of freedom felt by black Americans. He ended his famous "I have a dream" speech in Washington quoting the words of the "negro spiritual, Free at last, my God, free at last." But to achieve that freedom, people had to act, and not simply preach. King chose "mass civil disobedience" as "a device of social action that is more difficult for a government to quell by superior force. . . . It is militant and defiant, not destructive."[20]

King had a genuine, if at times naïve[21] belief in the way of non-violence. But the mood of many of his fellow campaigners was not so conciliatory. Many of them were in favor of more direct action. In resisting their demands for more proactivity, King demonstrated the self-reliance of the Adventurer. "Ultimately a genuine leader is not a searcher for consensus but a molder of consensus. If every Negro in the United States turns to violence, I will choose to be that one lone voice preaching that this is the wrong way. Maybe this sounds like arrogance. But it is not intended that way. It is simply my way of saying that I would rather be a man of conviction than a man of conformity."[22]

Never before in American history had anyone sought to bring about change in the conditions of an underprivileged class through peaceful means. Faced with considerable brutality from both police and civilians, it would have been easy for any leaders of the black civil rights movement to revert to retaliation. King was successful because, having adopted a technique that he believed would work, he persisted in changing the civil rights paradigm.

He stepped out alone, inviting criticism and scepticism. "I came to the conclusion that there is an existential moment in your life when you must decide to speak for yourself; nobody else can speak for you."[23]

In brief, an Adventurer strategy is: **liberate people and change paradigms**.

Four stages in the development of leadership strategy

In Part 1 of the book, I explored four sets of values associated with four kinds of character. Home Base is a combination of two of these. In most cases, one of the pair of value sets is more closely aligned with a person's character than the other. A Guardian/Warrior may be more Warrior than Guardian, or more Guardian than Warrior.

Although you may feel equally drawn to each of your "preferred" elements of character, I believe that, for the purposes of developing your leadership strategy, it helps to identify the one set that is most significant to who you are. Building strategy will be helped if you can sort out for yourself how each value set relates in rank order to the others. For example, you may be mostly drawn to the Warrior, but also clearly Guardian. This probably means that Sage is the least significant part of your core character, while Adventurer fits into third place:

1. Warrior
2. Guardian
3. Adventurer
4. Sage

In the process of developing your leadership strategy, think of these four as:

1. Your primary driver
2. Your secondary driver
3. Your footbrake
4. Your hand brake

Because of the inherently contradictory nature of the value sets, those you believe in will act as drivers for your life and strategy; those you do not believe in so fundamentally may act as brakes on your behavior: things you want to avoid doing. Guardians, for example, will avoid acting "irresponsibly"; Warriors will try to avoid being "wimps"; Sages will step away from being "aggressive"; while Adventurers won't want to be "bossy."

It is likely, also, that your "hand brake" will lie at the opposite end of the spectrum from your primary driver, while your secondary driver and "footbrake" will also be opposites on the same dimensions.

Developing your strategy means starting with your primary driver. Until you have comfortably established how to use this element of character as the bedrock for your leadership style, it may be better not to try to develop other, often contradictory, techniques. Despite the day to day complexity of the leadership styles of our four political examples, what made them effective and memorable was the simplicity and consistency of how they behaved and spoke.

In our daily lives, we often weigh up the pros and cons of various contrary ways of going about things. To establish a clear leadership strategy, it may be best to start by focusing on your primary driver, and actively to put aside, at least until you have established yourself, any influences from your "hand brake." What made our political leaders notable was the consistency of their leadership **styles** (not their strategies) throughout their lives. As the following chapters will show, the same can be said of notable leaders in organizational life. Bill Gates, for example, is not the only Warrior leader in industry. But as his story will show, it is his Warrior that clearly marks him out even from those around him who were also Warriors, but who may not have been so uncompromising in the pursuit of their Warrior goals.

There is an argument that it is this kind of simplicity that explains the successes of some famous brands as well as people.

In *The Hero and the Outlaw: Building Extraordinary Brands Through the Power of Archetypes*,[24] the authors argue that many famous brands have been associated in people's minds with particular archetypes. "No matter how effective the company's manufacturing and distribution systems . . . its competitors could imitate or duplicate them. In this circumstance, businesses found they had only two broad strategic routes to go: reduce their prices or imbue their products with meaning."[25]

Anyone can manufacture good motorcycles, they say, but no-one else can make a Harley-Davidson. And it is not its mechanics, its price, or its distribution system that makes a Harley-Davidson unique; it is its association with the rebel, the freedom-lover, the "biker." "By promoting the personality of the brand . . . the firm was able to expand from building motorcycles to selling a line of clothing and accessories linked not by function, but by archetype."[26] In achieving such a successful association with a particular archetype, or meaning, smart organizations make sure that the association remains clear and unambiguous. If you change what a brand means, they say, you stand to lose your business.

In Chapter 2, I suggested that leaders have to manage meaning at least as well as they manage facts. In many respects, it is not what leaders do that is significant, it is what their words and actions mean. Building a strategy for leadership implies making sure that what you mean by what you do is understood and consistent. Although, as you become established as a leader, you will need to take on and develop leadership capabilities that come from other parts of your character, until and unless the foundations are solid, what you think may be a well-rounded and balanced approach may appear to others as ill-defined, inconsistent, and not to be trusted. Inadvertently, you could be sending out mixed messages.

In other words, the strategy for developing a clear and consistent leadership style is to make sure that, in the first instance, you have created what your leadership means; by building a strategy based on your primary driver;

and then, step by step, add to your toolkit aspects of leadership that come from, in turn, your secondary driver, your footbrake, and your handbrake.

Leading from a good place

Chapters 11 to 15 suggest ways for you to develop a strategy for leadership that will align closely with your character, and thereby enable you to be affective in leadership, and to experience leadership as part of the way you are, rather than as a set of techniques that you may have picked up along the way, but which don't hang together.

To have any chance of leading effectively, you need to be working in a context that is in line with your values and character. In each chapter, I shall outline, with examples, the "ideal" job role for each of the four characters, and then suggest elements of strategy that can emerge from and depend upon such a job role. How you experience the work environment will have a major influence on how you lead.

CHAPTER 11

Developing a Warrior strategy

How much of this can you see in yourself?

"Perhaps the most damaging accusation made against me . . . was that I do not listen. Like most allegations which stick, this contained a grain of truth. Once I begin to follow a train of thought I am not easily stopped. This has its advantages. It means that I can concentrate on a tricky point almost no matter what is going on in the background. . . . But it does, of course, mean that I am inclined to talk over people and ignore timid or inarticulate objection and arguments. People who do not know me and how I work conclude that I have not taken in what has been said to me. Those who know me better will confirm, however, that this is generally not the case. I will often go away afterward to revise my views in the light of what I have heard. Indeed, I have even been accused by some supporters of taking too much notice of those who do not agree with me. The suggestion that I do not listen . . . can, however, simply mean that I do not agree with their views."[1]

This is the Warrior in action. Strong, decisive, and certain, the Warrior can be intimidating to others, and can be misunderstood in his or her determination to get results. For a Warrior to have the chance to excel, he or she needs to be in an environment that is conducive to his or her values and style.

The ideal job role for a Warrior

A role you took on because it would stretch you

For the Warrior, life is a challenge, or a series of challenges. The worst job role for him or her is one that allows for mediocrity. The best is one that is openly and assertively competitive. Some companies are renowned for their Warrior values, and provide people with fantastic opportunities to test themselves out.

The first words of Bill Gates' book, *Business @ the Speed of Thought* are: "I have a simple but strong belief. The most meaningful way to differentiate your company from your competition, the best way to put distance between you and the crowd, is to do an outstanding job with information."[2] Within these few sentences, Gates sets an agenda that is clearly competitive, and exemplifies the Warrior ethos: It's about beating the competition, and putting distance between yourself and the merely ordinary. If you are a Warrior, this is the kind of language that will excite and stretch you.

Opportunities to be successful

Success is not an abstract or static notion. What has been achieved once before is no longer enough, and each new day, week, month or year sets new goals. The world changes, and with it the definition of success. Microsoft was so successful in the 1990s that it faced antitrust suits in the United States and Europe. Bill Gates denied the charges levelled against him and the company. He was simply being more successful than anyone else, and they were jealous.

During this period, Microsoft had significantly eclipsed its predecessor as the giant of the information technology world. When he started out, IBM was "the environment." Its sales and profits were bigger then those of all its competitors put together. But in the short space of a few years, it had become "history." Talking privately with another of the industry's top CEOs, who had asked him if Microsoft was taking sufficient precautions to ward off government scrutiny, Gates said flatly, "The minute we start worrying too much about antitrust, we become IBM."[3]

In other words, last year's aspirational goal (to be as good or as big as IBM) is this year's turkey. The Warrior needs a role that keeps pushing up the standards.

Being in a position to achieve successful outcomes

You need to be able personally to contribute to success. One of the reasons for choosing Bill Gates as our example of a Warrior leader is the way in which he, personally, shaped the destiny and culture of Microsoft. "Until [1999] the Microsoft management style had not been invented, in the sense of deliberate planning. It inevitably reflected the personality of its founders, Gates in particular."[4]

Not everyone will have the same chance to establish the world's most successful company, but the Warrior needs his or her own arena to take on the challenges that drive him or her. Few things will frustrate the Warrior more in his or her job role than petty rules and restrictions. You need to be given the tools and be free to get on with the job.

The satisfaction of closing deals/contracts against the competition

The job needs to offer, at least in a large degree, the chance to compete and to win. Late in 1981 Bill Gates surveyed the competitive environment of the time. " 'We're going to put Digital Research out of business,' he told Leeds, slamming his fist into the palm of his other hand. He would issue a similar vow twice more during the next year, according to Leeds, promising to put MicroPro and Lotus out of business, each time emphasizing his promise by smashing his fist into his hand."[5]

The adrenaline buzz of such victories is vital to the job role of the Warrior, even if, at times, such single-mindedness attracts attention from competitors or others who worry that you may be getting "too successful."[6]

Established ways of getting over failures

In the real world, not every battle can be won. Fear of failure is a constant for Warriors[7] although most know that showing such fear is a weakness.[8] The Olympic Gold Medallist, Daley Thompson says, "He remembers all his successes, and how success reinforced success. Probably more importantly, if he was beaten – and he concedes that he may well have lost sometimes – he doesn't remember the defeats. He recalls only the positive experiences; always, a failure or a defeat would have been registered, learnt from and then forgotten. Defeat never preyed on his mind, as happens with many people."[9]

The Warrior does not want a job role that prevents him or her adopting this kind of tactic for wiping out the failures and getting on with the next challenge.

An organization that values the attainment of goals

Just as the failures need to be quickly erased from memory, so attainment of goals needs to be valued. The trophies of sport are ideally replicated in organizations. Successful deals are commemorated in the Warrior environment by certificates, plaques or other signs of recognition. And the size of the annual bonus, if you have one, should reflect attainment, not just effort.

The chance to excel

The Warrior in organizations, like the sportsperson, needs to win. Carling and Heller make this plain in the first line of their book, *The Way to Win: Strategies for Success in Business and Sport*: "Success in management and success in sports have the same roots." Throughout any book or article on Bill Gates, the message is clear: what drives him ever onward, despite having achieved phenomenal success and wealth, is the competitive spirit that emerged so early in his life.[10]

The spirit of competition has to be celebrated, individuals competing against individuals, team against team.

Challenge, challenge, challenge

The Warrior is looking neither for a quiet life nor a regulated one. For those who do not fully understand the Warrior mentality, it can come as a surprise to learn that it is not the taking part that counts, it's the winning. Steven Smith learnt this soon after he was taken on by Microsoft in July 1979 as their first marketing director and genuine business manager. Assuming that his contribution was to be the introduction of some discipline into the fledgling company, he was soon confronted by Bill Gates who, shouted at him about the length of time he was taking over a contract. He was told to "just get it done!" As he later said:

"I think what I realized was that I needed to focus, that the money and the opportunities were simply there, [and I needed] to close contracts with customers. So I focused on personal performance over management. Initially, I was dealing more with management issues, as a guy with an academic background coming out of a large company. But it only took a couple of meetings to realize that personal performance was what mattered."[11]

An organization that reward achievement

Awards ceremonies have become part of the fabric of almost every industry, many of them highly publicized in the media. Rewards and recognition are important to the Warrior. Sir John Egan, for example, was a hero while heading up Jaguar: "Through the early 1980s the tributes of success were heaped upon John Egan's shoulders. The influential Institute of the Motor Industry awarded him its 1982 Gold Medal. In 1983 he was named Midlander of the Year. When the new XJ40 was launched the Institute of Marketing named him Man of the Year and in 1986, Industry Year, came Mrs Thatcher's grateful accolade. John Egan received a knighthood."[12]

When you do a good job, it is important that this is recognized and rewarded.

A thirst for further recognition and reward

Ricardo Semler, our example of the Sage leader in commerce, went to Harvard to learn business. He took little away from this experience that he applied at Semco. But he does remember his classmates, many of whom told him that they clearly had thoughts of selling their business once they had made enough money, and retire. "In the intervening years a few did cash in, trading their companies for a chance to realize dreams of an island, a sailboat, and maybe even golf every day. But by the time the second session at Harvard came along a few of these liberated souls were already a bit bored. And by the third session nearly all those who had sold their businesses had started or acquired new ones and were happily back on the job."[13]

The Warrior who knows himself or herself knows that a life of quiet contemplation is not a reward for years of hard work and success; it is like a prison in which the punishment is invisibility and wasted time. For the Warrior, like those Semler met at Harvard, goals, once reached, have to be replaced by new challenges.

Warrior leadership

Lead from the front

The Warrior leader demonstrates his or her leadership by doing the job he or she expects of others, and doing it better. John Egan was a typical example of this at Jaguar: "He expects everyone to have the same total commitment to Jaguar that he has got and he can't understand why they haven't."[14] And Bill Gates led the way by being personally involved in all the deals that established Microsoft as the leader in the industry.[15]

Leading from the front means that you may, at times, have to put a check even on your own people if they are trying to take too much authority from you. Michael Heseltine was renowned for being ambitious, and his dissent was one major cause of his crossing swords with Margaret Thatcher. "I knew from Michael's behavior that unless he were checked there were no limits to what he would do to secure his objectives. . . . Cabinet collective responsibility was being ignored and my own authority as Prime Minister was being publicly flouted. This had to stop."[16]

The Warrior leader may adopt a consultative style, but there is room only for one at the top. In the words of Robert Herbold, recruited from Procter & Gamble to be COO of Microsoft in 1994, "Remember, no-one has ever accused Microsoft of being a democracy."[17]

Fight for what you believe in

"One of Gates's major principles is that you never give up without a fight, and, if you fight well enough, you won't need to give up at all."[18] In the capitalist economy, the battle is constant and shifting. Set your goals and go for them, even if you make a few enemies along the way.

Enemies you will have. Margaret Thatcher made many enemies, but, until 1990, was able to fight them off. When she went, what pained her was not that she had lost a fight, but that she felt betrayed: "I was sick at heart. I could have resisted the opposition of opponents and potential rivals and even respected them for it; but what grieved me was the desertion of those I had always considered friends and allies and the weasel words whereby they had transmuted their betrayal into frank advice and concern for my fate."[19]

Believing in yourself, your products and services, and your superiority is a key part of success. When Steve Ballmer, who became Bill Gates's number two at Microsoft after Paul Allen's departure, described the people employed at Sun Microsystems (one of Microsoft's main rivals) as "those sub-50-IQ people"[20] he was demonstrating the art of leadership by comparing them unfavorably with his own people. You have to believe you are the best if you are going to win.

And what you believe in has to be tangible. You need more than just a vision. As Bill Gates points out, "vision is free. And it's therefore not a competitive advantage in any way, shape or form." In other words, "Unless your vision translates into a marketable product or service, it has no value."[21]

Be assertive

In the constant battle for supremacy, it is a weakness to waver. One of Margaret Thatcher's strengths was her certainty: "Margaret had always seen things in black and white. She would become quite irritated if people complicated the issue with grey. What she saw, she spoke about quite bluntly, and what she said, she stuck to."[22] Warriors can weigh up the pros and cons of an argument, but when it comes to action, it is vital that the conclusion of any debate is pursued without hesitation or "dithering."

Bill Gates has always been known for his assertiveness, although many people who have based their expectations of him on first impressions have found his assertiveness surprising. Microsoft was established in the summer of 1975 when Bill Gates and Paul Allen moved to Albuquerque to write software for the world's first microcomputer, the Altair, that had been developed by Ed Roberts. Bill Gates and Ed Roberts did not always see eye to eye. "Although he wasn't old enough to order a beer legally, the 5-feet-11 Gates stood his ground with Roberts, often going jaw to jaw with the huge, gruff man 13 years his senior. Roberts weighed close to 300 pounds, and at 6-feet-4 towered over Gates."[23] Many other people have found Bill Gates to be similarly assertive with them, irrespective of their physical stature or their "importance."

Such assertiveness takes guts. The Warrior leader has to have guts, and anyone who doesn't is seen as weak by the true Warrior. Referring to Campbell Adamson, the Director General of the CBI calling for the repeal of the Industrial Relations Act just before the election of February 1974, Margaret Thatcher wrote, "It was all too typical of the way in which Britain's industrial leaders were full of bravado before battle was joined, but lacked the stomach for a fight."[24]

Be strong and decisive

"I didn't ring up the EC when I was with George Bush when the Iraqis went into Kuwait. What has happened that people have to have someone else holding their hand before they will take a courageous decision?"[25] Here, Margaret Thatcher shows why she is so revered. The Warrior must have the strength to carry out those actions that are necessary but which may be unpopular. For the Warrior leader, you have to make difficult decisions, but, once made, you have to carry them out decisively and quickly.

Thatcher did the same over the Falklands, a situation which was likely to be popular with the electorate, but also when she agreed to support the American attack on Libya: "However unpopular, no-one could doubt that our action had been strong and decisive. I had set my course and stuck to it."[26]

Among the central principles in Gates's theory and practice of management are:

- The boss is the boss
- As boss, he listens to all opposing arguments, and then makes a clear, unarguable decision
- He makes sure that the decision is followed through.[27]

For the Warrior leader, these are the principles that will keep you on track.

Be tough and resilient

Although there are many famous Warrior business leaders, some are more famous than others. One reason for this may be the way in which the ones who become more famous are unequivocal in their drive for success. Paul Allen, who set up Microsoft with Bill Gates retired when he became ill, so it is not surprising that it is Gates who is the better known. But had Paul Allen remained healthy, would he have still been running alongside Gates?

Allen was a Warrior, too: "He, too, was very ambitious, and very competitive. But Paul tended to be a lot more patient about things than Bill."[28] My guess is that Bill gates is so successful and famous because his Warrior is so dominant.

"They have very different personalities," Bunnell[29] said of Gates and Allen. "Paul was always much more laid back. All along, I thought Paul wanted to enjoy the fruits of his success a lot more than Bill. Bill wanted to drive on and on. I think Paul really wanted to not work so hard. . . . He had a lot more interest in just enjoying life."[30] In other words, the Sage part of Paul Allen's character, his handbrake, was a more effective handbrake than the Sage in Bill Gates.

From one point of view, tempering your Warrior with a bit of your Sage may produce a more balanced personality. But it may also weaken your resolve and water down your leadership. During the Falklands War people and circumstances contrived to make the pursuit of her chosen strategy very difficult for Margaret Thatcher, who wrote, "At such a time almost everything and everyone seems to combine to deflect you from what you know has to be done."[31]

Resilience means the strength of character that enables you to keep on the path you have chosen despite barriers, blocks, and detractors. Like Margaret Thatcher, the effective Warrior leader "can never be defeated by attrition."[32] The Warrior's approach to leadership, then, is tough. But it does not have to be unfair.

Stretch people

The Warrior leader sets people "big, hairy, audacious goals."[33] At times, this can go wrong: "Too often, Gates set unrealistic goals for product development."[34] But the Warrior leader does not take a failure to reach stretching goals as evidence of the goals being too big; he or she merely encourages greater effort to reach the goals. Scaling down is the thin end of the wedge.

The Warrior leader stretches at all levels, from the individual to the corporation. Early in 1983, Rowland Hanson was brought in as vice president of corporate communications. He wanted to stretch Microsoft from being simply a product company to being a household name. "The brand is the hero," he said, "We decided that we needed to make Microsoft the hero."[35]

The brand acts, in the same way as a fighting force's "colors" or a sporting team's flag, as the symbol of heroism each individual is fighting for. The "stretch goals, or targets are each individual's or team's contribution to the success of that symbol." Although targets are stretched, "The target shouldn't exceed the manager's abilities, but should exploit them to the full, closing the gap between potential and performance."[36] The good Warrior leader knows that setting impossible targets is pointless. It guarantees the failure that will sap the strength of the most dedicated of fighting forces.

Set standards and measure everything

The adage "what gets measured gets done" is music to the ears of the Warrior leader. If it is not measured, it is not seen, and cannot be rewarded. At Microsoft, "In performance reviews product managers are graded on the speed and quality of their team's responses to field queries, and salespeople are graded on how well they maintain up-to-date information in our customer tracking system."[37]

When people meet standards (especially those that stretch them) you need to make their successes known, and make sure they are rewarded. The trophy chest can never be too full.

Maintain a challenging style

To be consistent in your Warrior leadership style, you need to be in challenge mode at all times. This may lead to short-term irritations. As Margaret Thatcher admits, "I am often impatient with people."[38] And Bill Gates is not admired for his tact and diplomacy. If you want to be liked, don't try to be a Warrior leader, but if you want the respect of other Warriors, you need to maintain the challenge, day in, day out.

At Microsoft, "Although the office atmosphere was casual, it could also be confrontational. Gates was very demanding and the work was intense. . . . But the Microkids expected to be challenged. And they expected to be able to challenge Gates. In fact, he wanted them to argue with him. His confrontational style of management helped Microsoft maintain its edge, its mental toughness. It made those who worked for him think things through. These are qualities that continue to distinguish Microsoft to this day. It is a culture that never gives employees a chance to get complacent because as soon as they do, someone is going to challenge them."[39]

Challenge your people

Warrior leaders can be so challenging that they can appear to be very rude. Lady Thatcher was reported to have told Mr Whittingdale (former member of the shadow cabinet) "The trouble with you, John, is that your spine does not reach your brain."[40]

But they know that it is precisely this kind of challenge that other Warriors thrive on. The close friendship and trust that grew between Bill Gates and Paul Allen started at school, and was fuelled by Allen challenging Gates time and again.[41] Since challenge is the life-blood of the Warrior, you do well to provide the nourishment that your Warrior people need.

And make sure that the challenges you set are really challenging. Bill Gates went to Harvard and met up with Henry Leitner, who took a graduate math class with Gates on the theory of computation. "Leitner, now a senior lecturer in computer science at Harvard, was a graduate student at the time. He and Gates sat next to each other in class, and were supposed to collaborate on homework problems. But Leitner couldn't get the younger Gates to work on problems the latter didn't think were worthy of his time. Gates only liked the challenge of the most difficult problems."[42]

Surround yourself with people who rise to the challenges

One of the most frustrating things for a Warrior leader is to have to deal with what Margaret Thatcher referred to as "mediocrities."[43] At best, Thatcher described those world leaders she found lacking in the same steely strengths she admired as "a safe pair of hands."[44] But she was more assertive in blaming the West for the rise of power of the Soviets, which, she said, "was not because of the strengths of communism but rather because of the weakness and cowardice of Western leaders."[45]

There is no point in issuing challenges if they cannot be met due to some infirmity in the character of those you challenge. Sir Paul Girolami (Glaxo's boss during its transformation) was confronted by the challenge of the competitive threat to Glaxo's success that was posed by the Americans. He said that their "different management style – 'rough, tough, used to competition' – posed a greater challenge than their know-how, but the challenge isn't what matters: it's rising to it that counts."[46]

In these days of employee choice, where people can choose to move on to new organizations if they feel undervalued, part of any leader's challenge is to acquire and retain good people. People are, to this extent, already empowered. Yet many organizations boast how they empower their people.

At Microsoft, part of this process of "empowerment" lies in recognizing that everyone in such an organization is, at least in part, a "knowledge worker," having the ability to add to the stock of knowledge that can enhance competitive edge. Bill Gates knows this, and sees it as part of his job to give people the tools to turn this into reality. But, he cautions, "If you don't believe that all workers have the potential to contribute to your company's success, all the technology in the world won't empower them. Once you assume that every employee should be a knowledge worker, technology will help every employee put his or her full abilities to work on the company's behalf."[47]

And what will encourage them to "work on the company's behalf" is the rewards and recognition that doing so will bring. Which means, of course, that you need people who are motivated by those rewards. If, like Margaret Thatcher, you "want to promote merit and excellence,"[48] then you'll need to have around you people who are, like you, ambitious and competitive.

Chapter 12

Developing a Sage strategy

Sage leadership is practised less commonly in western commerce than other leadership styles. Western capitalism is essentially competitive, and is more congenial to the Warrior mentality, while the growth of the "market economy" in public services also encourages Warrior leadership styles.

Also, since it is inimical to the Sage to seek fame, fortune, and achievement in the outer world, it is not surprising that few business leaders are immediately obvious candidates as case examples. Even my Adventurer example, Richard Branson has Warrior as his secondary driver, as does our Guardian example, John Harvey-Jones. But the Sage cannot have Warrior as his or her secondary driver. For the Sage, the Warrior part of his or her character is the hand brake.

Living by values such as humility and inner harmony, the Sage leader is unlikely to develop his or her strategy quickly and assertively. For the Sage, leadership is a long and complex process of self-discovery, and is often adopted only later in life, after many years of appearing to be heading for a more assertive or competitive style. The two cases in this chapter, like Gandhi, behaved much more like Warriors than Sages in their early years.

But a note of caution here. Clues to their core values are there in the early lives (and biographies) of true Sage leaders. They did not evolve into Sages; they discovered their true selves later in life.

The ideal job role for a Sage

An organization or role you can believe in

Sages want to make a difference, according to their own values. For the Sage, a job is not a means to earning money or other material rewards; it is his or her chance to contribute to bringing about the "ideal" society. Many Sages who only recognize who they are later in life find themselves frustrated (some even say "cheapened") if they have taken on a career in an organization whose prime or sole "purpose" is to make money.

This is why many Sages gravitate to the public sector. The lower pay is not an issue, as they feel that it is the essence of what they do that counts, not the financial inducement to do it.

But there is room for the Sage in commerce, even though what they do as leaders may appear unconventional. Ricardo Semler, for example, is the CEO of Semco, a complex of businesses that started out as a marine manufacturing company in Brazil. Semler was the founder's son, and was at first reluctant to take over the reins of the company, feeling that a life in commerce was not what he craved.

So instead of seeking an organization he could believe in, Semler made one from the raw materials of the traditional company he inherited.[1]

An organization that values quality of life

Organizations are not only about products and services, designed to make more profit. They are also about the benefits they can provide to all stakeholders, including those who work there. And by the word "values" in the heading, I do not mean paternalistic or materialistic rewards for "good ideas."

Some organizations and their employees have an almost exclusively pecuniary relationship; the organization buys the employee's time and energy. The deal is that what the employee contributes is paid for, and the more the employee works and contributes, the more the organization pays him or her. But the Sage organization **is** its people. In Semco, for example, workers make the decisions previously made by their managers. They don't do it to get prizes or bonuses, but because their ideas and innovations have a direct and immediate impact on their own experience as part of the company.

When there is a conflict in a Sage organization between profit and the quality of life of their **primary** stakeholders, the employees, it is the latter that takes priority.

An organization that rewards knowledge, wisdom, and understanding

"If the cause was right, the means would follow."[2] Sage organizations do things because they are "right," not because they will achieve profits. Many business leaders use the "bottom line" as the ultimate measure of utility. Good ideas or knowledge are only as good as the increase in financial value to the company they produce. Sage leaders do not. They measure the value of ideas and knowledge against the values for which they stand. If those ideas produce financial benefit, that is a bonus.

Semler argues that "No company can be successful, in the long run anyway, if profits are its principal goal."[3] The Sage leader, then, is driven to leadership because of what he or she believes in. If he or she has the misfortune of failing to find an organization that is in line with those values, this can often be the spur to setting up in business from scratch. Semler inherited a company, other Sage leaders have had to start from nothing. As another Sage leader, Steve Shirley, founder of the FI Group (FI became a model of staff participation in the 1970s) says, "I felt that with my own company I could create a future that suited me, control my own business life and actually achieve something for other women."[4]

A place for learning

Learning is not simply the acquisition of knowledge; it is about changing how you do things.[5] In Chapter 15 I will look at some of the ways in which the idea of a "learning organization" have come and gone, and how such an idea relates differently to the four key leadership styles.

For the Sage, lifelong learning is a value; learning not for some other purpose, but for its own sake. This kind of learning is inevitably exploratory: if you know what you want to learn, in some sense, you already know it. So a place for learning is a place that is open, receptive and does not rely on preconceptions. Sometimes learning takes place simply because of a sense that something is not in line with what you truly believe in.

In his early days of leading Semco, Ricardo Semler did not have a grand scheme for its transformation. What he had was a sense of unease: "Our middle managers had studied at schools that taught traditional organizational discipline and the importance of structure and supervision. They had been reared on competition and trained to accumulate symbols of power, such as parking spaces near the door and embossed business cards. They enjoyed saying things like, 'See that four-door out there, the one with the graphite paint-job? That's my company car.' But democracy cannot be reconciled with expensive and unnecessary icons, especially those that come with radial tyres."[6]

At that stage of his learning, Semler valued democracy, but was not aware of how to make such an idea a reality within a workplace. He learnt by trying it out.

The opportunity to understand yourself and others

For the Sage, work is not simply a means of acquiring the money to survive. It has to have meaning in itself. And, given the significance of self-awareness and of understanding to the Sage, the ideal job role is one that allows opportunities for understanding oneself and others.

Part of the development of Semco involved splitting off parts of the company when units became too large – more than 150 people. This was known as the Satellite Program. At the time, this was unknown territory. "Sometimes it seemed foolish even to me. But we went ahead anyway, basing our decision on two feelings corporate managers are usually afraid to trust: Intuition and faith."[7]

Pedants may say that there is nothing new under the sun, but for the Sage, learning something new often means unlearning something old. Sages can irritate others by their apparent willingness to change their minds. Seen as a weakness by some, the Sage thrives on an environment that celebrates "U-turns."

In his early days as a leader of Semco, Semler did what he thought he had to do to make the organizational efficient and effective. He built systems and procedures to control everything, but "Workers just didn't seem to care. As I thought about it I realized the tough guys had taken over. And while I initially liked the idea of a disciplined, hard-driven company, run by aggressive managers armed with innumerable statistics, I was starting to have second thoughts. Work hard or get fired. That was the ethic of the new Semco. People were being pushed forward. But how much better to have a self-propelled workforce."[8]

By unlearning the received wisdom he grew up with, Semler was able to make the radical changes to the workplace that have become legendary.

Thought leadership

The medium in which the Sage operates is language, and the contribution is thought leadership. All leaders lead to some extent through what they say, their ideas. But for the Sage it is not the person who leads, but the thought – true "thought leadership." In other words, the Sage leader steps aside from ownership of the thought, and allows the thought, the spirit, the idea to lead.

Stepping aside from the front line is a common element in the stories of many Sage leaders, like Ricardo Semler, who watched the development of Semco from its traditional beginnings to its (at the time) radical transformation, and said, "The truth is, the company hardly needs me now in its day-to-day operations. And the ideas Semco is built on aren't mine, either. They flow from the company's culture, and that belongs to everyone at Semco."[9]

The chance to develop yourself

If other leaders are effective because of what they do, the Sage leader is so because of who he or she is, or what he or she stands for. In this sense, the ideal Sage job role is developmental, not just in the sense that it provides opportunities for learning job-related skills, but how it allows for true personal development. Having stepped back from full-time on-site work at Semco, Ricardo Semler continued to read and learn – for its own sake.[10]

It's a bad day if you've learnt nothing new

It is a classic symptom of a Sage mentality that the more you know, the more you realize how much more there is to learn. For the Sage leader, learning is not a by-product of work, it is what makes work worthwhile – it is the core of work.

The satisfaction of doing something worthwhile

Doing a good job is never enough for the Sage. The job has to be something that has worth beyond the task itself. The changes Semler brought about in Semco were not put in place because they would enhance productivity or profit, but because, intrinsically, they were right, according to Semler's values. The fact that they (or some of them) did produce business benefits was an added bonus.

Many Sage organizations owe their existence to the pursuit of a purpose more "worthy" (from the Sage point of view) than merely providing goods and services as a means of gaining profit. When a Warrior organization says, "the customer is king" it means that by treating customers well, they will keep buying, and the business will thrive. When similar sentiments are expressed in a Sage organization, it is because providing benefit for the "customer" is an end in itself, a principle that drove the Cheshire Homes for disabled people we will look at shortly. This was the classic Sage organization that, were it to have been set up to make a profit, would have died a death almost before its birth.

Becoming more contented with yourself or what life has to offer

The word "contented" may worry some readers. It conjures up complacency, and in commerce, complacency spells doom. In business, you have to keep striving and growing, or the competition will get you. Sage leaders have to face up to commercial realities as well as their search for inner harmony. As Semler views it: "Of course, some growth is necessary for any business to keep up with competitors and provide new opportunities for its people. But so often it is power and greed and just plain stubbornness that makes bigger automatically seem better."[11]

Business growth, for the Sage leader, is not a goal, but a necessary part of survival.

The Sage value of inner harmony, and his or her lack of interest in the material rewards of work, explain why the goal for a Sage leader is neither the product or service, nor the financial rewards, but how the experience of working enhances the spirit. This is one reason why Ricardo Semler decided not to hand down the company to his children. "I've already seen to it that none of my offspring can be promoted without the approval of three-quarters of the Semco board. Not even my death will change their circumstances, since outstanding shares in Semco will revert to the foundation that Irene Tubertini started."[12] Providing people like their children with sufficient material wealth to remove the need to work is, for the Sage, denying them of the opportunity to learn and grow; it is not a gift, but a curse.

The search for truth and inner harmony is central to the experience of the Sage. The ideal job role is one in which these values can be lived without apology, and that means that the organization in which the role sits cannot be driven by values that subsume the needs of the Sage under a drive for business growth and for profit.

As a teenager, another Sage leader had a memorable moment of peace in the countryside that "conjured up an image of all that a young heart hopes from life, of a future filled with nothing but happiness and promise."[13] This was Leonard Cheshire, VC OM.

Leonard Cheshire

"Today, it is not difficult to find a young person who has never heard of Leonard Cheshire. In the 1950s and 1960s it would have been virtually impossible."[14] Cheshire was a famous bomber pilot in the Second World War who went on to establish the Cheshire Homes, a charitable institution for disabled people. As a Sage leader outside of the commercial sector, his story provides a good contrast and comparison to the Sage leadership in business.

Like many Sage leaders, Cheshire spent his earlier years behaving in ways that belied his underlying Sage values. As an undergraduate, for example, "Cheshire passed through Oxford less in a blaze of rebellious individualism than as part of a genre. He became a model of what in his own eyes an undergraduate should be. . . . This was a kind of conformism."[15] And becoming the most celebrated bomber pilot in the war hardly suggests a Sage approach to life.

But even at Oxford, his concern for the city's "beggars and limbless ex-servicemen who hobbled the streets or offered their caps from doorways" was clear.[16] And in his first attempt at fiction, "Jill for a day lives Jack's life: she sees the welcome he gets wherever he goes: she meets his friends – the ordinary man in the street: and she realizes that this welcome, more powerful than any dinner of honour, is not because of what he has done, but because of what he is to his friends."[17] Essence, not achievement.

"If we seek a point of departure for Cheshire's search for universal meaning it is here, in the death of Frank Long."[18] It may have taken a few years after this unexpected death of a young man's hero – the apparently indestructible pilot Cheshire learnt so much from about staying alive in the most dangerous of situations – but Cheshire began to wonder about the meaning of it all while still flying missions in war.

What speeded up the process of self-discovery was the achievement of material goals he had set himself while "conforming" to undergraduate life. "By the end of 1945, as if in a dark folk tale, Cheshire had been granted his four wishes. He was universally admired, driving a Bentley, wearing Savile Row suits and had access to wealth. Then having gained what he imagined he wanted most, he found it joyless."[19]

Soon after, finding himself almost by chance nursing a stranger through to death, Cheshire began to exhibit more and more of the Sage, setting up home after home, shunning the publicity that he had previously courted as a war hero,[20] and deciding that: "I am going to hand everything I have to the new trust and receive back only the minimum and necessary expenses."[21]

"Cheshire's entrepreneurial strengths lay on a narrow front. He was a leader rather than a manager, and while inventive and persuasive, he displayed little of the merciless streak needed for the hard sell nor the realism to recognize what was practicable."[22] A classic Sage leader, Cheshire's success certainly did not come from any organizational capability; time after time the fund was hit by financial crisis, and none of his ventures was costed and planned. But he struggled through constant ill-health to set up a loose network of homes for the disabled across many countries, relying not on his own skills, but upon attracting to him people who believed in what he stood for.

Sage leadership

Engage in dialogue

All leaders talk. What makes the dialogue of the Sage leader different is its genuinely participative nature. As Ricardo Semler puts it: "What people call participative management is usually just consultative management. There's nothing new to that. Managers have been consulting employees for centuries. How progressive do you have to be, after all, to ask someone else's opinion? And to listen to that opinion – well that's a start. But it's only when the bosses give up decision-making and let their employees govern themselves that the possibility exists for a business jointly managed by workers and executives. And that is true participative management, not just lip-service to it."[23]

Many people who occupy senior positions often talk to people, but they hang on to the responsibility for making the final decisions. Anything else is abdication. Being the boss, it goes with the territory that you take on the role of final arbiter. But for the Sage leader, it is not seniority that gives you authority; it is how people respond to you as a person, not as a boss. Even as a senior officer, Cheshire " 'suggested' things rather then ordered them, and people did them as much because they were responding to him as a person as because an instruction had been given."[24]

For the Sage leader, true dialogue is between people, not roles. As Semler explains: "In these days of the new world order, almost everyone believes people have a right to vote for those who lead them, at least in the public sector. But democracy has yet to penetrate the work place. Dictators and despots are alive and well in offices and factories all over the world."[25]

Treat people as equals

The Sage leader lets go of the potential power over others that comes with seniority. He or she realizes that having such power over others (the power to fire someone, or to punish them) is a significant barrier to establishing mature relationships; the subordinate who is subservient is not a fully committed partner in dialogue. Sage leaders share with Ricardo Semler "the conviction that our employees are adults, and should always be treated as such".[26]

But if the Sage leader does relinquish the authority of rank, how does he or she actually **lead**, as opposed to simply joining in? Once again, it is not what a Sage leader does that makes him or her a leader; it is who they are, and how that character impacts on others. This is exemplified in one of "Cheshire's most powerful gifts: he made people feel better simply for being near him, and stirred desire for good because of it."[27] The Sage leader leads because people believe in him or her.

Listen and learn

The Sage leader may embody or symbolize an idea or vision, but he or she does not "own" it. For such an idea or vision to engage people, they have to share in its ownership (just as employees at Semco share the ownership of the company). Essential to good dialogue is the ability to listen as well as to speak. Cheshire "was a good listener – 'he drew you in' – and all kinds of people found themselves talking to him. His gift of making anyone feel they mattered invited confidences and forthrightness."[28] In other words, the openness and honesty of mature dialogue.

But simply to listen is not enough. You have to be able to learn, and some things you learn may be critical of you. Relinquishing the power of rank means being able to emulate "the imperturbable way in which Cheshire accepted criticism."[29] Managers at Semco learn about themselves every six months through 'reverse evaluation,' a comprehensive feedback method that allows employees to let managers know how they are doing as leaders.[30]

Create a developmental climate

"It has been rooted in the corporate consciousness that profits belong to those who invest in the capital."[31] But for the Sage leader, it is neither the profits nor the capital that define an organization; it is the people. The purpose of an organization, even a business, is to meet the needs of those who are the organization. And as an organization grows or changes, so, too, may those needs. The essence of Sage leadership lies in development for and of people.

Semco grew. But as organizations grow, the human touch can get lost, and needs can come into conflict. To counter this, Semco adopted an approach that spun off any part of the company that grew beyond about 150 people. They called this the Satellite Program.

"In a more fundamental sense, the Satellite Program is an extension of our philosophy of empowerment. After all, our new entrepreneurs have complete control over their work place – at least the control any owner has. They make all the decisions, including deciding how many decisions their workers should make. They are almost always even more productive than they were at Semco."[32]

This spirit of local involvement – keeping units small enough to enable those involved in their management to be responsible for their development – was a principle also adopted, almost by default, by Cheshire. "Ultimately, homes were founded and run not because of Cheshire's connections or anyone else's, but because local people believed in them, understood the particular needs of their communities, raised the funds, and did the work."[33]

A developmental climate means letting go of control. People don't always develop according to preconceived notions, and some of the Satellites of Semco went down different paths: "Semco has so far helped form more than two dozen Satellite companies. . . . To this day, no Satellite has closed. . . . Some are little Semcos, organized around the ideals of democracy, transparency, and trust. Some are utterly traditional, tiny Fords or IBMs (a temporary affliction, we hope)."[34]

Ricardo Semler's hope may not come true. There is no guarantee that those who lead the Satellites are all Sages. It is unlikely that Sage methods will graft neatly onto organizations that are not, themselves, led by Sages. Take, for example, "rounding the pyramid."[35]

In an attempt to rid Semco of the constraints of hierarchy, they did away with the organization chart, imagined the organization as a series of circles, and renamed people as Counsellors, Partners, and Associates. In the past fifteen years or so I have come across a number of organizations that have liked these ideas and tried to adopt them. In the following two examples, the names of the organizations have been changed to save embarrassment.

A major subsidiary of a global energy firm tried to do away with their hierarchy, and redrew their organization as "baskets of eggs." Soon afterward, they moved to new premises, an octagonal building on several floors. Despite the espoused democratization of the company, the outer edges of the building, next to the windows, were turned into offices, each occupied by a (always male) senior manager, and each with a little fenced-off area outside the office for the (always female) secretary. Everyone else sat in an open plan area in the centre of each floor. The hierarchy was designed back in.

About a year after being taken over by a new parent company for $17 billion, a global information technology company acquired a new CEO who had read all the right books. He went through the renaming of roles, and preached Sage methods. But few, if any, of the existing managers were Sages. They tried to become "Coaches," and to make sense of the bizarre ideas of the new CEO. But it didn't work. He lasted fifteen months, and after his departure, the parent company was forced to sell off its ailing new subsidiary. They received $8 billion for it.

In neither of these cases could Sage leadership work, because only true Sages can lead as Sages. Sage leadership is not about adopting trendy methods, and trying to graft them onto an organizational philosophy that is built on a desire to direct and control. A developmental climate drives a Sage organization, not a strategy.

As the history of the Cheshire homes shows, a developmental climate means putting the future into the hands of people and fate: "So often his projects had taken unforeseen turns, which nevertheless made perfect sense when viewed in retrospect, and cumulatively. Imposed strategies limited the context in which such things could happen."[36]

Adopt a developmental style

Development is not training, which is hierarchical in nature: the trainee climbing towards pre-defined skill levels. Trainer and trainee are not in the kind of democratic relationship that is the essence of the Sage. The trainee is subordinate to the trainer, much as a child is subordinate to a parent, and a worker is subordinate to a boss. At Semco, "we don't want to turn our managers into Father Figures, even if it makes them feel warm and cuddly inside. We don't want to be a big, happy family. We want to be a business. That's the flip side of paternalism. Employees give these owners a lease on their soul for their working lives, and that can be an expensive proposition."[37]

Even in the rigidly hierarchical environment of the wartime RAF, Cheshire seemed to be drawn to this kind of developmental style: "One of Cheshire's many morale-building steps was the inauguration of a monthly meeting in which all the aircrews would entertain all the ground crews. Another was 'The Plumbers' Meeting,' a monthly conference attended by every member of the ground crew for discussion of their experiences, suggestions and complaints. A third was his realization that relaxation and humour were not alternatives to efficiency but prerequisites to it."[38]

Encourage belief

People often look to leaders to sort things out, like "roles and responsibilities." Sage leaders do not sort out such things. They help people develop, and encourage belief in the values and causes that will provide answers to everyday questions, such as "what should I do in this situation?" When people embrace the values or the cause, the answers will be clear; you don't need the leader to tell you.

As employees at Semco came to believe in Semler's vision, they had the courage and belief to carry the process forward themselves. For Cheshire, with his non-commercial vision ("the oneness, the essential and organic solidarity of the human family. The dream, that we each in our way make our personal contribution towards building unity and peace among us."), "the way to contribute toward the peace of the world is to bring peace into your own surroundings, into someone else's life – first, of course, your own."[39]

Encourage self-discovery

Sage leaders, therefore, do not lay down rules or standards. When Ricardo Semler began to discover for himself that what he had inherited was not what he wanted, he said of the establishment of rules and procedures: "Sounds sensible, right? And it works fine for an army or a prison system. But not, I believe, for a business. And certainly not for a business that wants people to think, innovate, and act as human beings."[40]

And how, for the Sage, human beings grow and develop is through self-discovery. Answers are not imposed from without; they come from within. This may seem like a recipe for organizational chaos. Indeed, Sage leadership can seem chaotic at times. One of Cheshire's first homes, Le Court, was certainly not run on orderly lines. "Yet in spite of the perpetual disorganization that seemed to reign, no-one appeared any the worse. Almost, one would be tempted to suppose, the better for it, the stronger even in body for having discovered that they were needed and that someone depended on them."[41]

Lead from behind

Sage leadership is a paradox in that it is best manifested by its absence. Sages achieve the pinnacle of their leadership when their people lead themselves. And if a great deal of what starts this process is the strength of character of the Sage leader, one of his or her key tasks is to remove the barrier to self-determination that his or her personality represents.

Sometimes this means removing yourself from the scene altogether, a step that Cheshire had to take. He wanted people to lead themselves, but, "this required the destruction of the personality cult which attended everything he did. Only by his absence would individual homes discover self-reliance."[42] Semler came to the same realization. Having set in motion the process of employee ownership and rule, he wanted to finish the job of making Semco a true democracy. "With this in mind, and with Semco restructured in a way that made it much less vulnerable to the economy, I decided it was time to virtually eliminate another level of our hierarchy: mine."[43]

Ricardo Semler has subsequently followed what he learnt at Semco. Some years later, "I was invited to join Brazil's imperious Federation of Industries of the State of Sao Paulo ... ." Where "I followed my usual approach to leadership and backed away from the department as it revived. There would be no cult of personality here."[44]

Encourage people to adapt and change

Because the Sage leader does not lay down a blueprint for the future, but helps people to learn and develop so as to manage their own futures, it is important to help people deal effectively with this freedom. Embedded in the development of Semco were many different methods of doing this, such as job rotation to help people learn new skills and perspectives.[45]

Any guidance the Sage leader can give in this direction is valuable. But, for many Sage leaders, what enables them to take the steps back they do is the recognition that people adapt, and they will change, but they will be helped along the way by the vision they will have shared with the leader. For Cheshire, this is summed up like this: "THE OBJECTIVE . . . to take those that are unwanted, and to make them wanted. Not to say to them, 'Now just lie back and be comfortably sick for the rest of your life,' but to give them a purpose to live for."[46]

Be a coach or mentor

The Sage leader has a constant struggle between trying to make his or her vision a reality and stepping back to allow people to develop and to take control of their own destinies. For Cheshire, this was always a dilemma: "How was it possible to be simultaneously self-effacing and assertive?"[47] How is it possible to influence without being present? "Cheshire's idealism was the adhesive that held them together. When he was away there was friction."[48]

The answer to such dilemmas lies in becoming a coach or mentor, and allowing the values and vision be the guide. As Semler says, "Semco is more than novel programmes or procedures. What is important is our open-mindedness, our trust in our employees and distrust of dogma."[49]

However, open-mindedness, trust in employees and distrust of dogma are attitudes that could be adopted elsewhere. At the heart of the Sage approach to leadership lies the fundamental issue of a sense of purpose. For example, reflecting on the benefits and dangers of the growth of the use of technology in Semco, Semler says: "There is no doubt in my mind: technology has gone through the roof since 1633, but quality of life has gone down the drain. All we have done is accelerate our malfunctions and increase the intensity of our mis-communication. Let me propose a new definition: the truly modern company avoids an obsession with technology and puts quality of life first."[50] If "quality of life" is the vision, then how you deal with organizational challenges such as the use of technology becomes clear. If "profit" is the vision, your answers may be very different.

Once again, however, it is important to remember that, as a Sage leader, it is not what you decide that is important. "Leaders there have to be, and these may appear to rise above their fellow men, but in their hearts they know only too well that what has been attributed to them is in fact the achievement of the team to which they belong."[51] The leader appears to rise above because of how he or she has been successful in coaching or mentoring mature adults to work together towards a shared vision or goal. To be successful in this, you have to "always [be] thinking the best of everyone."[52]

Sage leadership is personal, but it rejects the "cult" of personality. Sage leadership demands that you step away, but it also requires you to develop mature and equal relationships with people. Sage leadership is egalitarian, and does not rely on status or rank for authority. "Only the respect of the led creates a leader."[53]

And this takes time. Some leaders achieve by being there and leading from the front – it is a **physical** presence. But the Sage achieves by instilling beliefs and allowing the **spirit** to drive. "Quick wins," as such a competitive phrase suggests, are not for the Sage leader. Be patient.

CHAPTER 13

Developing an Adventurer strategy

The ideal job role for an Adventurer

A sense of independence

The successful Adventurer leader needs to feel a sense of independence in his or her daily experience of work. Political Adventurer leaders, like Martin Luther King, often operate outside of the framework of organized political parties. The same is true of many Adventurer leaders in industry and commerce.

The most visible of these Adventurer type leaders is Richard Branson, who never took a job in an organization. From the start, he needed to be free from authority, and built his career around the entrepreneurial spirit typical of the Adventurer. Branson has a competitive streak. He is as famous for his world–record breaking attempts in boats and balloons. His secondary driver must be Warrior. But he typifies the lifestyle and attitudes of the Adventurer more than those of the Warrior.

Building the Virgin Group has enabled him to remain free from the authority of bosses, and from the rules and regulations of organizations owned by someone else. Being your own boss is a desire expressed by many people who may not be Adventurers; it is the deep-seated need to be independent that is the characteristic of the Adventurer.

An organization that rewards self-reliance

Although the Adventurer can become a good team player, his or her need for self-reliance often leads to a preference to operate alone. In some respects this comes from the natural reluctance of the Adventurer to shoulder the burdens of responsibility. People feel responsible for their team mates.

Adventurers will take on responsibilities, but even the indomitable Martin Luther King "was clearly intimidated by his new-found responsibilities"[1] when first elected as President of the MIA (Montgomery Improvement Association). And although, eventually, Richard Branson became a devoted father, he says,

"I think lots of men would happily drift through life without having children unless their partners forced the issue."[2]

Branson clearly does rely on input and collaboration from many people in his life. But in most situations he goes his own way. When, for example, he decided to use a Virgin plane to take part in the rescue of the hostages of Saddam Hussein in Iraq, it was not due to pressure from anyone else. As he says, "I had no idea how I would set about helping bring these hostages home. . . . It struck me that, in the same way in which I had been able to help the crisis in Jordan, I might be able to provide the vehicle for releasing these hostages."[3]

Most Adventurer leaders may not be in a position to do anything quite so dramatic, but the level of freedom they have to decide what to do, and how, is an important measure of how well they fit into the organizational culture.

Bucking the system

Adventurers hate rules. As Richard Branson says, "I have always thought rules were there to be broken."[4] And just as Martin Luther King cheated in his doctoral degree[5] Branson cheated in his one A-level exam.[6] Throughout their lives, Adventurers look for ways to circumvent systems and break rules.

Some organizations allow people to "act first and seek permission afterwards." Others are far less forgiving, and therefore less congenial to the Adventurer.

In my experience, of course, the degree of freedom to break rules an organization gives you is to a significant extent a matter of how you see it. I have often interviewed people whose formal position within the same organisation is the same. But individuals see the degree of freedom they have very differently. For example, I worked with two Country Managers in the same organization. One felt he was very closely governed by people from Head Office. He described himself as "no more than an NCO." The other saw his area of discretion much more broadly, and found ways round what the other saw as non-negotiable constraints.

Getting away with it

It is a fact of life for Adventurers that they will find themselves being reprimanded when they break rules. Those who develop into leaders find ways of dealing with this. Many, like Martin Luther King, become highly resilient. "King was seen by most whites as a troublemaker throughout his career."[7] He was beaten, imprisoned, had his home bombed, and he died at the hands of the second person to make an attempt on his life.

In business, people may need this kind of resilience, but they may also need to learn how to temper their Adventurer rebelliousness. In his early years, Richard Branson got into trouble with the law, but learnt one of the key lessons of his life: how to remain an Adventurer, while not suffering consequences that are worse than being free to break any rule going. Arrested for the illegal export of records to Europe, he found himself in prison over night.

"That night was one of the best things that has ever happened to me. As I lay in the cell and stared at the ceiling I felt complete claustrophobia. I have never enjoyed being accountable to anyone else or not being in control of my own destiny. I have always enjoyed breaking rules. . . . As a twenty year old I had lived life entirely on my own terms, following my own instincts. But to be in prison meant that all that freedom was taken away."[8]

It has to be a matter of personal judgment how much an Adventurer needs to modify his or her natural Adventurer tendency to rebel in order to fit in with his or her organization's rules. As with so many of these judgments, it is better to be honest than naively optimistic.

Doing your own thing

One reason why so many Adventurers become entrepreneurs is that they can follow their inclinations to do their own thing. As Richard Branson explains concerning his corporate "strategy," "I am continually trying to broaden the Group so we are not dependent on a narrow source of income, but I suspect this is more down to inquisitiveness and restlessness than sound financial sense."[9]

Within organizations, Adventurers often spend time keeping an eye out for new opportunities to try something out. As risk-takers, they have no concern that, at times, they will be exposed and alone. In some respects, being out of the mainstream is a comfort to the Adventurer who has concerns about "group-think." Doing your own thing allows you the freedom from what often seem petty concerns within groups.

Martin Luther King expressed similar doubts when he wrote, "groups tend to be more immoral than individuals."[10] As an Adventurer, it is what you feel you can do by yourself that is most important; being part of a community can feel more smothering than comforting.

Finding new ways of doing things

Richard Branson says, "I lived by the dangerous (and sometimes rather foolish) maxim that I was prepared to try anything once."[11] When Martin Luther

King adopted Gandhi's way of passive resistance, he brought to the civil rights movement an approach that was unexpected by his friends and enemies alike.

To some extent, everyone likes to be creative and innovative. It is the **radical** nature of any novelty that excites the Adventurer. In an environment that is open to such radical shifts, the Adventurer will be that much more able to develop and apply an Adventurer leadership strategy.

Freedom

Many of the elements of the job described above are about freedom, but they are specific kinds of freedom. Beyond these, there is that overall sense an Adventurer gets when he or she is in a good place, that he or she is able to be him or herself. It is not just about rules and methods of work; it is about a liberal atmosphere, free from the kinds of conventions that are commonplace in many organizations.

Richard Branson sums this up in a series of advertisements for the Virgin Group, in the autumn of 2005. He says, "To me, business isn't about wearing suits or pleasing stockholders. It's about being true to yourself, your ideas and focussing on the essentials."

An organization that values fun

In some of the organizations I visit I hear laughter; in others, laughter is for outside the office. Richard Branson has proved that business and fun can mix. "I can honestly say that I have never gone into any business purely to make money. If that is the sole motive then I believe you are better off not doing it. A business has to be involving; it has to be fun."[12]

Doing it because it seems like a good idea (at the time)

In the early days of the Virgin business, Richard Branson knew he wanted a recording studio. As he happened to be passing the Manor in Oxfordshire on the way back from Wales, and found it was for sale, he bought it. It seemed like a good idea at the time. It could have been a disaster; it wasn't.[13]

Many of the Adventurers I have worked with tell me that the reason they are in the job they currently occupy is that "it seemed like a good idea at the time, and I wanted a change." It is not so often that this reason is recorded in their curricula vitae.

What next? "No idea"

Facing an uncertain future is frightening for some people, who make investments and plans to minimize risk. The Adventurer finds such uncertainty exhilarating. Organizations in which career paths are planned for years ahead are not for an Adventurer.

Adventurer leadership

Be a radical mould-breaker

Adventurers break the mould. Not just once, but again and again. As if Virgin Music and Virgin Airlines were not enough, along came Virgin financial services. Why?

"The idea of setting up Virgin life insurance and a Virgin bank would have horrified our original staff at Albion Street, or our customers who lounged about on beanbags at the record shop. . . . The maverick in me was . . . quietly amused that the guy who brought you The Sex Pistols could sort out your pension too. Another part of me was equally amused by the idea that we were going to set up our own bank to give those very banks that nearly foreclosed on us a run for their money."[14]

Being an Adventurer leader demands a questioning attitude to everything. You don't just tweak things; you change paradigms.[15] It is an approach to leadership that is risky and unpredictable. You need to be like Richard Branson who says that, "Happily I have always thrived on havoc and adrenaline."[16] For every successful Virgin or Easyjet, there are hundreds of great ideas that have crashed and burnt.

To be successful, the Adventurer leader needs to attract to him or her people who are willing to take the same level of risk. The Adventurer leader needs to make sure his or her people understand that, with them, it will be a bumpy ride, and that they are not going to be provided with stability or certainty.

Challenge convention

Changing paradigms means a series of big steps. But these are fuelled by continuously challenging conventions. The Adventurer leader will make him or herself an irritant, constantly questioning why things have to be done "this way." He or she takes nothing for granted. Martin Luther King challenged the convention of segregation; Nelson Mandela challenged the convention of apartheid; and Richard Branson challenged most of the conventions of his day.

For the true Adventurer, this tendency persists whatever the outcomes. After many years of uncertainty and near-financial disaster, Richard Branson made his fortune. He writes, "At this point I could of course have retired and concentrated my energies on learning how to paint watercolours or how to beat my mum at golf. It wasn't in my nature to do so. People asked me, 'Why don't you have some fun now?' but they were missing the point. As far as I was concerned this was fun. . . . I am aware that the idea of business being fun and creative goes right against the grain of convention."[17]

Because convention is the tried and tested way, the Adventurer leader is going to be subject to a great deal of criticism. Martin Luther king was a "trouble maker"; Richard Branson was a significant problem to Lord King and British Airways, and came close to losing everything for his impertinence. Unlike the Warrior (which was not Branson's primary style), the Adventurer is unlikely to fight fire with fire, and Branson's constant appeal for fairness in the "dirty tricks" affair was described by many as "naïve."[18]

To be consistent in Adventurer leadership, he or she needs to avoid being dragged into wars. His or her role is to challenge convention, not people.

Be prepared to break the rules

It is also to challenge rules, especially where they limit freedom. The Adventurer leader acts first and if necessary asks for forgiveness later. It is sometimes frustrating for the Adventurer to understand why others are content to follow rules. To the Adventurer, this smacks not only of a lack of imagination, but also of becoming focused on the means more than the ends.

To the Adventurer leader, the ends justify the means, especially if the means cut across rules and conventions that get in the way of achieving those ends.

Encourage people to challenge your authority

The Adventurer leader may need to let people challenge **his or her** rules and conventions, too. If the Adventurer leader surrounds himself or herself with people who are not Adventurers, they will despair at his or her apparent lack of concern for their futures, and at the risks he or she takes with their lives. On the other hand if he or she does surround himself or herself with Adventurers, they will be rule-breakers and convention-challengers too. The Adventurer leader needs, like Richard Branson, to "thrive on mavericks."[19]

To do this sincerely, the Adventurer leader has to be able, like Martin Luther King, to admit to his or her weaknesses. As an Adventurer leader, one does not have to project an image of infallibility. Indeed, as King discovered, his open admission that he wondered whether he was adequate for the job, or able to face the challenges and responsibilities, was one of the reasons they followed him. He did not pretend he was a strong figure of authority (the Guardian), or that he was a tough fighter (the Warrior). Yet people loved him.

Dealing with the paradox of following your own ideas while giving your people freedom to challenge you is always hard, even for successful Adventurers like Richard Branson. He says, "Although I listen carefully to everyone, there are times when I make up my mind and I'll just go and do it. At times like those, the more people disagree with me, the more obstinate I become."[20]

Share

The Adventurer leader does a great deal of sharing to deal consistently with the paradox of challenge to his or her authority. The Adventurers in his or her following will hate hierarchies and authority. Like the leader, they will want to change things, to challenge. Many of them will be a significant source of the ideas the Adventurer leader thrives on.

He or she encourages them to share the risk. The Adventurer leader creates an environment in which people feel equals as pioneers in a shared adventure. The Adventurer needs to surround himself or herself with people who feel like Richard Branson, who says, "I love to experience as much as I can of life."[21]

Explore together

The chaos that goes with a whole bunch of Adventurers trying to change everything can get out of hand. To avoid too many acrimonious splits, it is a key part of the Adventurer leadership strategy that people explore all options openly and together.

When asked about his "formula" for success in business, Richard Branson said, "It's not that simple: to be successful, you have to be out there, you have to hit the ground running, and if you have a good team around you and more than your fair share of luck you might make something happen. But you certainly can't guarantee it just by following someone else's formula."[22]

Martin Luther King followed a similar line. For him, "a good team" meant experienced advisors who had been involved in movements in the past. Bringing them together to plan next steps, he said very little in strategy meetings. He listened to everyone's ideas first, waiting for solutions to emerge, until what were often heated and complex discussions were almost exhausted. He then summarized what he had heard, bringing disparate ideas together, and synthesizing the best. This enabled him to offer a view, as leader, that clearly took into account what each advisor had said. It was what the group needed: a synthesis of their ideas, not an imposed solution by a figure of authority.

Empower

I find many organizations these days that say they follow the route of empowerment, and some do this well. But in organizations where few of the people in senior positions are Adventurers, I see cynicism amongst those who are supposed to be empowered.

Some senior people in such organizations delegate and call it empowerment. In practice, this means giving a subordinate a job to do, and then judging the work according to the senior's own standards and methods. Maintaining the Parent-Child transactional relationship,[23] the essentially positive motivation for such delegation is to help the subordinate to learn responsibility, to learn by experience, and to learn from the feedback from such judgement. These are all highly positive behaviors, but they are Guardian-oriented, and are not empowerment.

For Guardians, "the buck stops with me." The responsibility for success or failure lies with the senior, no matter what the outcome of the delegation. For Adventurer leaders, empowerment means handing over both the task and the responsibility. In organizations that are not amenable to Adventurer leadership, this handing over of responsibility is interpreted as "abdication," a term that clearly demonstrates the essential inequality of hierarchical power.

For Guardians, that essential inequality is both necessary and positive. It is responsible. For Adventurers, it gets in the way of what they see as genuine empowerment, because it is built precisely on inequality, and such inequality implies that the subordinate is constrained by the senior.

Liberate

For the Adventurer leader, this poses another challenge. In the Virgin businesses, for example, Richard Branson is the boss. Relationships between him and employees are unequal. And such unequal relationships will naturally take on some of the flavour of the unequal relationship between parent and child. How we approach parenting may give us a clue as to how we might approach leadership.

Towards the end of his autobiography, Richard Branson gives an insight into his approach to being a parent. Sitting and watching his children, Holly and Sam, at play, he muses, "I wonder what the future holds for all the kids here. I look over at Holly and Sam and realize that I don't want to plan their lives for them. I just want them to be happy. . . . I know that other businessmen like Rupert Murdoch and Robert Maxwell had their children reading annual reports and financial accounts before breakfast, but I want none of that."[24]

Both as parents and as leaders, Adventurers face a dilemma. Each role carries with it the kinds of responsibility that Martin Luther King found daunting. Yet responsibility limits personal freedom. If you want your children and your people to be free, what happens when they mess up?

There are inherent weaknesses in each of the leadership models. How one deals with a person's failure is a question that confronts all Adventurer leaders. As Richard Branson admits, "I hate criticizing people who work with me, and I try to avoid doing so. Ever since then I have always tried to avoid the issue by asking someone else to wield the axe. I admit that this is a weakness, but I am simply unable to cope with it."[25]

Leave people alone to get on with it

Despite this kind of limitation, being an Adventurer leader means putting trust in people, giving them "enough rope," and letting them do the job both have agreed is theirs. Recall some of the Adventurer values:

- Freedom
- Challenging convention
- "You only live once"
- Change and variety
- Fast living
- Fun, excitement, adventure, and playfulness
- Self-reliance

The Adventurer is primarily motivated by freedom and adventure. Being an Adventurer leader is, in itself, an adventure because by leaving people alone to get on with it, he or she is being true to what he or she believes in, but it means taking risks, and relying on others to be successful doing it their way.

Let the future take care of itself

Life, for the Adventurer, is not something to be controlled. As an Adventurer, Richard Branson remembered one very important maxim from his parents: "Live for the present and the future will look after itself."[26] Similarly, leadership, for the Adventurer, is an adventure. You feel free to challenge convention, saying, for example, "And I think there is such a thing as a free lunch. We'll trade out of trouble."[27]

Conclusions

Being an Adventurer leader like Richard Branson or Martin Luther King is a very different experience from being a Warrior, Guardian, or Sage leader. It is a roller-coaster, and depends a great deal on luck and the quality of the people around the leader. Subordinates who are not Adventurers will despair of the Adventurer leader's irresponsibility and lack of seriousness. They will feel he or she is failing in leadership.

On the other hand, any Adventurers that an Adventurer leads will relish the freedom he or she provides for them. So long as they are up to the job, they will join in the fun and make it happen. The leader won't be able to control them, but won't want to. In their eyes, the leader really will be leading.

Chapter 14

Developing a Guardian strategy

The ideal job role for a Guardian

A role that represents a step up in life

"I've been promoted." "That's wonderful." The notion of a career for the Guardian is one of progression, mostly upwards. For some people, like Archie Norman, early in life they set themselves an objective, and this is often to run a company.[1] For the Guardian, it is through taking more and more senior roles that they have the greater chance to live out their Guardian values.

If you are a Guardian, you will be happier if your current role represents a step up in life. It is part of the career progression that is aimed at your ultimate objective. Every step should be "A major step up the ladder."[2]

An organization that rewards responsibility

For the Guardian, a place of work is a place in which one provides a service responsibly. Our primary example of the Guardian in corporate life is Sir John Harvey-Jones, who, in his book, *Making it Happen*, describes the "lessons I have learnt in my service in this world [of industry]."[3] He spent his entire career in one company, ICI, but his success in turning the huge company round has made him a very well-respected authority on leadership. ICI certainly did reward responsibility.

Despite his significant contributions to ICI, Harvey-Jones entered an organization that demonstrated values with which he was very comfortable, even if he had not fully expected, at first, how much in line his and the company's values were: "Looking back I am constantly amazed and grateful for the high risks that others took by giving me responsibility in my early years in ICI."[4]

He soon learnt that ICI was an organization that valued openness, respect for others, and plain speaking. But, as he points out, "Plain speaking and tolerance are tender flowers which have to be nurtured and helped to grow.

One 'hangover ridden' shortness of response, or a snappy turn-off to views you don't like causes infinite harm."[5] Responsibility, in this sense, includes responsibility for one's own behavior, day in day out.

A role where the best thing is the responsibility you have

And that is what the Guardian wants in a role – responsibility for things. This means that the tendency some organizations fall into of formalizing things to avoid risk (to create bureaucracy, in other words) is something that the Guardian's ideal organization resists. "Unless there is a really determined effort to 'burn the books,' and reduce this tangle of bureaucracy, the people at the bottom of the organization on whom everything depends feel an increasing lack of responsibility."[6] Entangling people in a web of rules and regulations is inherently disrespectful, as it implies that people cannot behave responsibly, and take responsibility away.

Similarly, if you are to take responsibility, it is important that you are involved in defining what you are expected to do. "In a good organization the objectives that have to be achieved are decided with considerable interaction between those who are going to carry them out, and those who ultimately have the responsibility for the leadership of the organization."[7] Good quality dialogue up and down the organization reduces risk, and means that the individual does not feel imposed upon or too immature to set his or her own goals in line with the overall strategy.

A role where you can take charge – especially in a crisis

Many well-researched works on how leaders develop agree that one of the most important elements for success is how an individual is exposed to difficult situations early in his or her career. In an organization that suits the Guardian, people are given opportunities to take charge, and to learn from their experiences. But this does not mean reckless abandon of responsibility on the part of people higher up the organization. Even where the individual is given scope to take charge, there has to be a safety net.

As Harvey-Jones says, "If the burden becomes too great, one must always feel that one can turn to somebody who is more knowledgeable, or has broader shoulders and who will share the burden. The burden should be shared but the burden should not be taken away. If it is taken away one will never grow."[8]

An organization in which professionalism is valued

The Guardian sets and lives by standards, and it is the accumulation of and adherence to these standards that is summed up in the concept of professionalism. Archie Norman says, "I'm a professional and my values are those of a professional."[9]

In 1990, John Harvey-Jones was asked by the BBC to engage in a program, called "Troubleshooter," in which he visited a number of companies to see if his experience and advice could be of help to them. He was at first slightly reluctant, as his own business experience was exclusively gained within ICI, a very large organization compared to those he worked with on the program. He did help the companies to varying degrees, but found out a lot at the same time about them. Each was different, with different problems and challenges. But, from his point of view, there were a number of common themes. "One area of omission which surprised me was the general lack of interest in professionalism."[10]

For Guardians, like Harvey-Jones, making it up as you go along is almost criminal when there is so much experience to draw on, and when it is clear that "everything in business is to do with balance, and the creation of the right balance of forces."[11] Professionalism means taking a mature and balanced approach, and avoiding the mistakes of tunnel-vision and single-mindedness.

Getting such balance, and being able to draw effectively on a wide range of experience and resources is far easier in a larger organization, and many Guardians thrive in such environments. To be sure, some gain some of their early experiences elsewhere, in consultancy, for example. But, as Archie Norman points out, "Consultants have strong professional values, a very strong sense of independence but they don't like being responsible for lots of people."[12] Guardians are temperamentally inclined to take responsibility for others.

A role where you can enjoy being responsible for people

In Chapter 3, I talked about the Guardian's instinct to self-sacrifice. It is not surprising, therefore, to hear that, in Harvey-Jones's view, "one of Britain's great national heroes was captain Oates, who sacrificed himself for the lives of the others on Scott's Polar expedition."[13] For the Guardian, responsibility for other people is not a burden, it is a pleasure and a privilege.

"Since in the last resort everything has to be achieved by people, the first thing we have to consider is the sort of environment in which people can give of their best."[14] For the Guardian, people are more than a resource, they are the future, and being responsible for the future careers of people is a key part of the enjoyment of work.

The opportunity to take care of people

This means that, to fulfil the working life of the Guardian, you have to be given people-responsibility. This means, in turn, putting people first. In some organizations, "putting people first" is a mantra that is hollow. The phrase "human resources" often gives this away, equating people with any other resources, be they physical or financial.

By contrast, the true Guardian organization is one in which people are expected to develop mature relationships as people, not as resources. As Harvey-Jones says, "The mutuality of respect for each other that we enjoy, the ability to discuss and differ openly and without rancour, and the total belief that we must look after each other are the most precious inheritance that any company can have."[15]

Guardian organizations are responsible, so they do not provide rest-homes for people who do not fit in. But when it is clear that there is such a lack of fit, it is also important to the Guardian that the needs of those who need to move out and take on a career elsewhere are met. "Fortunately, in many large organizations like ICI, there are enough people who genuinely care for others and will take this sort of work on, and indeed derive much justified pleasure from successfully rehabilitating people into a new way of life."[16]

It's a bad day if you let someone down

Other kinds of organization can seem excessively individualistic to the Guardian, for whom the "natural" habitat is the family. Within the family, the Guardian does best not by dictating, nor by abdicating responsibility, but by helping others to find a way forward they can all sign up to. Harvey-Jones exemplified this on his appointment as deputy chairman responsible for ICI's Wilton site in the late 1960s.

The situation there was poor, and many ways had been tried to improve things; none had worked. Harvey-Jones encouraged the people at the site to work with him and to develop a way forward they all felt they shared responsibility for. "From that day on things got better. We spent hours discussing the tactics until we were sure that we could live with them, and at no time, no matter what the pressures, did any of the team let the others down."[17]

A sense of belonging

The family atmosphere preferred by the Guardian engenders a sense of belonging. This is one reason why, on balance, Guardians feel more at home in organizations that have a history. It gives a sense of permanence and the prospect of a future – a legacy to develop and maintain.

In such organizations, as all else changes – products, services, markets, competitors, locations, systems, structure, and so on – the values of the organization provide the continuity the Guardian looks for. "These values are usually traceable to individuals much further back in the history of the company, and, if they are of the right intrinsic worth, they have been preserved, built upon, and transmitted through generations of people. The great belief in the primacy of people over technology in ICI derives from its founders and is directly traceable to them."[18]

But there have to be rewards apart from feeling good. The Guardian wants to develop a legacy for his or her family as well as enjoy the environment of work. In line with this, Harvey-Jones, a good Guardian leader, is "very much in favour of share option schemes. Apart from anything else, this gives the individual manager the best chance of building some capital. . . . Capital accumulation is a relatively easy matter for the self-employed but is almost impossible for the professional manager to achieve out of income."[19]

Chances for promotion

Many Guardians, like Harvey-Jones, prefer to remain for extended periods of time with the same organization, gaining career progression through promotion within the company. Ideally, the Guardian's job role should set him or her up for the next one or more steps in his or her career progression.

If this is not the case, in the words of Harvey-Jones, "You owe it to yourself and to your family to move on elsewhere if you are not satisfied that the objectives are worthwhile or if the prospects are insufficiently good."[20] For the Guardian, it is important to be able to look ahead, beyond the scope of the current job role, and to long-term aspirations for advancement and promotion. Good Guardian organizations recognize the importance of career progression, and focus on development that takes this longer-term perspective.

"My company," says Harvey-Jones, "has gone to the extent of retraining individuals and not just for the skills that we want, but for the skills we know will enable those who cannot stay with us to get good jobs elsewhere."[21]

Developing a Guardian strategy

Think ahead

Although it is the Warrior that represents the competitive drive for more and more success, the Guardian does not shrink from doing what it takes to establish and maintain a thriving organization. The Guardian leader knows that you have to stay ahead of the competition to survive. Harvey-Jones

expresses the Guardian attitude to the world of competition like this:
"Everyone prefers the safety of what they know to the uncertainty and possible excess of excitement in the unknown. And yet the greatest risk of all is not to change, for the world doesn't want the laggards, and the cut-throat competition from overseas has never even heard of the Marquess of Queensbury rules."[22]

But if the motivation may be different, the need to plan how to stay ahead is just as strong for the Guardian: "increasingly we are asked, and indeed ask ourselves, how much we need before we are satisfied. The answer is, of course, that the industrial manager will never be satisfied, and should not be, because the more money that is earned the more opportunities are open to one, the more chance of creating an uncatchable lead over the competition, of developing tomorrow's world and managing our own futures for ourselves, our shareholders and our people."[23]

The Guardian leader, more than any other, is expected to be able to light the path forward to the long term future. This is the legacy.

Give people clear direction

The vision for the future cascades down the organization, enabling everyone to be aware of his or her contribution to the realization of that future. From the perspective of the Guardian, "People work best when they know what is expected of them."[24]

This does not imply a dictatorial approach. The dialogue that takes place between the leadership and others is the means by which people accept responsibility for their contribution. It is important to give people ownership of areas of responsibility, "and this ownership must be transferred methodically and skilfully from the leader to his team."[25]

Surround yourself with people who take responsibility

"The job of top management is to allocate the responsibility for their contribution to the achievement of the whole to each part of the outfit."[26] And then to step back, be supportive, but have faith in the sense of responsibility of those who will make it happen. It is an essential part of the Guardian ethos that people are treated with mature respect, and a significant part of this respect is symbolized by the leader's faith that those under him or her will respond positively and competently.

"The key to tactical success is really in the ownership of the tactics, and the absolute determination and commitment of those carrying them out."[27]

Take responsibility

If part of the Guardian leadership lies in allocating responsibility, another is role-modelling responsibility. People will take their cues from the leadership, and, unless you are seen to take responsibility yourself, why should they?

The Guardian leader feels, like Harvey-Jones, that when they attain seniority, that "the future of my people and my business rested entirely on my shoulders, as indeed to a large extent it did."[28] But this feeling has to be backed up by the attitude that "the buck stops here," along with the actions that go with this attitude.

This means that, when things go wrong, "the leader can help most by 'throwing himself across the wire.' " "It is far better that you take upon yourself both the responsibility for the failure and the need for re-routing. Curiously, provided this responsibility is shouldered generously and with conviction, the invariable result is a strengthening of the leader's position rather than the reverse."[29] In the Guardian environment, having the ability to take responsibility, even for failures, is a sign of strength of character, not one of weakness.

If ultimate responsibility is to be shown by the Guardian leader, he or she has to accept that even the failings of an employee are to some degree a failure of leadership. "I have tried never to fire anyone without attempting to make them feel that the fault was more mine than theirs, that in some way the problem lay in my lack of ability to utilize their skills, rather than being any deficiency in them."[30] If they are not up to the job, you should never have put them there in the first place.

Be conscientious

In leadership, there are no right answers. When people look to a leader to define the "right" strategy, the "right" structure, and so on, he or she cannot give them answers that are in any way scientifically provable. Leaders make choices, and these choices have to be based as much on what they believe in than any magic foresight into the future.

The guiding light has to be your values, and for the Guardian, these values are conscientious values. "We in industry have the opportunity to have interesting and broadening careers: to help people to grow, and at the same time to enhance their capabilities and expectations; to help produce many of the devices and conditions which will enable tomorrow's world to be better than yesterday's, and to enjoy the task of their creation."[31]

Pragmatic though most Guardian leaders are, they do not allow expediency, short-term profit, unnecessary risk, or dissenting voices to get in the way of their values.

Create a sense of community

One of which is the value of community: "The best people involve themselves in their communities."[32] Guardians like a sense of belonging, and this extends to the workplace as well as the outside world. Treating people as innately valuable, and not just for the wealth they help to create, is a key part of the creation of this sense of belonging, and of community. People are not just a resource, they are more than a resource, a value often overlooked by leaders.

"Machinery would be inspected, listened to, oiled and maintained. Time is spent on each and every mechanical part. How is it that so many people begrudge giving the same degree of attention to the individuals who make up the company as they would give to a chunk of inanimate capital goods?"[33]

It is people who get things done. Success in making things happen, "is achieved by teamwork and the commitment, skill and mutual respect of the team. Creating that is the leader's job."[34] And the leader does that through his or her own ability to make each and every member of the corporate community feel valued and known personally. This means everyone, from the top of the organization to the bottom.

"I wonder how often chairmen visit their telephone exchanges, or actually thank those on the switchboard for the way in which they respond for the company."[35] Harvey-Jones's success is due, in no small part, to this preparedness to recognize the vital contributions of everyone, no matter how "invisible" they may appear in other organizations.

Care for people

Clearly, it is vital, if the Guardian leader is going to create this inclusive sense of belonging and community, that he or she does care for people and show it. Little things can mean a lot: "I make a habit of sending a certain number of cases of wine each year to individuals at any level of the company who have done something which I have come across which seems to be particularly meritorious. I send it to the individual's home and I include a personal note from me thanking him for his achievement."[36]

Time and again, a leader has to introduce change into his or her organization, because not to change is to invite disaster. What some leaders forget is that most of their people have not had the luxury of thinking about, planning, and deciding on change. The Guardian leader takes time to look at change from the perspective of those upon whom change is being imposed, rather than that of the leaders who have instigated it. Rather than see the worries of people as negative "resistance to change," the Guardian leader recognizes that people need help through change.

"Although intellectually we may accept the forces that are at play and we may recognize that we cannot 'go on' in the way we have been doing, in the end for most of us it boils down to the more personal questions such as 'What is going to happen to me?' and 'Can I manage to cope?' It is sadly true that not everybody *can* cope, although we are often guilty of assuming that people are less adaptable than they prove to be, and indeed they think they can be. I have been fascinated over the years to see the unbelievable changes that people can manage in their personal and professional lives, providing only that they are given help and the time to adjust."[37]

Some changes mean that people have to leave the organization, but helping people means caring for them, even if they are on the way out. When change is necessary, "Not everybody can be retrained, not everybody is still young enough to adjust and not everybody actually wants to. Many people will seize the opportunity to follow some other way of life but even they do not wish to be shown the door with a shotgun. They have the right to be treated with dignity, to be respected, understood and helped."[38]

For the Guardian leader, focus on caring for people is not an auxiliary part of the job: it is the essence of leadership. People who are cared for, given responsibility, and treated with respect are the means of achieving success. Caring for people is not a "nice to have"; it is the only way to survive. As Harvey-Jones says, "It is only the caring companies that will survive, and caring cannot be a 'con'; it has to be a genuine attitude of mind and an absolutely fundamental belief in every single person."[39]

Teach people

People do not come to their jobs fully competent. Everyone can improve, gain new skills, and become more competent. The Guardian leader recognizes his or her own experience as a vital raw material in the development of these skills and competences in his or her people. "This is the reward of industrial leadership: to see people, who do not think they have the capability of being a winning team, gaining confidence and effectiveness and morale, and the respect not only of their peers but also of their competitors and the world outside."[40]

These rewards come from a teaching relationship, in which the leader recognizes the individual development paths of each of his or her people.

Putting people first and skills second means agreeing that, "It is the responsibility of the leadership and the management to give opportunities and put demands on people which enable them to grow as human beings in their work environment."[41]

Protect people from politics

The Guardian leader strives for harmony within his or her organization, but also recognizes that, in the real world, the kinds of conflict discussed in chapter 5 will never disappear completely. Leaders develop political "savvy"[42].

Included in such maturity is the recognition that "the best, if sought in absolute terms, is the enemy of the good."[43] But not everyone in an organization will have the complex skills and knowledge to deal with the kinds of conflict that can turn into the appearance of self-serving "office politics." People with less experience of the world, and with fewer skills will recognize that: "Business and industry is not about internal politicking and sharp practice. It is about decent men and women trying to earn a reasonable return by following the honourable calling which, during the industrial revolution, propelled our country from a tiny offshore island to a world power."[44]

Until people learn this, it is vital that the Guardian leader protects them from being dragged into battles that can turn into wars that, in turn, undermine the mutual respect that the Guardian organization needs for success.

Develop an air of "natural authority"

On becoming chairman of ICI, tradition dictated that Harvey-Jones should take possession of a brand new Rolls Royce. He felt, at first, that this was an expense that was unnecessary, overly ostentatious, and that would send out completely the wrong message in a period of austerity in the company. Reluctantly, and after a great deal of soul-searching, he went along with the tradition. "Some time later I was talking to some of my shop stewards, and mentioned that this was a problem that had worried me. To my surprise they said they were glad that I had decided to buy it, as they did not want to have the feeling that they belonged to a company that was in such a poor way that it couldn't afford a Rolls Royce for its chairman!"[45]

Within the Guardian organization, seniority gains respect, so long as the leader does not lose that respect through his or her crassness. For many people, a Guardian leader is the psychological equivalent of the father-figure, creating a sense in those s/he leads of a kind of awe – the leader, like a parent in one's childhood, has the potential to be omnipotent. This is one of the components of "charisma," or "natural authority."

In reality, of course, no leader is omnipotent, or perfect. Yet good Guardian leaders build on the potential their position gives them. For example, he or she capitalizes on the fact that other people may have ideas or suggestions that will enhance success. "It should be possible for anybody in the organization at any level to make such a suggestion. Even if the suggestion that is made is not feasible, it should be listened to with courtesy and responded to with the respect that such an offer demands. It is not easy in a country as hierarchically inclined as ours to continually question authority in a constructive way. It requires a lot of faith to believe that such questioning will actually be recognized, liked and rewarded."[46]

Recognizing and rewarding others for their contributions could weaken a leader's image of perfection; but, as Harvey-Jones shows, the Guardian leader takes and retains responsibility for ensuring the acceptance with grace of suggestions that will work, while dealing courteously with those that will not. He or she is still in charge.

He or she is also likely to have developed a significant "feel" for things, based on experience. "There is no manual or book on how to do it – it is more a question of having seen large numbers of operations, and having a 'sixth sense.' "[47] The ease with which you manifest such "sixth sense" helps you to maintain the confidence of your people. The more you can do what seems almost "magical," the more you will maintain the respect for your "natural authority" that is a key element in Guardian leadership.

But it is not all about such skills and competence; it is not all about the Guardian's "strategy" for leadership. The theme of this book is character first, strategy second. "Eventually you rely on your ideals, and the picture in your mind of the sort of person you would like to be and would like to remain."[48] And then the Guardian leads by being that person, by being true to who he or she is, not by adopting a number of clever management techniques.

CHAPTER 15

Organizational culture and leadership

Organizational culture is not a tangible object you can accurately measure. It is something you experience. It is also something you can influence. In some respects, the degree to which you influence culture as opposed to simply experiencing it is a measure of your leadership effectiveness. The more you influence culture, the more you are leading.

There is a direct link between culture and character. This is obvious in cases such as Microsoft and Virgin, where the organizational cultures grew out of the characters of Bill Gates and Richard Branson respectively. It can, however, be overlooked.

An organizational culture is, in one respect, the aggregation of the values of the people within it. People tend to gravitate to organizations where personal values align with organizational values, although clearly, there is a great deal of room for diversity. The fact that people often realize only late in the day that they just don't fit into their current organization shows how easy it is to miss this link.

It also explains a great deal about why so many 'culture change' programmes just don't work. If an organization has evolved that has attracted, for the most part, Warrior/Adventurers, it is unlikely that these people will work diligently to help create a Guardian/Sage culture, no matter how much they are exhorted to do so.

For most people, the scales are weighted heavily toward the culture. Few individuals create or change cultures. Most people try, as far as is possible or comfortable, to adapt to the peer pressure that makes most people want to fit in. Unless you are another Bill Gates or Richard Branson, your experience is likely to be one of some degree of compromise.

But this book is about leadership, not about how to fit in.

Competence and style

People receive feedback on their performance. Some organizations offer a great deal of feedback, others less. Some believe that the best feedback comes from a wide range of people (often referred to as 360° feedback), others that only the boss needs to assess performance.

When you receive feedback that is critical, you can respond in a number of ways, from total acceptance ("after all, it's how I impact on others that counts, not what I think of myself") to total rejection. ("I don't respect that person's views; they don't know me.") It's all about perception, and, although 'perception is reality', opinions, as we discussed in chapter 2, are not factually right. They may say more about the person providing the feedback than about you.

So what should you do with negative feedback?

The first thing to remember is that, because how people interpret behavior as subjective, and that Warriors will interpret behavior differently from Sages, one key influence on feedback will come from the evaluator's and the recipient's potentially different starting points. If you are accused of being "too aggressive" is this because you "really" are too aggressive, or because the person telling you this interprets your assertiveness, which is good from your point of view, as excessive aggression, clearly a bad thing for him or her?

So before we explore your options regarding feedback, let's review some of the negative feedback you may be liable to receive from people whose Home Base is diametrically opposed to yours. As in chapter 5, these will not always be people's perceptions. But, in my experience, they do pop up quite often in people's appraisals.

Given that I have said that leadership is about character first, style second, in each case, I have first given examples of feedback relating to an individual's character, and then feedback more directly focused on his or her leadership style.

The Adventurer's character through the eyes of the Guardian

- Too selfish; doesn't think of others
- Not a team-player
- Bucks the system; lacks respect for how we do things around here
- Thinks success is what he or she can get away with
- Does his or her own thing; not a corporate citizen
- Disruptive; always reinventing the wheel
- Thinks of self more than others
- Never takes things sufficiently seriously; everything is a big joke to him or her
- Poor forward planning
- Works by expediency, not by strategy

The Adventurer's leadership style through the eyes of the Guardian

- Keeps moving the goalposts
- Fails to respect the wisdom of others
- Doesn't toe the line; a loose cannon
- Lacks authority
- Over-familiar with subordinates
- Can't decide without checking with his or her own staff
- Abdicates responsibility
- Allows people to get away with murder
- Offers no guidance; doesn't care for his or her people

The Sage's character through the eyes of the Warrior

- Not focused on the bottom line
- More interested in products and services than sales or profits
- Not pragmatic
- A perennial course-attender
- A navel-gazer
- Lacks follow-through
- Over-intellectualizes everything
- Lacks ambition
- Lacks motivation
- Content with second best; doesn't pursue excellence

The Sage's leadership style through the eyes of the Warrior

- "Analysis-paralysis"
- Rewards mediocre performance
- Lacking in confidence and strength of character
- Doesn't drive people
- Has lax standards and poor measurement of performance
- Impractical and theoretical
- Fails to judge people's competence
- Lacks guts
- Inconsistent
- Wants to be everyone's friend

The Guardian's character in the eyes of the Adventurer

- Only interested in climbing the 'greasy pole' of the hierarchy
- Takes life too seriously
- Always wants to be involved in everything
- A control freak
- Stickler for bureaucracy and the rules and procedures
- Self-righteous
- Patronizing
- Over-anxious to be seen to be toeing the line
- Tries to tie one down
- Always sucking up to the bosses

The Guardian's leadership style in the eyes of the Adventurer

- Inflexible and lacking in imagination
- Domineering and authoritarian
- Favours those who creep round those in authority
- Makes and admits to too many mistakes
- Pokes his or her nose into too many activities
- Never lets people alone to get on with the job
- Can become intrusive, even with personal life
- Always thinks he or she knows best
- Acts as a gatekeeper
- Has a high opinion of his or her own worth

The Warrior's character in the eyes of the Sage

- Over ambitious
- Always seeking glory for himself or herself
- Pushes himself or herself forward, in front of others
- Tunnel-vision; the deal overshadows everything, including people's feelings
- Never admits he or she is wrong
- Too aggressive
- Does not realize that there's more to life than work
- Driven to succeed at all costs
- Excessively competitive
- Wants to be noticed, especially by people in charge of the bonus

The Warrior's leadership style in the eyes of the Sage

- Micro manages; pokes his or her nose into every deal
- Always looking for a fight
- Doesn't care who he or she hurts
- Doesn't listen
- Thick-skinned
- Puts people under enormous pressure
- Pits people against one another for fun
- Makes people feel small and incompetent
- A bully
- Has favorites

Over the many years I have been working with leaders, I have seen all of these 80 kinds of feedback, and more, and have had to help the recipients work out how best to deal with it. In each of these cases, there remains an open question. Is the feedback an accurate assessment of the recipient's competence as a leader, or is it a criticism of his or her style?

It may help to look at another case study.

Pat's story

In his early forties, Pat joined an organization that seemed to be just right for him. As an Adventurer/Sage, Pat had tried many different jobs, in many different organizational cultures, and had never yet felt satisfied. Now he could be free to develop new services and ideas, and quickly became a highly valued member of a small team of consultants.

For the next few years, Pat gained the trust and respect of his colleagues. Creative and insightful, he introduced new ways of thinking that people quickly adopted, and his coaching style was frequently cited as a powerful development tool for the younger team members. Pat soon became a vital resource, as team members dropped into his office to talk about their assignments. He soon gained a reputation for being able to turn round failing projects, and became involved in much of the business of the team.

During this time, Pat asked for feedback from the team, using a robust and respectable instrument he had often thought to be very helpful in assessing leadership capability. The feedback was glowing. It seemed he could do no wrong.

For a while, the Unit was managed by an interim manager, and, although Pat was happy with this situation, others felt unsettled by the lack of continuity and stability in the formal leadership of the Unit. Pressure mounted for Pat to take charge.

Pat was flattered. Before he acted, however, he talked to people both within the team and outside. He had a dotted line to one of the most senior people in the organization, Colin, from whom he went to ask for support and advice. He got both.

He got support from Colin, but only grudgingly, because Colin knew Pat better than Pat did himself. Colin told Pat that it was a very bad move. Pat didn't listen to Colin; the pressure from his closer colleagues outweighed Colin's scepticism.

On the day that the CEO offered him the job of running the Unit, Pat went back to the office, called everyone round, and told them his news. A cheer went up from everyone. Things were going to be great for them all.

Pat wanted the Unit to add considerably more value to the organization than previously, and, to help in this, he started to recruit more consultants. Reluctantly, he had to get rid of one of the existing consultants who seemed very stressed out by the work she was trying to do. It was possible that others of the original team were also unlikely to be able to adapt to the new ways of working, and Pat was wondering whether he could help turn them round or would have to let them go as well.

He didn't have to wonder too long. Less than a year after formally taking over, Pat was summoned to the CEO's office and taken off the job.

Pat had made two common mistakes. The first was to assume that everyone around him would continue to value his Adventurer/Sage style of leadership as a boss rather than a colleague. The second was to assume that he would enjoy the responsibilities of being the boss.

Until his promotion, Pat had led from behind. He waited for people to approach him, and shared their problems. He coached people, but never took their problems from them. Work was play, and he made light of the difficulties people were facing, enabling them to appreciate the ease with which apparently intractable problems could be turned round. Pat was a leader through the influence of his skills and capabilities.

Once he was the boss, Pat had formal authority. And because not everyone in the team (and outside the team) was an Adventurer/Sage, Pat was now expected to lead from the front, and to take responsibility for people's problems and difficulties. But he carried on as before. It had worked then, why should it not work now?

Within Pat's organization, the culture was not Adventurer/Sage. While he was just another team member, he could "hide" behind the interim manager and lead people through his character and skills. As the boss, he became exposed. Now a member of the senior management team of the organization, Pat's style became a matter of concern to his new peers. They were Guardian/Warriors.

The CEO first began to suspect Pat's lack of fit when the Chief Accountant reported back on her first budget meeting with Pat after his promotion. Pat treated the meeting with what she saw as flippancy. He asked for a massive increase in the budget for travel and subsistence (to allow the consultants to get out and about more, building the business), and when the Chief Accountant asked how he was going to pay for such an increase, Pat replied that he'd cover it many times over through increased business. ("We'll trade out of trouble.")

As it happens, business did pick up very fast, and one feature of Pat's tenure was the best revenue and profit figures the Unit had ever recorded. But he had established a reputation for being uncommitted to the bottom line.

Pat was rapidly introducing very significant changes to the role and contribution of the Unit to the business of the organization as a whole. He believed passionately in what he was doing, and expected everyone else to see the value of his new approach. They didn't, and he soon began to be regarded by the other seniors in the business with deep suspicion. He was clearly not a corporate citizen. His reforms were, implicitly, a criticism of the status quo that they had established.

Furthermore, Pat did not take things seriously. His attitude to the budget was just one example. He was clearly far too familiar with his subordinates, undermining his authority as their boss. He was fast becoming a loose cannon. Despite dire warnings, he did not respect the wisdom of his elders, and, as far as the senior management team was concerned, he was not a team player.

Seen through the eyes of the other seniors in the business, Pat lacked the strength of character it takes to do the job properly. They attacked him and his team. He did not fight back. His own team (or many members of it) began to believe that Pat lacked the guts for a fight. The Unit's reputation was under threat, and Pat was not doing anything about it. Now he had been promoted, team members began to believe, like the seniors in the business, that Pat thought only about himself, and not of others. He abdicated responsibility for the Unit's declining status.

More than that, he abdicated responsibility for people's problems. Now he was the boss, it was, they felt, his job to take on their problems. That's what he was paid for. But when they asked for clarification about their roles, responsibilities, lines of demarcation, and how to deal with problem colleagues, Pat didn't seem to care. His staff turned against him. They started to complain to the CEO. Morale was very low.

The CEO was puzzled by Pat's apparent lack of motivation to deal with what were, surely, the issues he was supposed to be managing. As the new boy on the senior team, Pat would have been expected to show drive and ambition. But he just carried on as if nothing was happening. Pat had to be removed.

Like so many other Adventurer/Sages, Pat was naïve. Which is why, when he received the negative feedback, it came as a shock to him. This chapter explores the "cultural" aspects of Pat's naiveté. We will look at his other mistake (the wrong career choice) in chapter 16.

Was Pat's problem one of competence or style? Clearly, Pat did demonstrate one kind of incompetence: cultural incompetence. But for the (admittedly few) Adventurer/Sages in his team, Pat was still "the best boss I've ever had." From their point of view, Pat had been very shabbily treated. And had Pat changed his behavior to suit the bosses and the "pathetic whiners" (as his supporters called the detractors) in the team, he would, in their eyes, have sold out.

So what has all this got to do with "culture"? And how will knowing more about an organization's culture help answer the question what to do with critical feedback? Let's deal with the first question first.

The (implicit) organizational model of leadership

The culture of an organization gives permission to offer some kinds of negative feedback more than others. It is unlikely that many "Microkids" have been accused of being "too competitive". In some cases, it goes further than the relatively amorphous (but still powerful) influence of "culture" and into the formalized "model" of leadership an organization adopts.

Sometimes referred to as "competency models" or more explicitly "leadership models," many organizations have tried to formalize how they see leadership in order to help assess existing and potential leaders. None that I have come across assess differently for the four kinds of leadership in this book. Nor do they explicitly say that their model is "Warrior" or "Guardian," "Sage" or "Adventurer." But look closely at any such model and, once you get past the (in some cases) "motherhood and apple pie" competences (honesty, trust, collaboration, and so on), you begin to see elements that are clearly associated with some or all of these kinds of leadership.

Some are consistently Warrior, Guardian, Sage, or Adventurer. Some are a mixture. And it is clear that, in those cases where the model is firmly based on the Guardian, for example, Guardians will thrive, while Adventurers will either have to make some major shifts in behavior, or be on the receiving end of a constant stream of negative feedback.

In Part 1 of this book, we saw the potentially disastrous consequences of people moving too far from their Home Base. Is it fair that competency models or leadership models should discriminate in this way against people whose characters do not fit the cultural model?

Diversity or shared values?

This is both a practical and a moral question. Let's deal with the practical first by looking at a couple of examples of leadership teams.

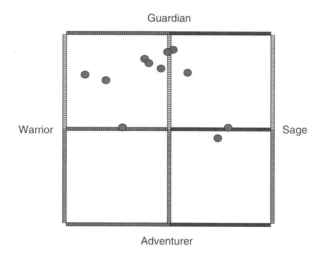

In this case, there is a fairly wide distribution of Home Bases. Although there are few Adventurers, three of the members of the team have well-pronounced Adventurer tendencies. But the stretch between Warrior and Sage is wide.

I have also worked with this team on their MBTI™ profiles, which are equally diverse. The diversity in their cognitive styles, as represented by their MBTI™ profiles, provides the team with a great deal of potential strength. There are outgoing people and reflectors; detail people and strategists; those who are task-oriented and others who consider the human context; and there are those who work in a disciplined and structured fashion, while others remain open to new possibilities and angles.

This diversity enables the team to cover all the bases, and, as long as they have the maturity and humility to blend together their respective strengths, they can get the job done highly effectively. The problem is that they find it hard to agree what the job should be in the first place.

The organization is rife with tension. Those who are primarily Warriors are all for going out and getting the business, beating off the competition, and building the business on the basis of excellence (they believe they are the best in the market). The people who are primarily Guardians are trying to build a community, to develop a legacy, and to avoid risk. The Sages are fascinated by the possibilities for new products, but find the ambition of the Warriors rather crass. They cannot get excited by the prospect of bigger and bigger targets, and often feel that a period of consolidation is what many of the stressed out employees need more than yet another major deal.

Most of the team members, when first I met them one by one told me that the biggest problem with the organization was its sense of identity. "What is our mission?" they asked (mostly rhetorically). The lack of clarity about their sense of purpose was of little **practical** importance, as everyone was busy with their day to day activities. But, as one or two of our earlier cases show, people have a need to find in their work the means of fulfilling themselves, according to the values their Home Bases identify. Working in ways that are not in line with one's Home Base can cause stress.

Most of the people in the organization, the senior team, thought that it was not their fault that there was not clarity about their mission, but that of the major shareholder, who, they said, kept sending them mixed messages. But I believe this, at least in part, to be another example of teams taking all the credit for their successes, but blaming external circumstances and agents for their failings. The constraints placed on their activities by the major shareholder did not, of themselves, prevent this team from hammering out their differences and arriving at a mission of their own. But this they could not and would not do.

If the members of this team can resolve, even gain strength from, their cognitive differences, why can't they do the same with their differences in their Home Bases? Primarily, for the reasons we discussed in chapter 5. It is **relatively** easy to respect the contributions of people with different ways of working; it is relatively difficult to respect people whose values are in conflict with one's own.

This is a rather large leadership team, which sometimes causes problems. One reason why a larger team can be problematic is that, statistically, it stands a greater chance of containing a wider variety of Home Bases.

By contrast, here is a different leadership team:

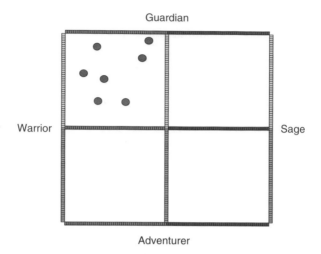

Members of this team have their fights; indeed, they enjoy them. They play hard, but they play fair. The one thing they don't fight about is a sense of purpose. Decisions are taken that all agree are in the best interest of achieving what they all want to achieve, and there is little, if any, agonizing about the ends. It's the means to get there that they disagree on, and this kind of disagreement they find energizing.

In a nutshell, this team has shared values, and from a purely practical point of view, they are significantly the better for having them. It may be, however, a very hard place for a Sage/Adventurer to get into.

Is it right (from a moral point of view) to operate such an implicitly closed shop? Since discrimination on the grounds of gender, ethnicity, or sexual orientation is now not only considered wrong, but also in many countries illegal, should there be any barriers to joining such a team?

In one sense, there are no such barriers. Membership of this tight, strong team is open to anyone who shows the competence and strength of character to earn his or her place at the table. But in another sense, entry is barred to those who are perceived to be lacking in ambition, drive, motivation, focus on success, and so the list goes on.

The point is that, since the differences between Warriors and Sages, Guardians and Adventurers are either never considered, or are about values such as membership of the community or personal freedom, it is much harder to avoid discrimination against people who are just not "our kind of people."

Getting into a team, or even getting a job in the first place often involves an interview, and it is the interview that this kind of implicit discrimination not only takes place, but is its primary purpose: to weed out people who, on paper may look good, but who do not present themselves in the right light. Take out factors concerning gender, ethnicity and sexual orientation, along with those job-related competences that cannot be adequately assessed within an interview, and what are you left with? Matt Ridley says, "Every job interview is about genetic discrimination. The . . . point of the interview is to take into consideration personality, and . . . personality is even more strongly heritable in this society than intelligence."[1]

To the extent that values, as opposed to potentially shifting attitudes, are a key part of our genetically inherited make-up (as we saw in chapter 3), interviews are about genes. They can be more or less effective or efficient ways of trying to determine the relative strength or influence of a candidate's "Guardian genes" versus his or her "Adventurer gene," and the same for the candidate's genetic response to the Warrior and Sage.

Some people may think that this only works if, during an interview, explicit questions are asked about a candidate's values, and this may not be appropriate. But this overlooks "gut reaction" of the kind I referred to briefly in chapter 2. It has been popularly known for some time that people tend to make up their minds about someone else, such as a candidate for a job, within a few minutes. They spend the rest of the interview justifying to themselves that their gut reaction was correct.

As so often with folk psychology, neuroscience has now discovered the source of this kind of reaction. The research shows that we do, in fact, have emotional reactions to people and situations before we have the chance to weigh up and understand what is going on.[2] Those emotional, but unconscious, reactions do influence the inferences we draw about someone. The fact that we do have an attitude to someone before we know anything about him or her means that as we listen to them speak, and watch their body language, we are potentially fighting against a prejudice most of us don't even know we have.

Someone we unconsciously take against in the first microseconds of meeting them doesn't stand much chance of conveying a contradictory impression, as people who came across Margaret Thatcher found out.

According to Penny Junor, she had a "tendency to judge a person at first sight, largely on nothing more scientific than whether she likes the look of them or not. If she does, she is friendly and relaxed, and the chances are the feeling will be mutual. If she takes against someone, she makes no attempt at pretence, and there is no frost more chilling than the brand reserved for people Margaret dislikes."[3]

It is not certain that people react positively in this unconscious way to others who have the same kind of character (Adventurers immediately liking other Adventurers, for example), but some research does suggest that we are immediately attracted to "like-minded people".[4] Maybe this is what people mean by "chemistry"? It is not infallible, but my guess is that our brains do have the innate capacity to discriminate between those people who are more likely to get on with us from those who may threaten our "integrity" by attacking what we believe in.

Should this kind of discrimination take place? Should you, as a leader, surround yourself with people like you, or try to create a community in which Warriors and Sages, Guardians and Adventurers have equal place? When this is a moral question, it has to be up to you. When it is posed as a practical question, the answer is clear. You will be better appreciated as a leader by people whose Home Base is very close to yours.

Kinds of organizational culture

As I said in chapter 8, many other writers have written on the subject of organizational culture. They offer different kinds of "definition" of "organizational culture." It is clear that my implicit definition of organizational culture centres on the values people hold, or imply through what they say, what they do, and the stories they tell. Stories have meaning.

Organizations are likely to have a mix of values, but I believe that, like successful leaders, organizations do well to avoid the "cognitive dissonance" that goes with too many mixed messages. You know where you stand in Microsoft. And if you are a Warrior, you probably enjoy it.

Indeed, it is my belief that organizations that jump on bandwagons, adopting the latest fad without checking it against their core value-set do themselves, their employees, and their other stakeholders no favors. I have seen time and again the introduction of a new management technique into organizations that looks good on paper, but which is doomed to fail within the context of everything else in the culture.

As with an individual, organizations with "strong" cultures are likely to have a primary set of values, with a secondary set in support. A Sage culture may be Sage/Adventurer or Sage/Guardian, and these will feel very different from each other. A person who is a Sage/Adventurer may be attracted to a Sage/Guardian organization because of their shared Sage values. But he or she may find, over time, the clash between the individual's Adventurer and the organization's Guardian becoming a barrier to happiness and even progression (in the individual's terms, of course).

In chapter 16, we will look more closely at this kind of situation, as we explore development and career progression. In this chapter, I shall look at the typical features of four kinds of organization: those that are, respectively primarily Warrior, Sage, Guardian, or Adventurer. To avoid repetition, I shall not look at the secondary drivers.

In each case, I shall identify only the key elements that typify each of the cultures. Rather than attempt a thorough, in-depth examination. For the purposes of understanding how best to factor organizational culture into your strategy for leadership development, all you need to know is, broadly, the kinds of ways each culture manifests itself in principle.

Because few real organizations exhibit a "pure" version of any of these four archetypal cultures, I shall not be using any case studies to describe culture.

The Warrior culture

The organization's heroes are Warriors

The Sage tries to avoid the cult of personality or hero-worship. But by contrast, in Warrior organizations, Warrior role-models set the standard to which aspirant heroes aspire. The public respect paid to heroes is manifested in the "employee of the month" kind of award, for without people being aware of what counts as success within the organization, they will be unable to strive to achieve it.

Less formal celebrations of the Warrior heroes abound in the stories (sometimes referred to by the social scientists as the "myths") that people tell, especially to new comers. The meanings conveyed by these stories (the "moral of the tale") inform new people about the culture and what is expected of them if they are going to do well around here.[5]

Personal renown

In Warrior cultures, you make a name for yourself by being successful. Here, as Oscar Wilde is reputed to have said, "There is only one thing worse than being talked about, and that is not being talked about." False humility does not ring true in the Warrior culture; if you have done something well, it is appropriate that you are recognized for it.

Because in some circles it has become unfashionable to boast (and because some people say that it is not British to be immodest, a view I am not convinced about myself), some less confident Warrior cultures espouse the primacy of teamwork over individual endeavor, often using homilies such as "there is no 'I' in 'team'." But as Carling and Heller show, Warrior organizations are run along lines analogous to sport[6]. In football, for example, good teamwork can make or break a side. But the best players get the best wages and awards, while it is rare for an entire team to transfer. Individual sportsmen and women may rely for success on the team's support and co-operation, but it is the individual who remains supreme.

Competition

A competitive culture taps into the competitive spirit of the Warrior, and enables him or her to find constant opportunities to pit themselves against others, or against targets. Individuals compete against individuals and teams against teams. Far from being the divisive influence claimed by the Sage, within a Warrior culture, competition brings people together. If an individual is not top of the league this time around, they will certainly be doing their best to be top next time.

In a Warrior culture, competition is the glue that binds people together. Here, there is no divisiveness in the publication of regular individual and team target achievement figures. It is an effective way of motivating people to do even better next time.

Defending your territory

Within the Warrior culture, people can be trusted to fight against threats to their patch. Non-Warriors often throw up their hands in despair at the internecine squabbling that characterizes the typical Warrior organization. What they fail to appreciate is that teams, groups, and departments are keeping each other on their toes. Nothing will make the Warrior more vigilant than the threat of being successfully attacked by "those guys from department x."

In the Warrior culture, so long as each part of the organization is defending itself from attack, the whole will be strong. Margaret Thatcher's battles within her own cabinet were, in some respects, a distraction. But she puts a great deal of her overall success down to her victories over the "wets."

Winning

Ideally, for the Warrior culture, out-and-out victories are reserved for battles against the formal competition: other organizations competing for the same business. But, to return to the sporting analogy, few individuals or teams can hope to be successful, to win, if they do not keep their winning edge between matches.

A winning culture means focus on winning at all times, and not just on the field of battle. A Warrior culture rewards the winners and not the losers. The trophy has to be a scarce resource, or the key motivator is weakened. The Warrior culture is not a democracy; it is a meritocracy.

Physical challenge

Physical fitness is a sine qua non for winners. The Warrior organization has its own gym. It does team-building by competitive outdoors activities. Keep fit, keep up, or drop out. In the Warrior culture, one of the key roles of HR is to keep a close eye on sickness leave, watching for signs of potential stress; many Warriors will not want to admit, even to themselves, that they are finding it tough, and few exit interviews, if the Warrior organization has them, will reveal this information, for the same reason. Warriors hate to admit to weakness, and most will feel weak if they cannot keep up the pace.

Advancement and promotion

Ambition must be rewarded in the Warrior culture. Last week's "personal best" is old news, so the Warrior organization must be geared up to setting new targets and standards for its people to strive for. And then it must have the means to reward success through enhancing the status of each and every winner.

This implies growth, often rapid growth. One reason for the success of Microsoft was that its very growth gave increasing scope to reward its Warrior people. The Warrior organization cannot stand still, so if organic growth is not enough to provide scope for advancement and promotion to its winners, it must acquire new companies to keep pace with the demand for advancement created by the success of its Warrior employees.

Achievement and accomplishment

One of the mistakes made by some managers in potentially successful Warrior cultures is to overlook the contributions of those in all parts of the organization. Sales people are the heroes because they bring in the revenue. The back office is simply there to support.

But a Warrior culture demands Warriors throughout. It is muddle-headed to develop a Warrior culture in sales, but to allow support to drift into Sage, or even an undifferentiated mish-mash of cultures. In a truly Warrior culture, every individual and department is set stretch targets, and is rewarded for achievement and accomplishment.

Fortune and material wealth

The Warrior culture pays well, but ideally it pays out the lion's share to its heroes in bonuses. The race goes to the swift, and nothing irritates the Warrior more than to see mediocre performance rewarded equally to excellence. Good financial rewards enable the achievers to wear their trophies with pride. The best suits, the best watches, the best cars, and so on are the gold medals in the Warrior culture.

The Sage culture

Humility

The Sage organization serves a cause that is very different from profit. Within the Sage culture, ego is subservient to that cause. There are no heroes, and anyone who seeks personal aggrandisement goes against the grain of the Sage culture.

Just as Gandhi enjoyed cleaning out latrines,[7] and Cheshire found his calling through personally nursing the terminally ill Arthur Dykes,[8] so Ricardo Semler strove to make himself redundant to the organization he inherited as CEO. In the Sage culture, there can be no cult of personality.

Quality of life

If the Warrior culture is a meritocracy, the Sage is a democracy, and within it, the quality of life of its members is of prime importance. Some are set up with that purpose, such as the FI Group described in chapter 12. Others, like Semco, evolve toward it. And whereas within the Warrior culture people serve the organization's goals, making personal sacrifices for the sake of the success of the organization, the Sage culture serves its people more than its markets. People first, profits second.

This will manifest itself in things like flexible working, home working, amenities designed for people not processes, and health and well-being provision. Some of these kinds of provision may also be a feature of the Guardian culture, where the organization looks after its people well. But in a Sage culture, all of these will be planned for and managed by people themselves, in co-operation with each other.

Co-operation

The Sage culture values co-operation. People solve problems together, resolve disputes together, and seek consensus before they act. Furthermore, there is no room in the Sage culture for people to "pull rank." The boss has no greater "voting right" than the most junior employee.

The physical environment will facilitate people meeting informally, and talking to each other. Meetings will happen as and when they are needed, will not necessarily follow an agenda, and will take as long as necessary for people to arrive at a fully agreed way forward. In many cases, few, if any, actions will come out of such a meeting. It's not the decision that's important; it's the dialogue. If people learn more and understand more as a result of such a meeting, but do not decide on a course of action, that's a good meeting in a Sage culture.

To the Warrior, the Sage culture can appear chaotic, inefficient and inconclusive. It is, if viewed as a process that is designed as a means to an end. But in the Sage culture, the co-operative spirit is, to a large extent, the end. So long as it is clear that it is alien to the Sage culture to be in constant pursuit of growth within a competitive market place, then it makes sense to focus more attention on the means than the ends.

In the Sage culture, there are no "stretch goals" where such goals would threaten the quality of life of the people, and where going for those goals would pit one individual or group against another. In the Sage culture, it is better to work together in harmony for a goal that is one tenth as ambitious as a goal that would threaten that harmony.

Spiritual well-being

The physical and financial rewards that are denied through the "inefficiency" of the Sage culture are not a loss to be regretted, since they are not the goal. People in a Sage culture are rewarded by feeling good about what they do and how they do it. At Semco, it was culturally appropriate for an entire factory to shut down production for a day to redecorate the workplace. Here, a better working environment is more valuable than the day's loss of production and the loss of revenue that ensued.

Celebrating others

The Warrior may shake hands at the start and end of a match, but while the match is playing, he or she is out to get you. He or she may say "congratulations" to someone they lose out to, but they wanted to win. The Sage wants others to win. Or, more accurately, he or she wants others to be successful whatever the other's goal.

But even if the other does not "win," the celebration continues. This is because the Sage culture celebrates being not doing. In Warrior cultures, one's worth is measured by what one achieves; indeed, in some sense, in a Warrior culture a person is defined by his or her achievements. In a Sage culture, what a person has achieved has no bearing on his or her worth. People are celebrated for who they are, not what they have done.

The Sage culture is a coaching culture in which helping others is more important than helping oneself. It is a personal culture in which the coach knows everyone personally, which is why it is also a small culture. Not only is growth (for its own sake) not an aim to the Sage culture, it is a threat. If it becomes too big, people cannot know each other personally, and cannot, therefore coach and celebrate the uniqueness of each individual.

The Satellite Program at Semco is a means to ensure that this personal culture has the chance to thrive, even when commercial success fosters organic growth. But because it is a Sage culture, organic growth is a by-product not a goal.

Mental and spiritual development

The Sage organization exists for the benefit of its members, not of some other group such as shareholders. And within the Sage culture, "benefit" does not equate to financial or material rewards. It equates to the way in which, simply by being part of the organization, and working within it, people attain mental and spiritual growth.

Again, this mental and spiritual development, in the true Sage organization, is not a by-product of its activities, but part of its purpose. In the Sage culture, people do not train so that they can produce more; they develop so as to become better people. In the Sage culture, departments set up for this purpose truly are "learning and development" departments, not training departments. Much of the budget will be spent on learning activities that have no direct bearing on the learner's job at all.

Learning and understanding

Within the Sage culture, people become better by learning and understanding. If a de-brief after a project in a Warrior organization is designed to make sure that the project is more successful next time, a debrief in a Sage organization is a chance for people to learn about themselves and others, and by so doing, achieve wisdom.

Wisdom

The goal of the Sage organization is not to add to the physical or technological stock of the world. It is to make the world a better place spiritually. In the Sage culture, wiser people are better people, and not because this enables them to produce more, but because, in the great scheme of things, it matters very little to the Sage whether this year's model is an improvement on last year's. It is a good day in a Sage culture if a person comes away at the end of the day that little bit wiser. If this is achieved by producing something, that is a bonus. But the production is the means, not the end. The end is inner harmony.

Inner harmony

The freneticism and sense of urgency that characterizes and energizes the Warrior culture would be destructive to the Sage organization. Within the Sage culture, finding someone sitting at his or her desk, feet up and gazing into space with a contented look is not a threat to civilization as we know it. Nor is it time off the job that will need to be made up later with some "real work."

Sage organizations do things. They produce goods (Semco) and services (The Cheshire Homes). How can they do anything if people are sitting all day contemplating their navels? In a Sage culture things get done because what is being done is, for the people who work there, innately worthwhile, either in the end-product (caring for the disabled) or in what the workplace provides for the workers (Semco). Sage cultures do not need to drive people; they drive themselves.

The Guardian culture

Organization before the individual

If the Warrior culture is a meritocracy, and the Sage culture a democracy, the Guardian culture is built around hierarchy. Like the physical buildings that symbolize the organization, solid and sheltering, in which people have places to work and identify with, the organization chart lets people know who fits where, who reports to whom, and where each person fits in the scheme of things.

In the Guardian culture, the organization chart is drawn up first, and people allocated to roles second. People may come and go, but the organization is designed for permanence. Within the Guardian culture, therefore, people know that they are part of something bigger, and that each has his or her unique contribution to make. Ideally, each person should be clear about where they fit, since it is within the organizational "map" that the Guardian individual finds his or her corporate identity.

Developing a legacy

The Guardian culture is not a "fly by night" one. Guardian organizations are here for the long haul. Tradition plays a key part, and continuity through change is important. Professionalism is a key part of that legacy. Each generation benefits from the skills and competences of the previous one, and, although all organizations have to change to survive, change in the Guardian culture is likely to be evolutionary rather than revolutionary. You don't throw the baby out with the bathwater.

Being at the centre of things

Although, as fashions change, a Guardian organization may go through periods of decentralization, the tendency is for power and decision-making to gravitate to the centre. This is where the most senior people are, and, in the Guardian culture, seniority equates to authority. The closer you are to the centre, the more you have the chance to influence and be seen.

Career progression

Within the Guardian culture, career progression is a matter of onwards and upwards. It is not uncommon for such organizations to have formalized career paths, or for individuals to be helped to develop their own career plans within the organization. The feeling in the Guardian culture is that people operate better when they know what is expected of them, not only in terms of activity, but also in terms of the development of their careers and long-term contributions to the organization's goals.

Because of the direct link between power and seniority in the Guardian culture, it is here that most emphasis is placed on job titles that signify where one fits in the hierarchy. Seniority carries status, and a great deal of attention is paid to ensuring that people's job titles reflect how successful they have been in gaining promotion through the ranks.

Economic security

The Guardian culture is relatively low risk. There are too many stakeholders dependent on the successful survival of the organization to put their financial well-being at risk. Investments are made for the sake of providing financial and economic security for all, be they employees or shareholders.

It will be in the Guardian culture that you will find the greatest attention paid to schemes such as pension provision and stock holding for employees. It is the responsibility of the organization to make sure that everyone is catered for well beyond their working lives. Once you commit to the Guardian culture, it commits to you. Loyalty here is two-way.

Protecting and providing

This loyalty goes beyond mere financial rewards. It is the Guardian organization that will take the lead in all kinds of benefits for the employees, be they health insurance or the provision of a crèche. And if an employee gets into trouble, the organization will do everything in its power to look after him or her.

Membership of the community

The Guardian organization is not just a place of work; it is a community, sometimes almost like an extended family. It is a relatively safe environment in which to grow and take on increasing responsibility for others as one matures. In any community, according to the Guardian culture, people have rights and they have responsibilities. Those rights and responsibilities are expected to be clear and fair. People are expected to look after each other and to do their level best to get on with each other.

In the Guardian culture, efforts are made to bring the lost sheep back into the fold. Of course, people are individuals, and space is made to accommodate a great deal of diversity; it is the right of each person to express his or her individuality. But this right has to be balanced against the individual's responsibility to ensure that the expression of his or her individuality is not at the expense of the well-being of the community.

Respect

It is a crucial part of the Guardian culture that people are treated with respect. People who struggle are helped to improve, not vilified or rejected out of hand. Mistakes are opportunities to learn, while those who cannot hope to climb far up the hierarchy are helped to feel good about their contribution, even if it remains a small one.

At the same time, those who do rise through the organization are accorded the respect that they deserve for their competence and for the responsibility they take on as managers and leaders. Due deference is paid to senior people. They have done their time in the lower ranks, and have proved their worth by being promoted to positions of power. They can be challenged, but it is expected that such challenges be made respectfully, and in consideration of the experience they will have accumulated on their journey to the top.

Maturity and responsibility

There is a place, in the Guardian culture, for healthy competition, for innovation, for democratic discussion, and for challenging the status quo. None of these is suppressed, as this would go against the principle of respect for others. But each of these has to be tempered by a mature and responsible approach. One does not try to win "at all costs" to take unnecessary risks with new ideas or approaches; to assume that putting forward ideas and suggestions means these will automatically be adopted; or to stage a palace revolution.

The Guardian culture makes room for diversity and for new ways of doing things. But it also provides protection from members of any "lunatic fringe" that, exciting though their ideas may be, fail to see the bigger picture. Guardian organizations are designed for longevity.

The Adventurer culture

Individual freedom

Many Adventurer organizations are loose amalgamations of individuals who come together not for mutual support, but to pool talents, resources or costs. They draw up the minimum of rules of engagement to capitalize on such pooling, but shy away from developing any structures or processes that would threaten each individual's freedom to do his or her own thing.

Change and variety

Anything within the Adventurer organization that does start to impinge on the freedom of the individual will quickly be abandoned. Consensus is temporary, not binding, and what has been agreed one day may be thrown away the next. Such a cavalier attitude may involve risk, but the Adventurer culture is deliberately high risk. There is no "cruise-control" button in the Adventurer organization.

Fast moving

Adventurers have little patience for lengthy discussion, so their culture is one of quick decisions with a preparedness to deal with the consequences when they happen (if they do). Because of the looseness of the organization, individuals often find that, in their absence, things have been changed by the others. In the Adventurer culture, one lives with that.

You only live once

The long-term planning of the Guardian culture is absent from the Adventurer organization. People within this culture live for the moment, and agree that making plans is pointless, since everything changes anyway, so plans become obsolete before they are put into operation.

As things do change, the new circumstances are opportunities to rethink how the organization is operating right now. If one doesn't seize the opportunity today, it may be too late tomorrow.

Moving on

People stick with an Adventurer organization for as long as it suits their purpose. People come and people go.

Good one-to-one relationships

While they are together, Adventurers have few procedures, structures or strategies to hold them together, apart from those that are informal and mostly unwritten. To comply with legislation, they will have procedures that are legally required, a statutory obligation for any organization. But these will be printed, published, and will gather dust on the shelf.

People in the Adventurer culture rely on good personal relationships to sustain them. There are no "rules of the community," either formal or informal, and "loyalty" is seen as other people's way of trying to paper over the cracks of relationships that cannot be held together by personal choice. While they like each other or can be of mutual benefit to each other, members of an Adventurer culture will stick together.

Self-reliance

Adventurers respect the strength that is shown through self-reliance. The Adventurer culture rejects the implicit paternalism of the Guardian, and expects each and every individual to take care of himself or herself. The Adventurer leader is delighted to help others if they ask for it. But he or she will not "impose" his help on others. In the Adventurer culture, direction is (broadly) set, and people then get on with it, in their own way, and at their own pace.

Challenging convention

Another common element of the Adventurer culture is its members habit of challenging convention, including their own. "Why are we doing this?" is a question that is constantly asked, and, unless there is a very good reason for it, it stops. A great deal of the success of the Adventurer business is built upon the fact that other kinds of organization rarely take this kind of challenge to such extremes.

Adventurer organizations often pop up suddenly in niches that were invisible to others. Once these niches become visible, they often get invaded by organization with non-Adventurer cultures. If this means that the niche becomes mainstream, the Adventurer organization moves on to another invisible niche.

Fun, adventure and playfulness

One reason for this constant shift to new opportunities is that the Adventurer culture has to be fun, adventurous, and playful. If it stops being fun doing one thing, the Adventurer organization, such as it is, moves onto a new game. Life is too short to take things too seriously.

Culture and consistency

In my experience, there are few organizations that demonstrate any of the "pure" cultural patterns I have described here. Most are a mixture of features from several of the models. Even though selection processes can tend to favor one kind of character than another, and interviewers may (possibly unconsciously) select out people whose values are different from their own, the fact is that, in most organizations, people do have different Home Bases, and each influences cultural development in his or her own way.

The most common source of this mix of cultures is that most organizations are a mix of two: these can be Warrior/Guardian, Guardian/Sage, Sage/Adventurer, or Adventurer/Warrior. In some situations, these can be complementary. These complementarities will ensure that such features become a deeply embedded part of the combined culture, and will be unshakeable.

In a Guardian/Sage organization, respect for the individual is a feature of both contributors to the mixed culture, as is caring for others, and a developmental approach to individuals, whether the teaching style of the Guardian or the coaching of the Sage.

When Sage is mixed with Adventurer, there will be a greater sense of individual freedom to develop along lines he or she chooses, while the perceived "paternalism" of the Guardian will be less prevalent.

As we swing round to the Adventurer/Warrior culture, people will look for freedom from barriers to winning, including any rules that appear to get in the way. "When your eyes are on the prize, rules are for fools."

In Warrior/Guardian cultures people play hard, but they play fair. Winners will gain respect, and, as winners will also rise in the organization, respect will be expected by anyone who is in a senior position.

But in the Warrior/Guardian culture, there are inherent conflicts between values of these two cultural styles. The "play hard" of the Warrior may clash with the family-orientation of the Guardian. Here, the "work-life balance" issue often remains unresolved.

In A Guardian/Sage culture, there can be continuing tension between the hierarchical orientation of the Guardian culture and the democratic ideals of the Sage. Issues such as the provision of car parking spaces on the basis of seniority will be contentious.

In Sage/Adventurer cultures, there are opposing forces at work regarding self-reliance and independence. The more Sage elements will seem intrusive to the more Adventurer members, while the people who are more clearly Adventurers may come across as being too self-centred, and not fully embracing the cause.

In Adventurer/Warrior cultures, the people who are more clearly Adventurers may want to change a winning formula, being told by the more Warrior elements, "If it ain't broke, don't fix it!"

My experience of working in organizations that have this kind of mix of cultures is that people often seek the resolution of this kind of tension in the fashion of the day. Sometimes there is a "see-saw" effect, with policies that have been adopted one year being reversed the next.

The fact that Microsoft has been so successful in retaining such a strong predominantly Warrior culture is partly due to its recruitment strategy: "We found it was easier to create a culture with people who were fresh out of school rather than hiring people from other companies and other cultures," Charles Simonyi, one of Microsoft's most senior and most revered programers, once said. "You can rely on it, you can measure it, you can predict it, you can optimize it: you can make a machine out of it."[9]

Another of the most common reasons for the mix of cultures in organizations is the way in which different parts of the organization develop different sub-cultures. Sales, for example, may be more inclined to develop a Warrior culture, while IT can sometimes feel much more Sage.

Given the innate conflicts between the values associated with each culture, it is not surprising that, in some organizations, there is conflict between departments or units that have, predominantly different cultures. This is not news. What may be helpful in this analysis, however, is this strong link between character, values and culture.

The reason this may be helpful is that it may help prevent initiatives designed to resolve internal conflicts that, well-meaning though they may be, are unlikely to be effective. This is especially the case when such initiatives are not designed to deal with the deep roots of much of the conflict.

Suppose you are confronted by a situation in which one department is predominantly Warrior and the other predominantly Sage. If you try to resolve this conflict simply by getting the two sides together to come up with a way forward and you do not recognize in that process the fundamental difference in the sense of purpose each party brings to the debate, any solution is likely to last only for a short time.

Solutions to this kind of challenge have to be sensitive to and commensurate with both cultures to be effective.

Many organizations have adopted an approach to this problem that sets up roles named "IT Account Managers," "HR Business Partners," or whatever the current terminology. In my experience, few people in such roles are fully aware of the fact that their key challenge is to mediate between potentially conflicting cultures. Even fewer, unfortunately, have the skills or capabilities to fulfil this cultural mission, and are often in the firing line from both sides.

This kind of leadership challenge is similar to many others. Consultants and business schools frequently come up with "the answer" to many of the challenges that face leaders and organizations. In many cases, the tool, technique, method, philosophy, or approach they advocate has been proven to work, and case studies of organizations that have utilized the method are cited as "proof."

But not every business school fad will work in every culture. When Ricardo Selmer published the book describing his approach in Semco, it created a storm, and the model was touted about as the answer to most of the problems facing most organizations. Ironically, for example, there is a chapter on Semco in Carling and Heller's otherwise thoroughly Warrior-oriented book, *The Way to Win*. They admit, however, that, although the principles adopted by Semler "should work anywhere. But very few other companies have followed Semler's preaching or practice."[10] The authors do not offer an explanation why.

My suggestion is that few truly Sage cultures exist in the commercial world, and that, unless an organization is pretty firmly in Sage territory, Semler's methods just won't work.

The same can be said of the once popular concept of the "learning organization." Back in the mid-1990s everyone was talking about this idea. Books were published and journals were set up specifically to research on it. It would be the way forward for any organization wishing to succeed because learning organizations are "where people continually expand their capacity to create the results they truly desire, where new and expansive patters of thinking are nurtured, where collective aspiration is set free, and where people are continually learning how to learn together."[11]

This is all very good Sage thinking. But, according to some observers, "Microsoft has been credited with being a genuine example of the 'learning organisation'." How can a truly Warrior organization successfully adopt such a Sage approach? The answer is they haven't. Looking more closely, we find that "learning organization" "is not a phrase used by Bill Gates, perhaps because of its vagueness."[12] Bill Gates himself "is less interested in the amorphous concept of 'learning organization' than in the harder notion of a 'knowledge company' "[13]

For the Sage, learning is an end in itself, not a tool to be used in the acquisition of profit. For the Warrior, knowledge is power, or, at least, a means of gaining some kind of advantage. There is no doubt that Bill Gates is a phenomenal learner. But, "The expenditure of his own time in the day-to-day business of Microsoft is justified by Gates as an investment in 'intellectual capital,' which he defines as, 'the intrinsic value of the intellectual property of your company and the knowledge your people have.' "[14]

The phrase "intellectual property" is telling. In a Warrior culture, learning has to lead directly to the bottom line. And if it doesn't, then it has no corporate worth.

A third example: "empowerment," currently a "good" word in almost all organizations, though it does not mean the same throughout. In the Sage culture, everyone has an equal say; people are inherently empowered. In a Warrior culture, empowerment means, "challenge the boss, and if you're right, that's what we'll do." For the Adventurer, empowerment means people are free to make their own way, and to make their own mistakes. In the Guardian culture, empowerment means respectful consultation with people before the boss, who is ultimately accountable, makes the final decision.

An Adventurer in a Guardian culture will not, therefore, feel empowered, no matter how much consultation goes on.

Organizations deal with things differently. In some cases, cultural phenomena, such as meetings, are part of almost every organization's activities, and will have evolved over time into patterns that generally fit in with the prevailing culture. One of the ways in which the culture of an organization can be assessed is by looking at the mood of meetings and how they are managed.

Warrior meetings will be brief, business-like, and focused on outcomes. Warriors do not value long, drawn-out discussions, and expect decisions to be taken quickly and on the basis of the strongest case. They may appear to non-Warriors as excessively confrontational, as the pros and cons of differing views are put up and knocked down. But within the Warrior culture, it is important that no idea or proposal is allowed through without rigorous and challenging examination.

Meetings in a Sage culture are more oriented to the discussion itself than the outcome. It will not be a disaster in a Sage meeting if no decisions are taken, so long as the discussion has helped participants gain deeper understanding of each other and where they are coming from. Meetings may last much longer here than elsewhere, Sages believing that meetings are not just a way of agreeing actions, but are also places where bonds are strengthened, and beliefs reinforced.

The Guardian culture will approach meetings in a professional manner, expecting people to take responsibility to come fully prepared, and to accord due deference and respect, especially to more senior participants. Information flow is an important part of the process, with seniors finding out from juniors the situations the latter will know more about, and with juniors accepting from seniors clear actions that enable them to fulfil their roles in contributing to the bigger picture in a responsible manner.

The ad hoc nature of the Adventurer culture spills over into how these cultures approach meetings. They are more commonly called at short notice, deal with one issue – the issue of the moment – and are often over quickly. However, this is not always the case. Sometimes an idea will be floated that comes from left field, and then the meeting will go off at a tangent, and may go on for several hours, as the new idea is thrashed out and explored. Occasionally, in Adventurer organizations, people suggest more regular and formal meetings. These tend to experience dwindling attendance, and soon peter out.

Apart from meetings and other "common" features of all organizations, other cultural phenomena may be new ideas or methods, introduced by senior managers, or by HR professionals. These newer ideas may fit well into the culture, and become effective parts of the way the organization operates. Others may need to be adapted to fit. Yet more are good ideas on paper, but go against the grain of the prevailing culture, and soon disappear, usually accompanied by huge sighs of relief from those who knew they would not work in the first place.

Sometimes this happens when people in HR have a different culture from those in the core business. In one organization I know the business culture is predominantly Warrior, with a fair amount of Guardian. HR, however, is far more Sage. Implicitly, they see their role, at least in part, as "humanising" the organization. But the organization does not, particularly see the value of this endeavour. From their point of view, HR's role is to recruit good people, train them up for the job, manage the personnel processes, provide them with statistics, and keep them abreast of what competitor organizations are doing.

When this organization faced a sudden need for cost-cutting, not surprisingly many of the victims of the ensuing cull were the HR professionals who were judged by the business not to be contributing directly to the bottom line.

The list of tools, methods, techniques, approaches, concepts, and philosophies an organization can adopt is potentially endless. Ideas such as share option schemes, "work-life balance," appraisal systems, quality circles, and others are explored further in the Appendix. These will either fit, as they are defined by the "gurus," with the prevailing culture, or be adapted to fit the prevailing culture, or die a death.

Responding to critical feedback

Which brings us back to negative feedback. If you are criticized for being too authoritarian in a Sage or Adventurer culture, rein back. If you are told you are being indecisive in a Warrior culture, get your act together. If you are seen as disrespectful in a Guardian culture, show some respect. Given that few cultures are "pure," you may, in reality, have to learn how to present yourself positively to a wide range of different types and styles. The focus, however, is primarily towards ensuring that, at the very least, your primary leadership style is delivered effectively, and is appreciated and understood by people around you.

And if you can't adapt, you may be in the wrong place.

In the final chapter, we will look at your own development. If you are culturally right for the organization, but are not being as effective as you could be as a leader, then focus on that development. If you are culturally out of place, then, like Pat, you may need to think of moving on to a place where you will fit, or like the right management technique in the wrong culture, you may have to say goodbye to any aspirations you have to be a leader.

CHAPTER 16

Developing your own leadership

The ideas in Chapter 15 are not meant to suggest that it's ok to exhibit bad behavior. Just because one is an Adventurer, this does not excuse letting people down. And being a Warrior does not mean it's ok to be a bully.

However, before trying to change behavior, it is worth taking time out to make sure that you are not doing what so many people are urged to do, and that is to change character. Development is about being the best possible version of who you are, not about trying to be someone else.

So when you do receive critical feedback you can do several things about it. You can, of course, simply ignore it. I would not advocate this.

The other two key choices you have depend upon your degree of fit with the culture of your organization, or of that part of the organization you work in. If you have decided that you and the organization are a good match, then focus on enhancing your behavior. If you feel you don't fit, you need to plan to move on. Let's deal with this option first.

Your career strategy

In Part 1 of this book, I invited you to explore your life story or stories, and consider how you have approached leadership so far in your career. In Chapter 6, I suggested that the idea of the "traditional" journey from Adventurer, through Warrior and Guardian to Sage may not be accurate, although for some people, society's pressures may have encouraged them to go along with it.

Throughout life most people are encouraged to make adjustments to their character. Warriors are told to be less competitive, Guardians to lighten up a little, Sages to be more ambitious, and Adventurers to grow up. A few people, none of whom I have met, may have responded to this kind of feedback in such a way that they have, effectively, worked their way round the model, apparently changing character to fit with the stereotypical life journey.

In my experience, few people actually do go through life like this. But few, also, have followed other paths that are so clear-cut. We do take notice of what people we care about tell us to do, and the changes we make affect both our self-awareness and our self-image, and these may differ in a number of respects. Some shifts of behavior make us more self-aware, others make understanding our true selves more difficult.

Sometimes, however, we have to step back and take stock, looking not so much at the next step in our careers, but at what our life story tells us about who we are and what this means for how we manage our careers henceforth.

This is what Pat had to do.

Pat's story continued

Pat joined the organization only a year or so after the CEO, who, at the time, had not had the impact on the organization's culture he was going to have. There was much more of an Adventurer feel to the organization when Pat joined, and his first boss before the interim manager, as an Adventurer/Warrior shared many of Pat's values. Neither, at the time, was aware of the leadership model described in this book.

A few years after Pat's appointment, Henry, his Adventurer/Warrior boss was sacked. He had broken too many rules. In the eyes of the CEO, Henry's disregard for the rules was a glaring example of the kind of lack of professionalism he was determined to weed out. Pat was concerned about Henry's dismissal, but did not feel it posed any threat to him. Henry's Warrior driver made him different from Pat, who, unlike Henry, would not contemplate competing with the organization for private work.

While Pat got on with the job of transforming the Unit through influence, the CEO got on with the job of eliminating, by various means, those seniors who were not sufficiently Guardian/Warrior for his taste. The CEO knew that you can only change the culture of an organization by changing its people, especially those at the top. By the time Pat was appointed Director of the Unit, the Adventurer elements of culture had been largely replaced by Guardian. Pat had either not noticed, or had disregarded it.

As he sat in his new office, having been removed from the Directorship, and invited to invent a new, less visible role within the organization, Pat finally took a long, hard look at himself and the organization. With the help of friends and colleagues he came to the conclusion that he had to move on. But where?

At these critical crossroads in a person's career, I believe that the best thing to do is what Pat, finally, did. He reviewed his beliefs and values, his life story, the job role he would thrive in, and the culture of the organization he wanted to belong to. Pat's story has a happy ending.

What Pat had learnt was this. If, like me, you are under 5 feet 10 inches tall, no amount of dedicated fitness training or development of ball-skills will guarantee success in life as a professional basketball player. But, for me, my height is only part of the reason. The more important one is that I lack the motivation to be fulfilled in life through sporting prowess. "You can be anything in life you want to be," goes the current mantra. But to make this true you really do have to be sure you want it. And if your motivations are those of the Sage, the killer-instinct of the Warrior, not being a key driver, they will be insufficient to enable you to go "from good to great."

I can build my muscle and skills, but I can't grow tall enough to make it in professional basketball. I can develop my attitudes, but I can't become the Warrior I'd need to be to do the same job. Pat learnt that he had been trying to be someone he wasn't. Now, in his career, he can be who he really is.

Taking stock of your career strategy

If, like Pat, you are considering moving on, you need to make sure you are not jumping from the frying pan into the fire. You may want to consider the following

- Your Home Base
- Your ideal job role
- The organizational culture within which you will be most effective

In the Appendix, there is an exercise you may want to go through that will help you look ahead to your next move.

Developing your leadership talents

If, however, you believe that your leadership talents will be best developed within your current job role and organization, this section may help pinpoint a development strategy that is right for you. Because of the uniqueness of your character this can only be a strategic overview, and may not, in every case, be directly relevant to you and your development needs. There are many other factors you will need to take into account: not every Adventurer is like every other. Ideally, before considering any of the steps I have listed below, you may want to explore what you think are your strengths and weaknesses with someone qualified to help. And once you have identified your own development needs, you may also want to consult the vast literature that already exists on personal and leadership development to select the specific development techniques that will suit you.

But do remember as you do so, to make sure that whatever development method you choose will feel right for and be helpful to you. Delightfully quirky though it may sound, a week's course contemplating your navel will have little lasting effect if you are a Warrior. If you are an Adventurer, no amount of good intentions will deliver much of a long-term return on investment from a time management programme. If you are a Sage, you may get a temporary buzz out of going away with your colleagues for several days' paintballing, but it is unlikely to make you a better leader. And if you are a Guardian, learning to tell everyone to go away, leave you alone, and get on with things without bothering you will not improve your strengths as the kind of leader you are destined to be.

Your Home Base forms the foundations of your character. You cannot change that. But you can change attitudes and behavior, so long as these are not in conflict with your character. If you are a Guardian, and have received negative feedback you want to respond to, the aim is to be a better Guardian, not someone or something else.

Developing leadership competence means differentiating between different sources of feedback. For people who share a Home Base close to yours, it is most probable that it is not what you do that is a problem, but how you do it. Guardians will value the responsible attitudes you take if you are also a Guardian; Warriors will not be, in principle, averse to your competitive nature, if you are a Warrior.

But for people with different Home Bases, it is more what you do that is the problem. As we saw in the previous chapter, Sages may be inherently averse to competition, and will be more uncomfortable with the essence of your leadership than your style.

So if your development strategy is a response to negative feedback of the kind we saw in Chapter 15, your first step is to make sure that your response is likely to be interpreted as you mean it to be. Is it a matter of style or substance? Is it about the way you do things, or the things you do?

It's not what you do it's the way that you do it

In the first instance, your development focus will need to be on how, more competently, to do the things you do naturally.

Increasing Warrior competence

The Warrior will naturally **lead from the front**. But other Warriors will want to "win their spurs," and can only do this if you give them projects or deals that they can also lead from the front. You will need to hang onto some of the more important deals and projects; this is what people respect you for. But tap into the energy and enthusiasm of your Warrior followers, and let them learn on the job, and gain the kudos they seek by stepping back and giving them their head.

When you **fight for what you believe in**, remember that sometimes, discretion is the better part of valour. Make sure that fighting does not become your sole means of achieving what you want. Consider which enemies may be potential allies, and develop a more collaborative approach to conflict handling. If you are at risk of becoming "drunk" with power, remember how embarrassing the fighter is who wants to take on everyone in the bar. Learning to manage your emotions[1] may be beneficial if this is an area of development for you.

It is natural to the Warrior to **be assertive**, but there is a difference between assertiveness and aggression. Aggressive behavior is characterized by the use of language and/or body language that inappropriately imposes solutions on others. Assertive behavior may result in the same solution, but assertive individuals ensure that they calmly explain their understanding of the situation, encourage others to share their points of view, and then identify ways forward.

The Warrior's tendency to **be strong and decisive** can erode his or her ability to listen. As leader, you may retain the right to take the final decisions, but Warriors around you will want to demonstrate their strength of character, too. Listening skills are harder than some people imagine, and you may want to explore the concept of "active listening" to ensure that people know that you recognize and appreciate their input.

Warriors learn from an early age how to **be tough and resilient**. Overplayed, this can evolve into insensitivity to constructive feedback. Nobody is perfect, but an inability to hear what you need to hear about the impact you are having on others is a dangerous weakness.

It is not a bad idea to **stretch people**, but each individual has his or her own limits of elasticity. As people experience more and more pressure, they are assisted in their endeavors by increasing levels of adrenaline in their systems. But at some point, positive pressure becomes negative stress, and the consequent secretions of cortisol can be very damaging. Tanya Arroba and Kim James[2] provide a clear set of guidelines to managing the stress levels that come from excessive pressure at work. You need to monitor carefully each individual's tolerance for the pressures you put him or her under, and make sure that you don't overstretch him or her.

What gets measured gets done, so you **set standards and measure everything**. But make sure that you keep the vital information at the centre of your radar. If people start to believe that you are more interested in the numbers than on the way they have worked hard to achieve the numbers, the measures become an end in themselves, rather than a motivational tool.

Information on performance can be used constructively to motivate people. But it can also become destructive, especially if you focus on the negative end of any league table you construct.

The Warrior is best when he or she **maintains a challenging style**. You should, as leader, be able to outperform your people. But it is important not to be like the "competitive Dad" who uses his superiority to humiliate rather than to motivate.

When you **challenge your people**, do it in such a way that they feel challenged and not bullied. Watch the body language, and read between the lines. Are they enthused by your challenges or daunted? Are you challenging them as adults, or treating them like children?[3]

If you are a Warrior, you will **surround yourself with people who rise to the challenges**. You will celebrate successes and reward those who perform well. They will gain a very positive reputation, especially with you. The problem with reputation is that it can become too influential in how people interpret what goes on day by day. Warrior leaders can sometimes be so convinced of the ineffectiveness of underperformers that they become blind to their progress. They can also cast high achievers in such a good light that they dismiss as unimportant any lapses the "stars" happen to fall into. You need to be doubly vigilant that your encouragement of and support for your highest achievers does not slip into favouritism.

Increasing Sage competence

Sages are democratic, and enjoy the Sage leader's willingness to **engage in dialogue**. But they also have firm beliefs, and generally want to make a difference. The good Sage leader will recognize that dialogue can vary in quality from highly constructive and effective debate to pointless meandering. Although it's good to talk, talk that fails to meet people's needs is time wasted when they could have been learning, or doing what they believe it is good to do. Monitor what is going on in the group, and make sure that everyone is engaged and contributing. When dialogue is over, it's over.

When you **treat people as equals**, remember that equality of rights does not equate to equality of competence. As a leader you have more to offer than making people feel important in themselves. You may have to help people learn. Sometimes, as leader, you may also have to make things happen.

As you **listen and learn** consider that excessive humility undermines your contribution to a debate. Active listening is not simply a matter of accepting every point of view as equally valid. Be strong, and use your wisdom as a guide to others, even as you learn from them. At the same time,

make sure that, like Gandhi at times, you are not fooling yourself into thinking you are listening and learning when, in fact, you are more dictatorial and
more self-indulgent than you think you are.[4]

The more you **create a developmental climate**, the more you may need
to make sure that it does not become self-indulgent. Unless you are running
a monastery, your organization needs to interact with others, and your mission has to be more than simply developing your people to the exclusion of
everything else. A reputation for self-righteousness will not endear you or
your people to anyone.

The phrase "**adopt a developmental style**" does not, as some Sage leaders
I have met seem to believe, mean adopt a style that tolerates people's weaknesses. Development can sometimes be uncomfortable, and less effective
Sage leaders can be so afraid of challenging people that they fail to help
them to develop at all, allowing them to remain hampered by a lack of skills
and competences that the leader, incorrectly, thinks they can never overcome. Developing people is not the same as wrapping them in cotton wool.

Encourage belief, but don't fall into the evangelical trap. Some otherwise
tolerant Sages I know can become dismissive of those who do not support the
cause with the same zeal as they do. They can also be intolerant of people
whose beliefs differ from their own. The word is "encourage" not "enforce."

In an attempt to **encourage self-discovery**, some less effective leaders
lose patience with those who appear to be reluctant to know themselves. It is
a common failing of well-meaning Sage leaders that they will try to force
this process by offering insights into the hearts and minds of their people,
instilling self-images that may or may not be accurate, but are hard to shift. I
have had to deal with countless numbers of people who have inherited from
others ideas about themselves that become so deeply ingrained that they can
become caricatures of either themselves, or, even more damaging, of someone else. Help people to find out who they are. Don't try to tell them.

If you **lead from behind**, you still lead. Or, to put it more accurately, the
cause you represent or advocate still leads. But until your people are truly
capable of self-determination, you need to be accessible when they really do
need guidance. Avoiding the cult of personality by creating physical distance between yourself and your people does not imply, and should not
make people feel, that you have abandoned what you believe in. Continue to
communicate your support even when they are doing it for themselves.

You **encourage people to adapt and change**, but do not forget how
changes can be unsettling. In many organizations, a great deal of what
makes change unsettling is a lack of involvement in planning and deciding
on a change. But if you are doing your Sage leadership well, this should not
be the case. What will still need to be managed, however, is the emotional

transition people go through in times of change. This transition generally is considered to go through seven stages shock, denial, acceptance, letting go, testing, searching for meaning, and moving forward. Known as the "transition curve," this model is useful for planning how to help people through significant change.

Be a coach or mentor, but recognize that your time is precious, and the more you take time with each individual, the less you will have to do anything else. Don't get so sucked into this part of your leadership that you become swamped. As Ricardo Semler discovered, good time management is vital to Sage leadership.[5]

Increasing Adventurer competence

Be a radical mould-breaker, but not an anarchist. It is easy for the Adventurer to fool himself or herself that it is breaking the mould that is the aim. It isn't. Breaking the mould is for an ulterior purpose, and unless both that purpose and how breaking the mould will achieve that purpose is clear, you will take yourself and your people down the same road as so many of the failed dot com companies that blossomed and shrivelled so quickly just a few years ago.

Challenge convention, but don't reject it just because it is convention. "Why should we do things like this?" is not, as many of the less effective Adventurers I have met think, a rhetorical question. Sometimes there are good reasons why. The skill of the good Adventurer leader is identifying conventions that can be done without, not just every convention willy-nilly.

The Adventurer will always **be prepared to break the rules**, but to be effective, you need both to consider the potential value of a rule and the consequences of breaking it. The driver who goes at 80 miles per hour through a residential street is not just breaking a rule, but is endangering innocent lives. And if you want to break a rule you don't believe is a good rule, like Martin Luther King and Richard Branson be prepared to take the punishment. Once again, the mature Adventurer only breaks the rules that he or she needs to, not just because they are there.

Encourage people to challenge your authority, but have the honesty, integrity and maturity to deal with this challenge well. It takes guts to challenge the leader, and if you get into the habit of pretending to accept the challenges while rejecting each one out of hand, then your people will back off and a valuable source of inspiration will dry up. On the other hand, agreeing with everyone's challenge will raise the inevitable question, "Who is the leader here?" Keep it fun, but keep it balanced.

The Adventurer's innate tendency is to **share**. How much to share, and how close you should get is a matter of personality that our model of leadership is not designed to answer. On this issue, as with many of the others in this chapter, it may be helpful to factor into the equation aspects of personality that are better dealt with by something like the Myers Briggs Type Indicator™. This tool explores differences in style that are not based on values and beliefs, but on preferences for different ways of operating and interacting. By considering this aspect of each individual's personality, you will be better able to understand how much, and in what way, you should share.[6]

For a group of Adventurers to **explore together** effectively, the leader needs to curb his or her enthusiasm sufficiently to allow others to have their say. This was a skill that Martin Luther King mastered, and it was his mastery of summing up the collected views of the people around him that played a crucial part in gaining commitment to courses of action that were risky and potentially unpopular.

Empower, but maintain an interest. Richard Branson, like many Adventurers, can lose interest in projects when they become more mainstream. But at the very least, the Virgin brand ensures some kind of continuity. The most important developmental challenge here for the Adventurer leader is to ensure that he or she does not give the impression that, by empowering others to pick up where he or she leaves off, those who do so are taking on something stale, boring, or of less importance than the newer activities.

When you truly **liberate**, you lose control. It is important that the Adventurer leader does not, by compensation for this loss, keep trying to interfere, peering critically over the shoulders of those now in charge, and, effectively, limiting the freedom that they need to operate most effectively.

Leave people alone to get on with it. The one-to-one relationships that characterize the Adventurer culture are predicated on mutual trust. The good Adventurer leader maintains personal interest and provides personal support and encouragement without impinging on people's freedom to do things their way. The trick is for the leader to be there when he or she is needed, but otherwise to keep well away.

Let the future take care of itself. There is an Adventurer joke: Question: "What makes God laugh?" Answer: "People making plans." Some Adventurer leaders see patterns emerging from their successes and failures.

Wanting to learn from these, and tempted to help others learn in the same way, they drift into more and more plans, built on the emergent patterns. The big risk is that these plans become the conventions, even the rules, by which the organization increasingly is run. The culture begins to change, and people start to get mixed messages. Strategy is great for the Guardian organization, but is a constraint to freedom and the opportunism that characterizes the Adventurer culture.

Increasing Guardian competence

It is important to the Guardian leader to **think ahead**, taking control of people's futures is one of the most obvious leadership duties. Some Guardian leaders take this responsibility so far that their plans become set in stone, and limit creativity. Make sure that your plans are constantly open to revision in the light of changing circumstances.

Having thought, communicate. One of the most common mistakes made by Guardian leaders I have known is the belief that, having communicated the vision, their job has been done. Communicate, communicate, communicate. As George Bernard Shaw once said, "The greatest problem with communication is the illusion that it has been accomplished."

Give people clear direction, but take into account that different people need different levels of detail. Insights into people's cognitive styles that you can get from MBTI™ are invaluable in helping to identify exactly how each individual prefers to receive such direction.

And remember that, within this direction, your fellow Guardians will need the space to develop their own areas of responsibility, and to work with the cognitive styles and individual strengths they possess. Setting direction does not mean taking away people's individuality.

Surround yourself with people who take responsibility, but avoid the temptation to allow sycophancy to develop. Focus on talent as well as conscientiousness so that people are not led to believe that mediocre performance is ok so long as people keep their noses clean.

Much of the recent literature on leadership has recognized that people can often take on much more responsibility than had been the norm in the past, and that, by taking on these extra responsibilities, people grow. Try not to take this too far. If you engender a culture in which people feel they have to take on more and more, it will be hard for individuals who feel the strain to admit they are overstretched.

Take responsibility, but don't interfere unless you are asked to pitch in. People learn from their mistakes, and if you never let people make them, their learning will be impaired.

Be conscientious, but not condescending or "holier than thou." Learn to role model your imperfections, too. Admitting weakness is a strength, and allows your people to be more honest about their own weaknesses and areas for personal development.

When you **create a sense of community**, remember that there are other communities, outside of the workplace, that people will feel loyal to as well. People need multiple identities, and, no matter how well they identify with the community you help to create, they will have other lives by which to make sense of themselves.

Even within the community you lead, tailor involvement to individual needs. Your introverts may want to express their sense of belonging in less overt ways than others, so depending solely on social activities to cement the sense of community may become stressful to them.

When you **care for people**, show it. You will already be aware of the differences in people enough to recognize that what one person receives as caring, another feels is intrusive. So how you show that you care will need to take into account what each individual will perceive as such.

As before, you can take caring too far, providing such protection from harm that people are denied the opportunity to learn how to take the knocks we all need from time to time.

Teach people, but sometimes, let them learn by themselves. Remember that one of the potential problems in teaching people how to do things is that it makes it less likely that they will discover new and better ways of operating. So, unless your way is the only way (according to the rules), or is undeniably the best way, keep some of the learning open.

In situations where you are in a position to teach, remember that teaching is a skill that needs constantly to be developed and enhanced, so make sure your teaching skills are up to scratch.

Protect people from politics. There are some heavyweight beasts in many organizations who can do real harm to people unless they are protected. But if your people are going to grow and develop, they may, at times, need to get stuck in. Teach them the political "savvy" they will need to operate at higher levels in the future.

Do make sure at the same time, that your protective cover does not become a barrier to the exposure to senior management your people need to build a name and reputation for themselves. They will need to feel that their success is down to their own endeavors, and this means gaining respect from seniors in their own right.

Develop an air of "natural authority." Before this becomes aloofness, keep a sense of perspective and humanity. Take into account that, in a Guardian culture, your seniority will carry with it the potential to strike fear into the hearts of more junior people. By all means maintain dignity and gravitas, but try not to abuse your position by making others feel small or insignificant.

It is what you do

When leading people who do not share your Home Base, it is often what you do, not how you do it that causes problems.

In Chapter 5, I explored the kinds of inherent conflict of values that can get in the way of good relationships. But although having a different Home Base from others can cause conflict, it doesn't have to.

In my experience, you reduce the chances of conflict, and enhance the positive impact of your leadership by moving into the other person's space, if only while you are directly interacting with them. This is how it works.

The first step is to recognize that people's values are not like their attitudes. You can change their attitudes, but not their values. Consequently, building good relationships depends upon you not trying to change other people's values. Not only can you not do it, but also trying to increases the chance of conflict rather than reduce it.

Second, although you may not agree with the other's values, you have to respect them. No matter how clear it may be to you that your own values are right (and by implication, theirs are not right), you cannot prove the rightness or otherwise of values.

Third, treating others' values with respect is neither betraying your own values, nor putting yourself at risk of "becoming one of them." I have met many people who have got stuck on this one, fearing that their integrity will be compromised if they do not keep the "aliens" at arm's length. Remember, just as you can't change their values, they can't change yours. Respect is not surrender.

Fourth, don't expect them to move into your space, unless they have the same insights into these different value sets as you do. They may not realize, as you do, the background to the differences between Warriors and Sages, Guardians and Adventurers. You need to make the effort.

Finally, moving into their space is not being dishonest, deceptive, or putting on a mask to hide your true nature. Remember, Sages have some Warrior in them, and Adventurers have Guardian instincts. When you move into someone else's space, you are simply allowing those parts of your character that are not the core of who you are to have a role in how you operate. A Sage who competes does not become a Warrior; s/he is a person who has switched into their Warrior for the purpose of fighting a battle.

But do bear in mind that by switching into a different mode, you will be using a part of your character that is less natural to you. Moving into a different Home Base is not play-acting. But as you will be relying on parts of your character that are less significant to your character, you may need to take more care in how you come across. If you are right-handed, think of it as doing something with your left hand; it is possible, but it needs more careful monitoring.

Life and leadership

Most people would agree that a balanced life is a good life. People who are all Warrior or all Sage, if such a person could exist, would be unbearable and socially inept. In their daily lives people, quite rightly, call upon behaviors that grow out of all four of these instinctive bases.

In some respects, this is also what good leaders do. They learn how to move into other people's spaces and lead them as they would like to be led. But as our examples have shown, it is often the clarity and simplicity of the core leadership style that separates the outstanding leader from the ordinary.

How much you focus your leadership style on your primary driver, to the exclusion of your secondary driver, your footbrake and handbrake is a matter of judgement, and good leaders need that above all else. The problem is that this judgement is not a matter of fact, but of opinion, and only by constantly monitoring how you are doing in leadership, through more or less informal processes of feedback, will tell you how accurate your judgement is. And as circumstances change, so will the degree to which your reliance on your primary strategy is going to be effective.

Like all leaders, you need to learn that what works today may not work tomorrow. That is why many of the people I work with go through the kinds of exercise I have included in the Appendix not once, but many times. Not only does this help them to make the subtle adjustments all good leaders need to make to maintain the relevance of their leadership style to the circumstances of the day, but it also helps enhance that self-awareness all good leaders need, but few people, if any, ever fully attain.

CHAPTER 17

Conclusions and health warning

When it comes to understanding people, including and especially ourselves, few answers come out of books alone. If this book can be of any help, it can only do so in conjunction with a great deal of honest self-evaluation, and even more robust feedback from others.

I was motivated to write this book by people I have worked with over the years who told me that it was a shame that the insights they found so valuable as we worked together on their character and leadership skills were not more widely available.

But this is only a book. I believe that it can in no way substitute for in-depth and challenging coaching. I am not a writer by profession. I am a coach, and even after this book is published, my work will not be over.

To augment the work I do with individuals and teams I use a series of questionnaires based on the concepts and model this book describes. It is, as I suggested in Chapter 1, more in the debriefing of the analyses from these questionnaires that the best leadership development emerges.

The health warning. Reading this book, and even completing faithfully all the exercises in the Appendix will not answer all the questions you need to answer about your own leadership capabilities and potential. It will help further if you continue your researches by accessing some or all of the books I have referred to in the bibliography. But don't stop there. Leadership development is a lifelong task.

If you do want to know more about the questionnaires, about coaching for yourself and/or others, please get in touch.

Best wishes and good luck.

Keith Patching

keith.patching@btinternet.com

Appendix: Your route map

Some people like to take notes as they go, along especially when they come across the kinds of questions I have been asking throughout the book. In the Appendix, I have brought together all those questions. If it helps, you may want to jot down some answers here.

Chapter 1   Introduction

Before going any further, you may find it useful to note here how you would describe your approach to leadership.

What kind of leader are you?

What makes you the kind of leader you are?

What are your leadership strengths?

What weaknesses are you aware of in how you lead?

Chapter 2 Stories

For each and any of the 16 stories in Chapter 2, which, if any, resonate with you?

Consider what it has taught you about leadership.

Did it tell you that you have to fight on and never give up fighting for what you believe in?

Did it teach you that failure is the best way to learn?

Did it tell you that people look to you for guidance and authority?

Did the lesson show you that people respond best to being free?

What kind of character is the hero of your own story?

Chapter 3   Science

Look back at the stories you have identified as important to the formation of your character.

Are the lessons you learnt from the stories the only lessons you could have learnt?

What conclusions do you draw from the meanings you have *actually* placed on the facts of the stories?

Chapter 4   Values

Which value set is closest to what you believe in? You may want to check through them to see whether, at this stage, they help clarify what is really important to you. Please be careful to look at what the value means, and not just at the attractiveness of the word or phrase alone.

Warrior

Value	*Comment*
Achievement and accomplishment	
Winning	
Competition	
Advancement and promotion	
Fame	
Fortune and material wealth	
Defending your territory	
Physical challenge	
Being a hero	

You are primarily motivated to win and achieve.

Comment

Adventurer

Value	Comment
Freedom	
Challenging convention	
Moving on	
"You only live once"	
Change and variety	
Fast living	
Fun, excitement, adventure and playfulness	
Self-reliance	
Having a playmate	

You are primarily motivated by freedom and adventure.

Comment

Guardian

Value	Comment
Having a family	
Being home	
Putting down roots	
Economic security	
Protecting and providing	
Respect	
Membership of the community	
Maturity and responsibility	
Developing a legacy	

You are primarily motivated to take responsibility for others.

Comment

Sage

Value	Comment
Wisdom	
Learning and understanding	
Search for truth	
Humility	
Celebrating others	
Mental and spiritual development	
Seeking spiritual inspiration	
Inner harmony	
Love of the arts	

You are primarily motivated to learn and understand.

Comment

Chapter 5   Conflict

There are times when you have to make choices. These may be questions that do not relate to your life, but even as hypothetical questions, they can help you to identify the kinds of response that would come naturally to you.

When a career opportunity comes along that conflicts with the needs of the family, what do you do?

When the pressures of your current job become an almost intolerable strain on you personally, but there is no alternative that will meet your financial commitments, what do you do?

When a rival threatens to take credit for work you have done, what do you do?

When you fall out of love with the father or mother of your children, what do you do?

Look back at the values, and the conflicts between the values and ask yourself, when the chips are down, when I have to stand up and be counted, where am I?

Chapter 6 Home base

In this chapter, I listed a number of dilemmas that people sometimes face. In each case, how would you resolve the dilemma? Which option would you choose?

You are at a career crossroads. You have two job offers. Job 1 is better paid, and is a significant challenge, so much so that it is likely that you will have to work very hard to make it a success. Job 2 you will certainly be able to do well, as you have proven in the past that you are capable of doing this kind of thing excellently. Although it pays significantly less, it delivers much more direct benefit to the community.

In this situation I would probably choose Job_____

Your organization operates a mentoring system. You have two possible mentors to work with. Mentor number 1 is a renowned high-flyer who is going places. He or she has made rapid progress up the organization, and, although he or she may have trod on a few toes to get there, many people recognize that "you can't make an omelette without breaking eggs." He or she has agreed to mentor you if you want it, but has warned that you will have to keep up a hectic pace, and that you will have to learn as you go, as he or she has little time for idle chatter. Mentor 2 is a well-established and wise person who has expressed an interest in helping your development. She/he has warned that it takes time to grow into good leadership, but that she/he will guide you all the way. The fact that this mentor has, as some people say, plateau-ed, means he or she will have much more time to devote to your development.

In this situation I would probably choose Mentor number_____

You find yourself mixed up in a political battle. Your opponent is known to be dangerous and a born fighter. Moreover, she/he has many people on his or her side. But you think they are doing something very wrong.

In this situation, I would fight/back off_____

You have experienced a spectacular failure in a job. In this situation I would go for something similar to prove myself/take a different route._____

Your job has become boring. But you have a mortgage, children to support, and very little chance of getting another job that will bring in anywhere near enough money to support your family to the standard they have become accustomed to.

In this situation I would probably stick with it/ quit.

_____

A lot of your time at work is spent on unproductive red tape. In this situation I would probably work towards gaining consensus for change/break the rules._____

You are offered the chance to start something new. The problem with the opportunity is that it is very high risk. It is a completely new direction for the organization, and the chances of it working are slim. You will be working with little support from the senior people, and if it goes wrong, there is no guarantee that there will be anything for you to go back to. Because of the risks, the organization wants you to keep the project under wraps, and you will have few, if any, people working with you. You will be on your own.

In this situation I would probably turn it down/go for it.
_____

You have worked hard and are offered a promotion. The new role carries with it considerable responsibility for budgets, people, and the direction of strategy. The salary increase is considerable, and your new title will reflect your new-found seniority. In your capacity as manager, you will have little, if any, time to do the kind of job you have been doing. It is a significant shift away from doing to managing.

In this situation I would probably accept the promotion/stay put._____

Values and principles

Are the values I most approved of really my values or are they a set of principles?

Are the lessons I say I learnt from the experiences of my past my lessons or those taught to me by others?

If there is a mismatch between my values and my stories, where does this come from?

Where is your Home Base?

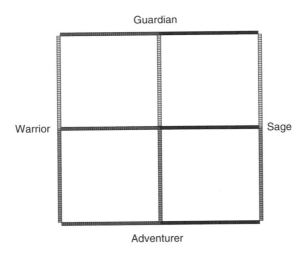

Chapter 7   Where you are now

Consider your current lifestyle and attitudes. What are you trying to become?

What do you spend your time on?

What switches you on, and what turns you off?

What would make you happier, and what do you try to avoid?

Who are your role models, and who do you have little time for?

Now compare what you have come up with to your values, and to the stories of your life. Are all these consistent with each other?

If you do find inconsistencies, then this may be the time to question where these inconsistencies come from. Are you striving for something someone else told you that you ought to go for?

If you are living a life currently that is out of step with what you really believe in, why are you doing this?

If you have made compromises, how long will you have to live with them?

If you are going through a stage in your life that has taken you away from your Home Base, but which is under your control, and you know the way back home, just pause and ask yourself if what you are looking at is a clear route home, or one of those rationalizations that are so artful in obscuring from you issues you really do know you should confront, but have told yourself is really not a problem. Not today, anyway.

Where are you now, compared to your Home Base?

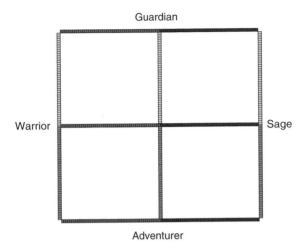

Chapter 8   Job role

Organizational culture

Do you at this stage feel that your organization's Home Base is the same as your Home Base?

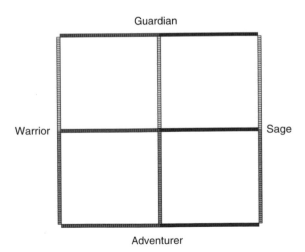

If the answer to the previous question is "no," you may want to go on to the following set of questions:

Are you sure that you have assessed both your Home Base and the organization's Home Base accurately?

How aware were you before you did this exercise that you and the organization are "out of step" with each other?

Has being out of step with the organization's culture caused you any problems in the past?

How are you currently managing to operate successfully in what is essentially an alien culture?

Can you continue to survive and thrive in an organization that is not in tune with your Home Base?

If so, what plans do you have in place to minimize the potentially negative impact of operating out of your Home Base on a daily basis?

If not, what should you do about it?

Your job role

How well is your current job role meeting your needs?

If you are a Warrior, does it provide you with the chance to win?

If you are a Sage, is it a true learning environment?

If you are a Guardian, does it provide a community you feel you belong to?

If you are an Adventurer, does it give you the freedom you need?

You may want to revisit the values you identified as most important to you, and check out how each of those values is provided for in your daily work.

If your Home Base and Job Role are far apart, what should you be doing about it?

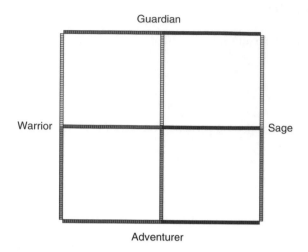

The relationships you have with people at work

Consider up to about half a dozen of the key relationships that are important to you. Although you may have to make guesses, where do you think their Home Bases may be?

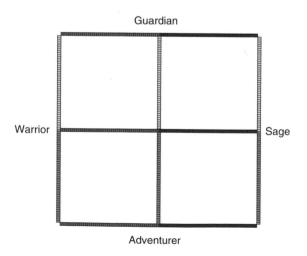

Does this exercise bring out any relationship issues you may have already been aware of?

Does it highlight differences you may have not been aware of?

Chapter 9   Your model of leadership

Consider your ideal model of leadership. Is it Warrior, Guardian, Sage, or Adventurer?

Does he or she lead from the front and fight for what is right?

Does he or she say "the buck stops with me," and take firm control of every situation?

Is he or she a teacher, a guide, a mentor, who gets things done through dialog?

Or is he or she a radical mould-breaker who challenges convention and redefines the rules of the business?

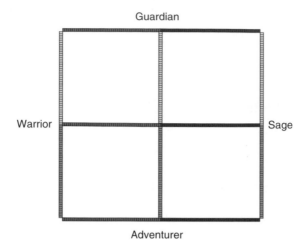

How you lead now

How would you describe your leadership style now?

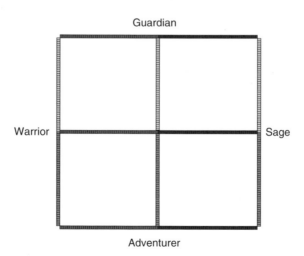

Are you a go-getter, a steady rock, a wise coach, or a rebel?

Do you lead most by challenging, directing, coaching, or empowering?

Where on the model is your leadership style in practice?

If you receive feedback from others, what is their view of how you lead?

Is it consistent with your intentions?

As you consider the key aspects of your reputation as defined through this feedback, are you seen as Warrior, Guardian, Sage or Adventurer?

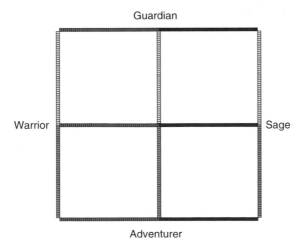

And if, on balance, it is a bit of all of these, is this because you are truly successful at being all things to all people, or are you working with a reputation of inconsistency? Is your leadership style an inconsistent mixture of all kinds of leadership attributes with no clear cohesion?

Your leadership model and your Home Base

Consider any difference between your Home Base and your Leadership Model. If it is significant, why has this come about?

What impact might this be having on how you are seen by others?

What impact might this be having on your effectiveness?

What impact might this be having on your inner sense of integrity?

Chapter 10   Strategy

Consider which of the following is closest to how you feel you lead.
In brief, a Warrior strategy is: **lead from the front and win**.

In brief, a Guardian strategy is: **create a community and build a future**.

In brief, a Sage strategy is: **develop people and foster personal growth**.

In brief, an Adventurer strategy is: **liberate people and change paradigms**.

My primary driver is_____

My secondary driver is_____

My footbrake is_____

My hand brake is_____

Chapter 11   Developing a warrior strategy

If you are a Warrior, you may want to assess how favorable your current job role is to you by scoring each of the following job role elements out of 5, where 5 means, "I get as much of this as I need," and 0 means your job provides none of this:

A role you took on because it would stretch you	
Opportunities to be successful	
Being in a position to achieve successful outcomes	
The satisfaction of closing deals/contracts against the competition	
Established ways of getting over failures	
An organization that values the attainment of goals	
The chance to excel	
Challenge, challenge, challenge	
An organization that rewards achievement	
A thirst for further recognition and reward	
Total suitability of your job for a Warrior	
Multiply the total by 2, leading to % fit	%

Key elements of the Warrior approach to leadership

If you are a Warrior, you may want to use this space to note ways in which you put into practice each of the following elements of the Warrior strategy for leadership.

If you are not a Warrior, you may want to reflect on any of these elements of strategy to check whether you may be sending out mixed messages by adopting them.

Lead from the front

Fight for what you believe in

Be assertive

Be strong and decisive

Be tough and resilient

Stretch people

Set standards and measure everything

Maintain a challenging style

Challenge your people

Surround yourself with people who rise to the challenges

Chapter 12 Developing a Sage Strategy

If you are a Sage, you may want to assess how favorable your current job role is to you by scoring each of the following job role elements out of 5, where 5 means, "I get as much of this as I need," and 0 means your job provides none of this:

An organization or role you can believe in	
An organization that values quality of life	
An organization that rewards knowledge, wisdom, and understanding	
A place for learning	
The opportunity to understand yourself and others	
Thought leadership	
The chance to develop yourself	
It's a bad day if you've learnt nothing new	
The satisfaction of doing something worthwhile	
Becoming more contented with yourself or what life has to offer	
Total suitability of your job for a Sage	
Multiply the total by 2, leading to % fit	%

Key elements of the Sage approach to leadership

If you are a Sage, you may want to use this space to note ways in which you put into practice each of the following elements of the Sage strategy for leadership.

If you are not a Sage, you may want to reflect on any of these elements of strategy to check whether you may be sending out mixed messages by adopting them.

Engage in dialogue

Treat people as equals

Listen and learn

Create a developmental climate

Adopt a developmental style

Encourage belief

Encourage self-discovery

Lead from behind

Encourage people to adapt and change

Be a coach or mentor

Chapter 13   Developing an Adventurer strategy

If you are an Adventurer, you may want to assess how favorable your current job role is to you by scoring each of the following job role elements out of 5, where 5 means, "I get as much of this as I need," and 0 means your job provides none of this:

A sense of independence	
An organization that rewards self-reliance	
Bucking the system	
Getting away with it	
Doing your own thing	
Finding new ways of doing things	
Freedom	
An organization that values fun	
Doing it because it seems like a good idea (at the time)	
What next? 'No idea'	
Total suitability of your job for an Adventurer	
Multiply the total by 2, leading to % fit	%

Key elements of the Adventurer approach to leadership

If you are an Adventurer, you may want to use this space to note ways in which you put into practice each of the following elements of the Adventurer strategy for leadership.

If you are not an Adventurer, you may want to reflect on any of these elements of strategy to check whether you may be sending out mixed messages by adopting them.

Be a radical mould-breaker

Challenge convention

Be prepared to break the rules

Encourage people to challenge your authority

Share

Explore together

Empower

Liberate

Leave people alone to get on with it

Let the future take care of itself

Chapter 14   Developing a guardian strategy

If you are a Guardian, you may want to assess how favorable your current job role is to you by scoring each of the following job role elements out of 5, where 5 means, "I get as much of this as I need," and 0 means your job provides none of this:

A role that represents a step up in life	
An organization that rewards responsibility	
A role where the best thing is the responsibility you have	
A role where you can take charge – especially in a crisis	
An organization in which professionalism is valued	

A role where you can enjoy being responsible for people	
The opportunity to take care of people	
It's a bad day if you let someone down	
A sense of belonging	
Chances for promotion	
Total suitability of your job for a Guardian	
Multiply the total by 2, leading to % fit	%

Key elements of the guardian approach to leadership

If you are a Guardian, you may want to use this space to note ways in which you put into practice each of the following elements of the Guardian strategy for leadership.

If you are not a Guardian, you may want to reflect on any of these elements of strategy to check whether you may be sending out mixed messages by adopting them.

Think ahead

Give people clear direction

Surround yourself with people who take responsibility

Take responsibility

Be conscientious

Create a sense of community

Care for people

Teach people

Protect people from politics

Develop an air of "natural authority"

Chapter 15 Organizational culture and leadership

The tables on the following pages contain lists of feedback that people I have worked with have received in real life. You may want to use these lists for two purposes.

The first is to check those comments you may have actually received (or feedback in different words that amount to the same criticism). They may help confirm how people have interpreted your behaviors, and confirm (or otherwise) the degree to which you may have been projecting to them elements of your character that align with Warrior, Adventurer, Guardian or Sage.

The other column in each table is for you to check items you feel are areas you would like to improve on. This will provide a greater degree of focus for how you read and respond to chapter 16.

The Adventurer's character through the eyes of the Guardian

Feedback	*Have had*	*Improve on*
Too selfish; doesn't think of others		
Not a team-player		
Bucks the system; lacks respect for how we do things around here		
Thinks success is what you can get away with		
Does his or her own thing; not a corporate citizen		
Disruptive; always reinventing the wheel		
Thinks of self more than others		
Never takes things sufficiently seriously; everything is a big joke to him or her		
Poor forward planning		
Works by expediency, not by strategy		

The Adventurer's leadership style through the eyes of the Guardian

Feedback	Have had	Improve on
Keeps moving the goalposts		
Fails to respect the wisdom of others		
Doesn't toe the line; a loose cannon		
Lacks authority		
Over-familiar with subordinates		
Can't decide without checking with his or her own staff		
Abdicates responsibility		
Allows people to get away with murder		
Offers no guidance; doesn't care for his or her people		

The Sage's character through the eyes of the Warrior

Feedback	Have had	Improve on
Not focused on the bottom line		
More interested in products and services than sales or profits		
Not pragmatic		
A perennial course-attender		
A navel-gazer		
Lacks follow-through		
Over-intellectualizes everything		
Lacks ambition		
Lacks motivation		
Content with second best; doesn't pursue excellence		

The Sage's leadership style through the eyes of the Warrior

Feedback	Have had	Improve on
"Analysis-paralysis"		
Rewards mediocre performance		
Lacking in confidence and strength of character		
Doesn't drive people		
Has lax standards and poor measurement of performance		
Impractical and theoretical		
Fails to judge people's competence		
Lacks guts		
Inconsistent		
Wants to be everyone's friend		

The Guardian's character in the eyes of the Adventurer

Feedback	Have had	Improve on
Only interested in climbing the "greasy pole" of the hierarchy		
Takes life too seriously		
Always wants to be involved in everything		
A control freak		
Stickler for bureaucracy and the rules and procedures		
Self-righteous		
Patronizing		
Over-anxious to be seen to be toeing the line		
Tries to tie one down		
Always sucking up to the bosses		

The Guardian's leadership style in the eyes of the Adventurer

Feedback	*Have had*	*Improve on*
Inflexible and lacking in imagination		
Domineering and authoritarian		
Favours those who creep round those in authority		
Makes and admits to too many mistakes		
Pokes his or her nose into too many activities		
Never lets people alone to get on with the job		
Can become intrusive, even with personal life		
Always thinks he or she knows best		
Acts as a gatekeeper		
Has a high opinion of his or her own worth		

The Warrior's character in the eyes of the Sage

Feedback	*Have had*	*Improve on*
Over ambitious		
Always seeking glory for himself or herself		
Pushes himself or herself forward, in front of others		
Tunnel-vision; the deal overshadows everything, including people's feelings		
Never admits he or she is wrong		
Too aggressive		
Does not realize that there's more to life than work		
Driven to succeed at all costs		
Excessively competitive		
Wants to be noticed, especially by people in charge of the bonus		

The Warrior's Leadership style in the eyes of the Sage

Feedback	Have had	Improve on
Micro manages; pokes his or her nose into every deal		
Always looking for a fight		
Doesn't care who he or she hurts		
Doesn't listen		
Thick-skinned		
Puts people under enormous pressure		
Pits people against one another for fun		
Makes people feel small and incompetent		
A bully		
Has favorites		

You may want to use this check-list to do a cultural assessment of your organization. For each pair of cultural characteristics, tick the one that you feel is most commonly adhered to or rewarded. For example, if you feel that people in your organization are rewarded for being a hero, tick that box; if, on the other hand, humility is rewarded more, tick that one.

The organization's heroes			Humility
Personal renown			Quality of life
Competition			Co-operation
Defending your territory			Spiritual well-being
Winning			Celebrating others
Physical challenge			Mental and spiritual development
Advancement and promotion			Learning and understanding
Achievement and accomplishment			Wisdom
Fortune and material wealth			Inner harmony
Total for Warrior			Total for Sage

Organization before the individual			Individual freedom
Developing a legacy			Change and variety
Being at the centre of things			Fast moving
Career progression			"You only live once"
Economic security			Moving on
Protecting and providing			Good 1-2-1 relationships
Membership of the community			Self-reliance
Respect			Challenging convention
Maturity and responsibility			Fun, adventure and playfulness
Total for Guardian			Total for Adventurer

On the next page, you may want to reassess the respective positions of your Home Base and the place on the model you have defined the organizational culture of where you work right now.

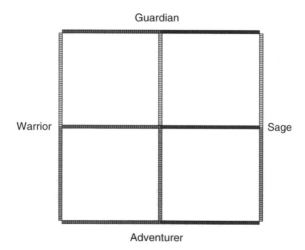

Are both plots close enough together for you to feel confident in your ability to be a successful leader within this culture?

Cultural Appropriateness

On the following pages, some cultural phenomena are explored in the context of the four prevailing organizational cultures. You may want to match these against your own organization's prevailing culture.

Chapter 16 Developing your own leadership

	WARRIOR	SAGE	GUARDIAN	ADVENTURER
Meetings	Short, focused, and aimed at getting decisions	Informal opportunities for learning and understanding	Formal and informative. Aimed at giving each attendee clear responsibilities for his or her contribution	frequent, informal, mostly unrecorded, with unpredictable outcomes
Appraisals	Regular objective measures of performance, aimed at providing commensurate rewards	Informal and constant, providing personal Appreciation of each individual's value to the organization	360° evaluation of progress towards development goals to enable career progression	Happen by chance when people tell each other how they feel. No formal system
Training and development	Skills-based and directly relevant to the individual's ability to do the job	Eclectic and designed for personal growth, as the individual chooses	Progressive and aimed at broadening the individual's capabilities to take on more	Ad hoc and at the individual's discretion
Discipline procedures	Three strikes and you're out	Informal peer pressure	formal and fair. Built to help the Individual avoid mistakes in the future	A necessary evil; ad hoc and seen as a chance for the individual to consider his or her options

	WARRIOR	SAGE	GUARDIAN	ADVENTURER
Car parking	The heroes deserve the best places, or first come first served to maintain competition	No policy at all	Seniors earn the best places; busy and influential, they need the convenience of rapid entry	First come, first served
Counselling	Is for wimps; a last resort	Everyone counsels everyone else	Provided as an important service to help employees deal with any problems that may be harming them	Invisible, and provided unconsciously through one-to-one relationships.
Career development	So long as an individual is winning, he or she will keep moving onwards and upwards	Self-managed within an essentially democratic environment. Position and rewards are agreed by everyone in consultation	A managed process that enables each individual to rise as high as his or her talents will allow	Opportunistic and unplanned
Awaydays and offsites	Opportunity for focused work on specifics. Clear outcomes needed, and with a good dose of golf, go-karting etc. to keep the adrenalin going	Quiet contemplation away from the distractions of work. Done as cheaply and simply as possible, and with open agendas	Well-planned in advance, and structured to make the most effective use of time and resources. Evenings are for socialising (often with spouses) to get to know one another	For fun and ideas generation, with business issues dealt with when people are in the mood.
Offices and environment	Prestigious appearance to impress clients. Space designed to release	The human touch. Environment belongs to the people, especially	Internal layout reflects the hierarchy. Needs to symbolize solidity and	Lots of open space, unorthodox layout, often more like a sports or social

	WARRIOR	SAGE	GUARDIAN	ADVENTURER
	energy.	one's own bit of space one can personalize	permanence	club. Tea, coffee, etc on tap. Desks shared on an ad hoc basis. Constant
Work-life balance	Long hours Culture means it's always a 'problem'	Life first, work second.	Family comes first, so long as family commitments don't let colleagues down too much	Work is fun, so not an issue

Chapter 16   Developing your own leadership

Taking stock of your career strategy

If you are considering moving on, you may want to consider the following

- Your Home Base
- Your ideal job role
- The organizational culture within which you will be most effective

Your Home Base

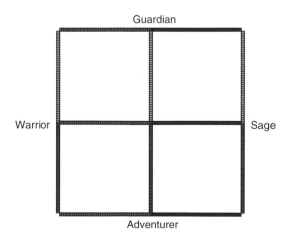

From the values you may have identified in the exercise in chapter 4, what are your four or five key values?

What kind of career move would enable you best to live those values in your work?

Your ideal job role.

Go through the following table, and identify, in rank order, the ten to twenty key elements of any job role that would be your ideal.

A role you took on because it would stretch you	
Opportunities to be successful	
Being in a position to achieve successful outcomes	
The satisfaction of closing deals/contracts against the competition	
Established ways of getting over failures	
An organization that values the attainment of goals	
The chance to excel	
Challenge, challenge, challenge	
An organization that rewards achievement	
A thirst for further recognition and reward	
An organization or role you can believe in	
An organization that values quality of life	
An organization that rewards knowledge, wisdom, and understanding	
A place for learning	
The opportunity to understand yourself and others	
The satisfaction of doing something worthwhile	
Thought leadership	
The chance to develop yourself	
It's a bad day if you've learnt nothing new	
Becoming more contented with yourself or what life has to offer	
A sense of independence	
An organization that rewards self-reliance	
Bucking the system	
Getting away with it	
Doing your own thing	
Finding new ways of doing things	
Freedom	
An organization that values fun	
Doing it because it seems like a good idea (at the time)	

What next? "No idea"	
A role that represents a step up in life	
An organization that rewards responsibility	
A role where the best thing is the responsibility you have	
A role where you can take charge – especially in a crisis	
An organization in which professionalism is valued	
A role where you can enjoy being responsible for people	
The opportunity to take care of people	
It's a bad day if you let someone down	
A sense of belonging	
Chances for promotion	

The organizational culture within which you will be most effective

For each of the following contrasting pairs of cultural elements of an organization, select the one pair that is most important to you as a feature of your ideal organizational culture.

The organization's heroes			Humility
Personal renown			Quality of life
Competition			Co-operation
Defending your territory			Spiritual well-being
Winning			Celebrating others
Physical challenge			Mental and spiritual development
Advancement and promotion			Learning and understanding
Achievement and accomplishment			Wisdom
Fortune and material wealth			Inner harmony
Organization before the individual			Individual freedom
Developing a legacy			Change and variety
Being at the centre of things			Fast moving
Career progression			"You only live once"
Economic security			Moving on
Protecting and providing			Good 1-2-1 relationships
Membership of the community			Self-reliance
Respect			Challenging convention
Maturity and responsibility			Fun, adventure and playfulness

You may want to translate your values, your ideal job role, and the organizational culture you are seeking into whatever format of c.v. you prefer. Good luck with your search.

Developing your competence in each Leadership style

In this final exercise, you may want to note in the following tables any specific leadership behaviors you would like to improve on, and what you think you will do to achieve this.

Increasing your Warrior competence

Leadership behavior	Development actions
Lead from the front	
Fight for what you believe in	
Be assertive	
Be strong and decisive	
Be tough and resilient	
Stretch people	
Set standards and measure everything	
Maintain a challenging style	
Challenge your people	
Surround yourself with people who rise to the challenges	

Increasing your Sage competence

Leadership behavior	Development Actions
Engage in dialogue	
Treat people as equals	
Listen and learn	
Create a developmental climate	
Adopt a developmental style	
Encourage belief	
Encourage self-discovery	
Lead from behind	
Encourage people to adapt and change	
Be a coach or mentor	

Increasing your Adventurer competence

Leadership behavior	Development actions
Be a radical mould-breaker	
Challenge convention	
Be prepared to break the rules	
Encourage people to challenge your authority	
Share	
Explore together	
Empower	
Liberate	
Leave people alone to get on with it	
Let the future take care of itself	

Increasing your Adventurer competence

Leadership behavior	Development actions
Think ahead	
Give people clear direction	
Surround yourself with people who take responsibility	
Take responsibility	
Be conscientious	
Create a sense of community	
Care for people	
Teach people	
Protect people from politics	
Develop an air of "natural authority"	

Notes

Chapter 1   Introduction

1. Tait 1995: 332.
2. Tait 1995: 363.
3. Pinker 2002: 264.
4. Goleman 1997: 132.
5. Goleman 1997: 120–22.

Chapter 2   Stories

1. Goleman 1995.
2. Pearson 1991: 289.
3. Stevens1996: 94–96 is a good summary of how evolution has shaped the process of selection of what we remember.
4. Mark & Pearson 2001: 31.
5. A scientific analysis of the neurological contrasts explored in this section can be found in Edelman's description of "primary consciousness" and "higher-order consciousness" (Edelman 1990, Chapter 11).
6. Thatcher, 1995: 470.
7. Abernathy 1989: xv.
8. Pinker 2002: 201–7.
9. Goleman 1995: 18.
10. Kuhn 1970.
11. Payne 1969: 568.
12. Bruner 1990 looks more closely at the importance of the meanings of the stories in our everyday lives.
13. Carson 1998: 228.
14. Kirk 2005: 172.
15. Mark & Pearson 2001: 1–2.

chapter 3   Science

1. Junor 1983: 86.
2. Renshaw 2004: 76.

3. Payne 1969: 56.
4. Ridley 2003: 52.
5. Pinker 2002: 47.
6. Ridley 1999: 172.
7. Ridley 2003: 165.
8. Ibid.: 248.
9. Ibid.: 158.
10. Ibid.: 251.
11. Ibid.: 255.
12. Ibid.: 257.
13. Ridley 1999: 85.
14. Arroba & James 1987: 22.
15. Stewart & Joines 1987.
16. Ridley 2003: 181.
17. Ibid.: 92.
18. Ridley 1999: 149–51.
19. Pearson 1991.
20. Donaldson 1992.
21. Ridley 1999: 164.
22. The model I am using has been developed from a number of different sources, most of which use different terms for the characters I am describing. Some of the works you may want to look at for different terminology are Guzie & Guzie, 1984; Pearson 1986; Gray 1996; Mitroff 1983; Thompson 1971; and Moore & Gillett.
23. Ridley 2003: 42–4.
24. Pinker 2002: 238.
25. Romer, cited in Pinker 2002: 238.
26. Pinker 2002: 238.
27. Thatcher 1995: 118.
28. Ridley 2003: 204.

Chapter 4   Values

1. Ridley 2003: 83.
2. Ibid.: 80.
3. Pinker 2002: 278.
4. Sergeant 2005: 39.
5. Ibid.: 57.
6. Ibid.: 122.
7. Junor 1983: 110.
8. Ibid.: 114.
9. Thatcher 1995: 465.
10. Ibid.: 466.

11. Junor 1983: 196.
12. Thatcher 1995: 316.
13. Thatcher 1993: 124.
14. Sergeant 2005: 17.
15. Junor 1983: 35.
16. Ibid.: 17–18.
17. Thatcher 1993: 626.
18. Sergeant 2005: 37.
19. Thatcher 1995: 100–1.
20. Ibid.: 1995: 10.
21. Ibid.: 24.
22. Ibid.: 230.
23. Ibid.: 832.
24. Ibid.: 104.
25. Ibid.: 10.
26. Junor 1983: 133.
27. Thatcher 1993: 57.
28. Thatcher 1995: 182.
29. Thatcher 1993: 181.
30. Thatcher 1995: 11.
31. Thatcher 1993: 469.
32. Carson 1998: 358.
33. King 1958: 150.
34. Carson 1998: 55.
35. Ibid.: 307.
36. Ibid.: 6.
37. Ibid.: 22.
38. King 1986: 49.
39. Carson 1998: 220.
40. Kirk 2005: 7.
41. Carson 1998: 56.
42. Dyson 2000: 52.
43. Ibid.: 120.
44. Ibid.: 211.
45. Carson 1998: 18.
46. Dyson 2000: 51.
47. King 1986: 267.
48. Dyson 2000: 5.
49. Carson 1998: 324.
50. Ibid.: 319.
51. Dyson 2000: 139.
52. Ibid.: 149.
53. Ibid.: 155.
54. Ibid.: 161.

55. Carson 1998: 182.
56. Ibid.: 335.
57. Ibid.: 88.
58. Ibid.: 85.
59. Ibid.: 342.
60. Ibid.: 340.
61. Tugwell 1967: 168.
62. Renshaw 2004: 190.
63. Tugwell 1967: 192.
64. Renshaw 2004: 4.
65. Ibid.: 180–1.
66. Tugwell 1967: 112.
67. Ibid.: 113.
68. Ibid.: 149.
69. Ibid.: 109.
70. Ibid.: 114.
71. Renshaw 2004: 86.
72. Tugwell 1967: 177.
73. Neustadt 1968: 162.
74. Schlesinger 1957: 386.
75. Tugwell 1967: 55.
76. Ibid.: 128.
77. Ibid.: 86.
78. Ibid.: 95.
79. Schlesinger 1957: 392.
80. Tugwell 1967: 83 – emphasis original.
81. Ibid.:123.
82. Renshaw 2004: 7.
83. Tugwell 1967: 11–12.
84. Ibid.: 18.
85. Ibid.: 27.
86. Renshaw 2004: 16.
87. Ibid.: 48.
88. Ibid.: 7.
89. Ibid.: 186.
90. Ibid.: 28.
91. Ibid.: 15.
92. Ibid.: 70.
93. Schlesinger 1958: 92.
94. Renshaw 2004: 107.
95. Tugwell 1967: xi.
96. Renshaw 2004: 14.
97. Ibid.: 26.
98. Ibid.: 189.

99. Tugwell 1967: 209.
100. Renshaw 2004: 40.
101. Schlesinger 1960: 577–8.
102. Payne 1969: 151.
103. Ibid.: 82.
104. Ibid.: 28.
105. Ibid.: 604.
106. Ibid.: 126.
107. Ibid.: 39.
108. Ibid.: 99.
109. Ibid.: 419.
110. Sitaramayya 1943: 178.
111. Gandhi 1958: Vol. XVI, 408.
112. Payne 1969: 312.
113. Gandhi 1958: Vol. XXIII, 114.
114. Ibid.: Vol. XII, 411–12.
115. Payne 1969: 249.
116. Ibid.: 15.
117. Gandhi 1958: Vol. II, 166.
118. Payne 1969: 323.
119. Gandhi 1958: Vol. IX, 479–80.
120. Ibid.: 509.
121. Payne 1969: 477.
122. Ibid.: 211.
123. Thoreau 1854.
124. Tendulkar 1951: Vol. VI, 39.

6 Home base

1. Ridley 1999: 147–60.
2. Ridley 2003: 92.
3. Sergeant 2005: 202.
4. Thatcher 1995: 81.
5. Sitaramayya: 1943: 180.
6. Renshaw 2004: 16.
7. Ibid.: 21.
8. Carson 1998: 68.

7 Where you are now

1. Pinker 2002: 283.

8   Job role

1. My favourites are Deal & Kennedy 1982, and Schein 1989.
2. Tait 1995: 334.

10   Developing strategy

1. Sergeant 2005: 209.
2. Thatcher 1993: 129.
3. Thatcher 1995: 259.
4. Junor 1983: 195.
5. Thatcher 1993: 516.
6. Thatcher 1995: 88.
7. Thatcher 1993: 449.
8. Renshaw 2004: 16.
9. Schlesinger 1957: 471–2.
10. Tugwell 1957: 128.
11. Ibid.: 70.
12. Ibid.: 113–4.
13. Ibid.: 84.
14. Payne 1969: 108.
15. Sitaramayya 1943: 178.
16. Payne 1969: 15.
17. Carson 1998: 24.
18. Ibid.: 27.
19. Ibid.: 240.
20. Dyson 2000: 86.
21. Carson 1998: 134.
22. Ibid.: 331.
23. Ibid.: 335.
24. Mark & Pearson 2001.
25. Ibid.: 8.
26. Ibid.: 134.

11   Developing a warrior strategy

1. Thatcher 1993: 560–1.
2. Gates 1999: 3.
3. Heilemann 2001: 63.
4. Heller 2000: 72.
5. Wallace & Erickson 1993: 211.

6. For the case against Microsoft and Bill Gates, see Rohm 1998 and Heilemann 2001.
7. For example, John Egan, the tough manager who took on the challenges of British Leyland admits, "I'm afraid of failure." Underwood 1989: 87.
8. As Margaret Thatcher once said, "I'm damned if I'm going to let them see I'm afraid." Junor 1993: 138.
9. Carling & Heller 1995: 44–5.
10. Wallace & Erickson 1993: 15–16.
11. Ibid.: 149.
12. Underwood 1989: 92.
13. Semler 1993: 229.
14. Underwood 1989: 68.
15. Wallace & Erickson 1993: 151.
16. Thatcher 1993: 431.
17. Heilemann 2001: 51.
18. Heller 2000: 84.
19. Thatcher 1993: 855.
20. Heilemann 2001: 47.
21. Heller 2000: 94.
22. Junor 1993: 115.
23. Wallace & Erickson 1993: 96.
24. Thatcher 1995: 237.
25. Sergeant 2005: 289.
26. Thatcher 1993: 449.
27. Heller 2000: 82.
28. David Bunnell was a technical writer who joined Microsoft in the very early days.
29. Wallace & Erickson 1993: 159.
30. Ibid.: 236.
31. Thatcher 1993: 213.
32. Ibid.: 517.
33. Heller 2000: 87.
34. Wallace & Erickson 1993: 120.
35. Ibid.: 244.
36. Carling & Heller 1995: 75.
37. Gates 1999: 284–5.
38. Thatcher 1995: 197.
39. Wallace & Erickson 1993: 128.
40. Sergeant 2005: 266.
41. Wallace & Erickson 1993: 24–5.
42. Ibid.: 64.
43. Thatcher 1995: 263.
44. Here, she was referring to President Gerald Ford. Thatcher 1995: 360.
45. Thatcher 1995: 364.

46. Carling & Heller 1995: 60–1.
47. Gates 1999: 317–8.
48. Junor 1993: 108.

12   Developing a sage strategy

1. A great deal has been written about Semco, including Case Studies at some of the most prestigious business schools. I still feel that the best way of understanding the development of Semler's Sage strategy is his book, "Maverick!".
2. Morris 2000: 416.
3. Semler 1993: 228.
4. Tait 1995: 242.
5. Patching 1999.
6. Semler 1993: 75.
7. Ibid.: 96.
8. Ibid.: 42.
9. Ibid.: 217.
10. Ibid.: 219.
11. Ibid.:191.
12. Ibid.: 217.
13. Cheshire 1985: 10.
14. Morris 2000: 377.
15. Ibid.: 23.
16. Ibid.: 5.
17. Ibid.: 95.
18. Ibid.: 73.
19. Ibid.: 247.
20. Ibid.: 258.
21. Ibid.: 286.
22. Ibid.: 230.
23. Semler 1993: 68.
24. Morris 2000: 147.
25. Semler 1993: 137.
26. Ibid.: 130.
27. Morris 2000: 61.
28. Ibid.: 187.
29. Ibid.: 298.
30. Semler 1993: 237–42.
31. Ibid.: 109.
32. Ibid.: 205.
33. Morris 2000: 381.
34. Semler 1993: 205.
35. Ibid.: 153.

36. Morris 2000: 420–1.
37. Semler 1993: 131.
38. Morris 2000: 101.
39. Ibid.: 334.
40. Semler 1993: 78.
41. Cheshire 1961: 155–6.
42. Morris 2000: 329.
43. Semler 1993: 214.
44. Ibid.: 224.
45. Ibid.: 125.
46. Morris 2000: 346.
47. Ibid.: 352.
48. Ibid.: 243.
49. Semler 1993: 233.
50. Ibid.: 228.
51. Cheshire 1981: 98.
52. Morris 2000: 282.
53. Semler 1993: 255.

13 Developing an adventurer strategy

1. Kirk 2005: 37.
2. Branson 1998: 178.
3. Ibid.: 281.
4. Ibid.: 36.
5. Dyson 2000: 139.
6. Branson 1998: 45.
7. Dyson 2000: 18.
8. Branson 1998: 90.
9. Ibid.: 180.
10. Carson 1998: 191.
11. Branson 1998: 81–2.
12. Ibid.: 53.
13. Ibid.: 78.
14. Ibid.: 438–9.
15. The idea of the "paradigm shift" was first suggested by Thomas Kuhn (Kuhn 1970). He discovered that scientific advance is best described as a series of sudden shifts rather than steady growth of knowledge and understanding.
16. Branson 1998: 185.
17. Ibid.: 431.
18. Ibid.: 423.
19. Ibid.: 440.
20. Ibid.: 258.
21. Ibid.: 213.

22. Ibid.: 432.
23. Stuart & Joins 1987.
24. Branson 1998: 449.
25. Ibid.: 68.
26. Ibid.: 409.
27. Ibid.: 175.

14   Developing a guardian strategy

1. Archie Norman's career and beliefs are described on pages 25 to 41 of Tait 1995.
2. Tait 1995: 31. This is how Archie Norman described his role as a consultant at McKinsey, before he joined Kingfisher plc as Group Finance Director.
3. Harvey-Jones 1989: 26.
4. Ibid.: 81.
5. Ibid.: 53.
6. Ibid.: 68.
7. Ibid.: 71.
8. Ibid.: 86.
9. Tait 1995: 27.
10. Harvey-Jones 1990: 182.
11. Ibid.: 1995: 311.
12. Tait 1995: 32.
13. Harvey-Jones 1989: 130.
14. Ibid.: 67.
15. Ibid.: 148.
16. Ibid.: 140.
17. Ibid.: 97.
18. Ibid.: 315.
19. Ibid.: 92.
20. Ibid.: 93.
21. Ibid.: 141.
22. Harvey-Jones 1990: 11.
23. Harvey-Jones 1989: 134.
24. Harvey-Jones 1990: 184.
25. Harvey-Jones 1989: 96.
26. Harvey-Jones 1990: 184.
27. Harvey-Jones 1989: 95.
28. Ibid.: 190.
29. Ibid.: 113.
30. Ibid.: 140.
31. Ibid.: 317.
32. Ibid.: 94.

33. Ibid.: 149.
34. Ibid.: 121.
35. Ibid.: 295.
36. Ibid.: 91.
37. Ibid.: 138.
38. Ibid.: 139.
39. Ibid.: 148–9.
40. Ibid.: 65.
41. Ibid.: 83.
42. One of the best introductions to the art of positive political management within organizations is DeLuca 1999.
43. Harvey-Jones 1989: 37.
44. Harvey-Jones 1990: 17.
45. Harvey-Jones 1989: 292–3.
46. Ibid.: 90.
47. Ibid.: 304–5.
48. Ibid.: 288.

15 Organizational culture and leadership

1. Ridley 2003: 262.
2. Goleman 1995: 17–20.
3. Junor 1983: 75.
4. Pinker 2002: 283.
5. Deal & Kennedy 1985 is a good source of further information about how stories inform corporate cultures.
6. Carling & Heller 1995: 1.
7. Payne 1969: 15.
8. Cheshire 1981: 11–29.
9. Heilemann 2001: 48.
10. Carling & Heller 1995: 150.
11. Senge 1990: 3.
12. Heller 2000: 30.
13. Ibid.: 30.
14. Ibid.: 7.

16 Developing your own leadership

1. Daniel Goleman's *Emotional Intelligence* (Goleman 1995: 56–77) is a good source of advice on this topic.
2. Arroba & James 1987.

3. Transactional Analysis is very helpful in identifying these kinds of behavioural cues. Stuart & Joines 1987 is a good introduction to this approach.
4. Payne 1969: 15.
5. Semler 1993 carries an appendix on time management.
6. There are hundreds of books on the MBTI™. My favourite is Hirsch 1991.

Bibliography

Abernathy, Ralph (1989) *And the Walls Came Tumbling Down: An Autobiography*. New York: Harper and Row.

Argyris, Chris (1978) *Organisational learning*. Reading, MA: Addison-Wesley.

Arroba, Tanya and James, Kim (1987) *Pressure at work: A Survival Guide*. London: McGraw-Hill.

Beslievre, June (2000) *Still the Candle Burns: A Collection of Reminiscences and Reflections of 'GC'*. Jersey NJ: J. B. Gencot, Publications.

Botton, Alain de (2004) *Status Anxiety*. London: Hamish Hamilton.

Branson, Richard (1998) *Losing My Virginity: The Autobiography*. London: Virgin Publishing.

Bruner, Jerome (1990) *Acts of Meaning*. Cambridge, MA: Harvard University Press.

Carling, Will and Heller, Robert (1995) *The Way to Win: Strategies for Success in Business and Sport*. London: Little, Brown and Co.

Carson, Clayborne (ed.) (1998) *The Autobiography of Martin Luther King, Jr*. New York: Little, Brown.

Cheshire, Leonard (1961) *The Face of Victory*. London: Hutchinson.

Cheshire, Leonard (1981) *The Hidden World*. London: Collins.

Cheshire, Leonard (1985) *The Light of Many Suns: The Meaning of the Bomb*. London: Methuen.

Dallek, Robert (1995) *Franklin D. Roosevelt and American Foreign Policy 1932–1945*. Oxford: Oxford University Press.

Deal, Terrence and Kennedy, Allen (1982) *Corporate Cultures: The Rites and Rituals of Corporate Life*. London: Penguin Business.

DeLuca, Joel R (1999) *Political Savvy: Systematic Approaches to Leadership Behind-The-Scenes*. Berwyn Pennsylvania: EBG Publications.

Donaldson, Margaret (1992) *Human Minds: An Exploration*. London: Penguin Books.

Dyson, Michael Eric (2000) *I May Not Get There With You: The True Martin Luther King, Jr*. New York: The Free Press.

Edelman, Gerald (1992) *Bright Air, Brilliant Fire, On the Matter of the Mind*. London: Penguin.

Gandhi, M.K. (1928) *Satyagraha in South Africa*. Ahmedabad: Navajivan Publishing House.

Gandhi, M.K. (1958) *The Collected Works*. New Delhi: Publication Division of the Government of India.

Gates, Bill (1999) *Business @ the Speed of Thought: Succeeding in the Digital Economy*. London: Collins.

Goleman, Daniel (1995) *Emotional Intelligence*. New York: Bantam Books.

Goleman, Daniel (1997) *Vital Lies, Simple Truths: The Psychology of Self-Deception*. London: Bloomsbury.

Gray, Richard (1996) *Archetypal Explorations: An Integrative Approach to Human Behaviour*. London: Routledge.

Guzie, T and Guzie, N.M (1984) *"Masculine and Feminine Archetypes: A Complement to the Psychological Types." Journal of Psychological Type*, 7: 3–11.

Harvey-Jones, John (1989) *Making it Happen: Reflections on Leadership*. London: Fontana.

Harvey-Jones, John and Masey, Anthea (1990) *Troubleshooter*. London: BBC Books.

Heilemann, John (2001) *Pride Before the Fall: The Trials of Bill Gates and the End of the Microsoft Era*. London: Harper Collins.

Heller, Robert (2000) *Bill Gates*. London: Dorling Kindersley.

Hirsh, Sandra (1991) *Using the Myers-Briggs Type Indicator™ in Organisations*. Consulting Psychologists Press Palo Alto, California.

Junor, Penny (1983) *Margaret Thatcher: Wife, Politician, Mother*. London: Sidgwick and Jackson.

King, Martin Luther, Jr (1958) *Stride Toward Freedom: The Montgomery Story*. New York: Harper.

King, Martin Luther, Jr (1986) *A Testament of Hope: Essential Writings of Martin Luther King, Jr*. New York: Harper and Row.

Kirk, John A (2005) *Martin Luther King Jr*. Harlow: UK, Pearson Education.

Kuhn, Thomas (1970) *The Structure of Scientific Revolutions*. Chicago, IL: Chicago University Press.

Ling, Peter J (2002) *Martin Luther King, Jr*. London:

Mark, Margaret and Pearson, Carol (2001) *The Hero and the Outlaw: Building Extraordinary Brands through the Power of Archetypes*. New York: McGraw-Hill.

McCall, Morgan, Lombardo, Michael, Morrison, Ann (1988) *The Lessons of Experience: How Successful Executives Develop on the Job.* New York: The Free Press

Mitroff, Ian (1983) *"Archetypal Social Systems Analysis: On the Deeper Structure of Human Systems." Academy of Management Review, 8,3,* 387–97.

Morris, Richard (2000) *Cheshire: The Biography of Leonard Cheshire VC, OM.* London: Penguin Books.

Neustadt, Richard E (1968) *Presidential Power: The Politics of Leadership.* New York: Wiley.

Patching, Keith (1999) *Management and Organisation Development: Beyond arrows, boxes and circles.* Basingstoke, UK: Macmillan Business.

Payne, Robert (1969) *The Life and Death of Mahatma Gandhi.* London: Bodley Head.

Pearman, Roger (1998) *Hard Wired Leadership: Unleashing the Power of Personality to Become a New Millennium Leader.* Palo Alto, CA: Davies-Black Publishing.

Pearson, Carol S (1986) *The Hero Within.* New York: Harper and Row.

Pearson, Carol S (1991) *Awakening the Heroes Within: Twelve Archetypes to Help Us Find Ourselves and Transform Our World.* San Francisco, CA: Harper.

Perry, Lee Tom (1990) *Offensive Strategy: Forging a New Competitiveness in the Fires of Head-to-Head Competition.* New York: Harper Business.

Pinker, Steven (1994) *The Language Instinct: How the Mind Creates Language.* New York: William Morrow and co. Inc.

Pinker, Steven (2002) *The Blank Slate: The Modern Denial of Human Nature.* London: Allen Lane.

Renshaw, Patrick (2004) *Franklin D. Roosevelt.* London: Pearson.

Ridley, Matt (1999) *Genome: The autobiography of a species in 23 chapters.* London: Fourth Estate.

Ridley, Matt (2003) *Nature via Nurture: Genes, Experience and What makes us Human.* London: Fourth Estate.

Rohm, Wendy Goldman (1998) *The Microsoft File: The Secret Case Against Bill Gates.* New York: Random Books Inc.

Schein, Edgar H (1989) *Organisational Culture and Leadership.* San Francisco, CA: Jossey-Bass.

Schlesinger, A. M (1957) *The Age of Roosevelt: The Crisis of the Old Order.* Boston: Heinemann.

Schlesinger, A. M (1958) *The Age of Roosevelt: The Coming of the New Deal*. Boston: Heinemann.

Schlesinger, A. M (1960) *The Age of Roosevelt: The Politics of Upheaval*. Boston: Heinemann.

Semler, Ricardo (1993) *Maverick! The Success Story Behind the World's Most Unusual Workplace*. London: Century.

Senge, Peter (1990) *The Fifth Discipline: The Art and Practice of the Learning Organisation*. London: Century Business.

Sergeant, John (2005) *Maggie; Her Fatal Legacy*. London: Macmillan.

Sitaramayya, B. P (1943) *Gandhi and Gandhism*. Allahabad: Kitabistan.

Stevens, Anthony (1996) *Private Myths, Dreams and Dreadimng*. London: Penguin.

Stewart, Ian and Joines, Vann (1987) *T A Today: A New Introduction to Transactional Analysis*. Nottingham: Lifespace Publishing.

Tait, Ruth (1995) *Roads to the Top: Career decisions and development of 18 business leaders*. London: Macmillan.

Tendulkar, D.G (1951) *Mahatma*. New Delhi: Publications Division of the Government of India.

Thatcher, Margaret (1993) *Margaret Thatcher, the Downing Street Years*. London: Harper Collins.

Thatcher, Margaret (1995) *Margaret Thatcher: the Path to Power*. London: Harper Collins.

Thompson, William Irwin (1971) *At the Edge of History*. New York: Harper and Row.

Thoreau, Henry, D (1854) *Walden: Life in the Woods*. Boston: Ticknor and Fields.

Tugwell, Rexford G (1967) *FDR: Architect of an Era*. New York: Macmillan.

Underwood, John (1989) *The Will to Win: John Egan and Jaguar*. London: W.H. Allen and Co.

Wallace, James and Erickson, Jim (1993) *Hard Drive: Bill Gates and the Making of the Microsoft Empire*. Chichester: UK, John Wiley and Sons Ltd.

Index